LUKE
A Gospel for Today

For Teddy and Margaret Saunders
who have shown me how to live out Luke's message

LKS

For J.W. Meiklejohn
whose influence has been lasting

WR

LUKE

A Gospel for Today

Linda Smith and William Raeper

LION EDUCATIONAL

Published by
Lion Publishing plc
Sandy Lane West, Oxford, England
ISBN 0 7459 1503 5
Albatross Books Pty Ltd
PO Box 320, Sutherland, NSW 2232, Australia
ISBN 0 7324 0061 9

First edition 1989
10 9 8 7

British Library Cataloguing in Publication Data

Smith, Linda
Luke: A Gospel for Today
1. Bible. N.T. Luke – Critical studies
I. Title II. Raeper, William, 1959–
226'.406
ISBN 0 7459 1503 5

Printed in Malta

Acknowledgements
Bible quotations are from the *Good News Bible*, copyright 1966, 1971 and 1976 American Bible Society, published by The Bible Societies and Collins.

Quotations on page 78 are from Janet Green, *Home-made Prayers*, Lion Publishing

Photographs
Associated Press, pages 113, 168 (above); Trustees of the British Museum, pages 109, 141; DAS Photography/David Simson, pages 58, 185 (all), 73; Chris Fairclough Colour Library, page 31 (above); Format, page 81; Greenpeace Communications, page 34; Sonia Halliday and Laura Lushington Photographs, pages 13, 38, 43, 62, 129, 132, 137 (below), 159, 161 (below) /F.H.C. Birch, pages 26, 178 /Sister Daniel IBVM, page 174 /Barry Searle, page 10 /Jane Taylor, page 161 (above) /T.C. Rising, page 133; Hulton Picture Company, page 111; Jewish Chronicle/Werner Braun, pages 107, 144 /Frank Dabba Smith, page 115; Lion Publishing/David Alexander, pages 14, 101, 125, 139 (above), 153, 158, 169, 189 /Jon Willcocks, pages 148/49; Mansell Collection, pages 146/47; Picturepoint, page 31 (below); Popperfoto, pages 35, 85, 168 (below), 190; Rex Features, page 90; Frank Spooner Pictures/Pierre Dupin, page 93; Scripture Union/John Haysom, page 104; Zefa (UK) Ltd, pages 37, 46, 126 /Richard Nowitz, page 117

Illustrations, maps and graphics
Simon Jenkins, pages 7, 15, 23, 36, 48, 78, 82, 97, 106, 118, 172
Lion Publishing, pages 11, 25, 66, 70, 77, 134, 136, 140, 164
Lion Publishing/Tony Cantale Graphics, pages 18, 21, 40, 51, 61, 64, 65, 92, 121, 124 (both), 130, 132, 157, 163, 182, 184, 188
Lion Publishing/Graham Round, pages 75, 104

Design by Tony Cantale Graphics

Contents

Introduction

You are about to enter someone else's world. You may never have heard of Luke or his Gospel. It may be a completely alien world to you. So, to learn about Luke we need to travel through time and space. Use your imagination just for a minute . . .

You go home tonight very anxious to set something straight. One of your best friends has been accused of theft. You know the story is not accurate, so you sit down to write out the facts clearly so that the Headteacher gets a true picture of what has happened. It takes a long time and you work late into the night. You have to think about your friend's character. You have to record the sort of things he/she does and says to back up your account. You even use other people's evidence to support your argument to convince the Head of his/her innocence.

Years and years later, in AD4000, a group of fourth-years are studying your account. It has been handed down over the years, reprinted again and again throughout the centuries because – amazingly – your friend turned out to be someone very important. Your account is one of the few remaining texts that tell the world anything about him/her. The fourth-years are puzzled: 'Who was the author?' 'When did he/she write this?' 'What does he/she want us to know?' 'Which stories are other people's evidence rather than the author's?' 'Why is this friend so special that someone takes all this trouble to write about him/her?'

These are the questions we are going to ask and try to answer about Luke's Gospel. He wrote it to set the record straight about Jesus. So we shall see Jesus through Luke's eyes.

UNIT 1.1

First-century Places: The Land of Israel

What is your world like? There is your external world, the world outside yourself, and there is your internal world, the world inside yourself.

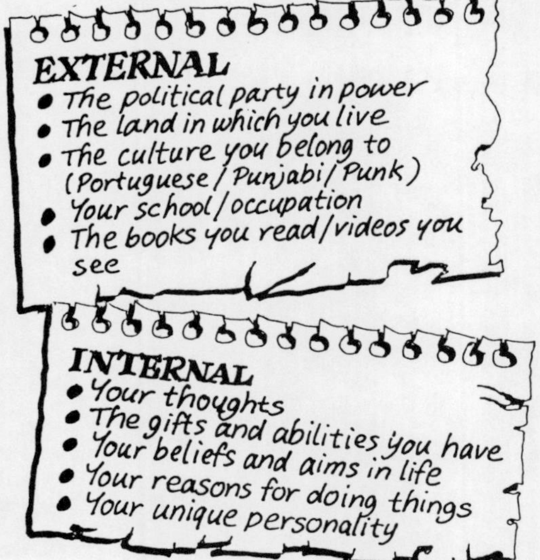

These and many more things make up the world in which you live. They give a sort of picture of the person you are. But what if we wanted to sketch a picture of Luke, someone who lived almost 2,000 years ago? Where would we go for information? Two sources are helpful: what others have written, and what Luke himself wrote.

By piecing together these ancient writings, and looking at different archaeological finds, we are able to form a picture of the world Luke lived in and the sort of person he was.

First, let's look at the **external world**. What was it like for Luke living in the first century? What was going on? What was news? Who was in power? What were the fashions? What sort of places did Luke write about in his Gospel?

Palestine in the first century

Hardly a day passes without there being some mention of Palestine on the TV news. Look at the map of Palestine in this unit. You'll notice that it's a small country. In fact, it's a strip of land sandwiched between the desert and the Mediterranean Sea, and it would fit into the size of Wales.

The coastal plain stretches for a distance of about 200 km/120 miles from the borders of Lebanon to Gaza.

The central hills cover some 320 km/200 miles from Northern Galilee to Sinai. These are made up of interlocking hills and plateaux.

The River Jordan slices through Palestine for over 100 km/60 miles where it follows the great Rift Valley. This stretches right down into Africa. Its northern sector includes *Lake Galilee* which is 200 metres below sea level. Although it is called a lake, Galilee is more like a sea because of its size (20 km/13 miles long). In Luke's Gospel it is also called *Lake Gennesaret* (Luke 5:1).

The River Jordan flows through Lake Galilee from north to south, so its waters are fresh. It is no wonder that fishing was a flourishing business there. In Jesus' lifetime the fisheries were famous throughout the Roman Empire for their export trade. Jesus spent a lot of his time in the area around this lake, especially on the northern shore in towns like Capernaum and Bethsaida.

The great Rift Valley is at its deepest at the Dead Sea. The Dead Sea is about 80km/50 miles long and 20km/12 miles wide. Tourists come from all over the world to visit the sea – it is the lowest point on earth. Because it lies so far below normal sea level (400 metres), streams flow in,

but they cannot flow out. The rate of evaporation is so great (temperatures often reach 43°C/110°F in summer) that the lake never increases. In fact, over recent years, the sea level has been slowly dropping. The water is very rich in minerals and salts, which make the sea buoyant. It takes no effort to float. The effects are fatal on fish however – they die within seconds if they swim in from the Jordan river.

Jerusalem is one of the world's most famous cities. People were living here over 1,500 years before Christ. Throughout the centuries Jerusalem has been inhabited, destroyed and re-occupied many times. It is a city with an ancient history.

Today Jerusalem is considered sacred

The Dead Sea is so salty that it's easy for anyone to float. But no fish can live in its waters.

by three great faiths: Judaism, Islam and Christianity. It lies in the southern part of the country. In Luke's Gospel, Jesus visited the city when he was twelve years old and then again at the end of his life.

The desert is mountainous dry land, especially in the south. In Luke 4 Jesus lived in the desert for a while and it was there that he was tempted. In modern Israel some of the desert places have been irrigated and transformed into gardens bearing citrus fruits, wheat and grapes or figs. Many of the farms or communities of people who work there are called *kibbutzes*.

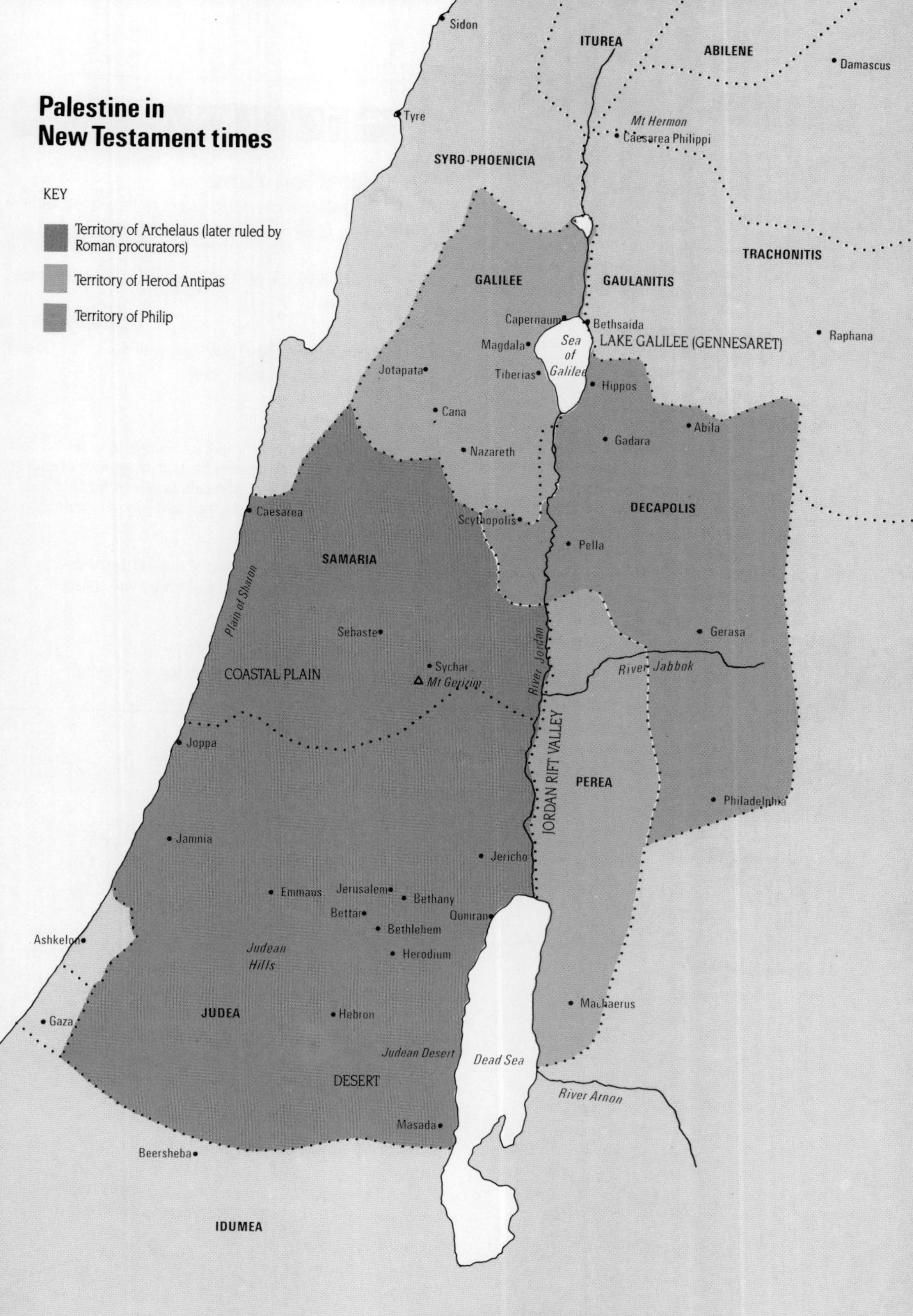

Palestine in New Testament times
KEY
Territory of Archelaus (later ruled by Roman procurators)
Territory of Herod Antipas
Territory of Philip
Sidon
ITUREA
ABILENE
Damascus
Tyre
Mt Hermon
Caesarea Philippi
SYRO-PHOENICIA
TRACHONITIS
GALILEE
GAULANITIS
Capernaum
Bethsaida
Raphana
Magdala
Sea of Galilee
LAKE GALILEE (GENNESARET)
Jotapata
Tiberias
Hippos
Cana
Abila
Gadara
Nazareth
DECAPOLIS
Caesarea
Scythopolis
Pella
SAMARIA
Plain of Sharon
Sebaste
Gerasa
Sychar
COASTAL PLAIN
Mt Gerizim
River Jordan
River Jabbok
JORDAN RIFT VALLEY
Joppa
PEREA
Philadelphia
Jamnia
Jericho
Emmaus
Jerusalem
Bethany
Bettar
Qumran
Bethlehem
Ashkelon
Judean Hills
Herodium
JUDEA
Hebron
Machaerus
Gaza
Judean Desert
Dead Sea
DESERT
River Arnon
Masada
Beersheba
IDUMEA
NABATEAN KINGDOM

FACT·FILE

Places and towns Jesus visited in Luke's Gospel

1. Born in **Bethlehem** (Luke 2:6)
2. Dedicated to God by his parents in **Jerusalem** (Luke 2:22)
3. Brought up in **Nazareth** (Luke 2:39–40)
4. Jesus aged twelve at Passover feast in **Jerusalem** (Luke 2:41–42)
5. Jesus baptized at **River Jordan** (Luke 3:21)
6. Jesus tempted in **the desert** (Luke 4:1–2)
7. Jesus begins his work at about the age of thirty in **Galilee** (Luke 4:14)
8. Jesus is rejected by his own people in **Nazareth** (Luke 4:16–30)
9. Jesus works in **Capernaum** (Luke 4:31–44)
10. Jesus calls his disciples to follow him at **Lake Gennesaret** (Galilee) (Luke 5:1–11)
11. Jesus heals a Roman officer's servant at **Capernaum** (Luke 7:1–9)
12. Jesus raises a widow's son from death at **Nain** (Luke 7:11–17)
13. Jesus calms a storm on **Lake Galilee** (Luke 8:22–25)
14. Jesus heals a man with demons at **Gerasa** (Luke 8:26–39)
15. Jesus is kept out of a **Samaritan village** (Luke 9:51–56)
16. Jesus heals ten men on the border between **Samaria** and **Galilee** (Luke 17:11–19)
17. Jesus heals a blind beggar **near Jericho** (Luke 18:35–43)
18. Jesus visits and speaks to Zacchaeus in **Jericho** (Luke 19:1–9)
19. Jesus tells his disciples to prepare for his visit to the capital **in or near Bethany** (Luke 19:28–30)
20. Jesus ends his life and is crucified at **Jerusalem** (Luke 23)
21. Jesus appears alive after death to two followers on the road to **Emmaus** (Luke 24:13–35)

Question time

1. Jerusalem is considered sacred by three great faiths. Can you name them?

2. What do you know about the land of Palestine at the time of Jesus?

3. Name three places that Jesus visited in Luke's Gospel and say what happened there.

To do

- Design a travel brochure for tourists to Israel. It could be a travel brochure from the time of Jesus or one for today. Use the information about places, features and history in an imaginative way, as if you were trying to attract visitors.

- Find out about the land of Israel today. Visit your local travel agent or the local library and collect information.

Talking-point

Is Jerusalem still important in the world today? If so, how?

First-century Life in Palestine: Romans and Jews

Every **country** is ruled by a person or a political party.

Then there is the **town, city or community** which is governed at a local level.

In every **school, business or shop** there is someone who is in charge.

In **families** there is usually someone who has the final word.

In **a group of two or three friends** there is often one person who makes most of the decisions.

Think for a minute how you respond to people in authority.
– Do you always respect them?
– Do you usually respect them, depending on who is in charge?
– Do you rarely respect them, because you are suspicious?
– Do you never respect authority?

Roman rule

In first-century Palestine the Romans were in charge. They had conquered the country in 63BC, and ruled in a harsh way. Although the Romans held the real power, they allowed the Jews to be ruled by local 'kings'. The most famous of these was Herod the Great, who ruled from 37BC until his death in AD4. After his death, the kingdom was divided between three of Herod's sons. However, these sons were poor rulers, and so the Romans stepped in and began to rule Judea directly. The men who now wielded ultimate power were called Procurators (Governors). One of them was Pontius Pilate, who appears later on in Luke's story.

The mountain fortress of Masada was the last stronghold of the Jewish resistance against the Romans, after the destruction of Jerusalem in AD70. The ruins of Herod's palace can be clearly seen.

The Jews responded to this new form of direct Roman authority in different ways . . .

- The *Sadducees* adapted to it.
- The *Pharisees* rejected it and put their energies into their religion.
- The *Essenes* reacted to it by opting out of society and into the desert.
- The *Zealots* opposed it and became a revolutionary force.

The Pharisees – the people's religious party

The term 'Pharisee' comes from the Hebrew word meaning 'separated' – but separated from what or whom is not known. The traditional view is that they tried very hard to obey the Jewish religious laws and so kept themselves apart from the ordinary people who were not as devout as they were. They also added their oral (spoken) teachings to the written Law. These were not written down but were spoken comments which applied the old written Law to every situation in life.

For instance, the Law said you had to have the seventh day of the week (the Sabbath, a Saturday) free from work. The Pharisees said what could and could not be counted as work on the Sabbath.

The Pharisees hoped for a Messiah. This meant they were waiting for a leader, specially chosen and empowered (or *anointed*) by God to set their country free from foreign rule. They thought this special leader would be like King David of old and descended from his family. The Pharisees also believed in a future Kingdom of God and the resurrection of the dead.

Most importantly, the Pharisees were well-organized and enthusiastic. They were laymen, not priests, and they defended the Law fiercely when the priests forgot it. The Pharisees created a specific sort of society with rules for membership. These groups were 'communities' which met for study, friendship and meals on Friday afternoons before the Sabbath day began. These communities were open to only a few people and some scholars think they had secret teachings.

Even if the Pharisees were exclusive, they were powerful because they were the people's religious party and they kept the Jewish faith alive in the towns and villages of first-century Palestine.

This orthodox Jew is wearing on his forehead a little box containing part of the Law. Phylacteries like these but smaller were worn by the Pharisees in Jesus' day.

Though the Gospels generally give a negative picture of the Pharisees, we need to remember that many of the Pharisees were sincere, devout people. Not all of them were opposed to Jesus, and several of them were his friends.

The Sadducees – the privileged party

The Sadducees were a party of wealthy property owners living in Jerusalem. Some were priests and some were laymen. They supported the status quo and worked in co-operation with the Romans. Centred on the great Temple in Jerusalem and all the influence that went with it, they were anxious not to upset the Romans who allowed them such power.

The Sadducees were enemies of the Pharisees and disagreed with them violently. Unlike the Pharisees, they were not expecting a Messiah to deliver them from Roman rule. They did not accept the oral law which had been added to the written Law (the Torah). They rejected the belief in a resurrection from the dead and did not believe in angels. They were quite content with the services of the Jerusalem Temple.

The Essenes – the desert party

A third group was the Essenes. They are not mentioned in the Bible, but they have become well known since the discovery of the Dead Sea Scrolls in 1947. These scrolls belonged to the Essene community who were monks at Qumran near the Dead Sea. The scrolls were hidden when the Romans invaded Judea in AD66 and they remained a secret for almost nineteen centuries.

The community at Qumran was founded after the Maccabean wars. Some Jews felt that religious life was being corrupted. People preferred winning wars and gaining fame rather than obeying God's laws. The community's aim was to prepare for the coming of God's Messiah. They believed that by living in their monastery in the desert they were obeying the word of the prophet Isaiah:

> 'Prepare in the wilderness a road for the Lord! Clear the way in the desert for our God' (Isaiah 40:3).

Three ancient historians tell us something about the Essenes.

Philo of Alexandria says:
There were about 4,000 of them.
They lived in villages working hard at agriculture and studying moral and religious questions.
All their property was shared.
They were celibate – i.e. they did not marry or have sex.
They did not keep slaves.
They would not fight or work for money.
They took care of the sick and the aged.

Pliny tells us:
The Essenes renounced women and money, yet their numbers kept up because so many others came regularly to join them. Pliny says that there were many like them who were tired of the ordinary way of living and were looking for something else.

Josephus says:
The Essenes were found in all the cities of Judea, including Jerusalem. They were very kind and hospitable, especially to other Essenes who had come from far away. They treated them as brothers.

To be an Essene you had to have a three-year training. At the end of the first year the novice was allowed to be involved in the ritual purification in water, but it took another two years to share the community meal. This meant you were a full member.

A typical Essene day recorded by the Jewish historian Josephus

- Get up before sunrise. Morning prayers.
- Work until noon at a given task.
- Bathe at noon and have a simple meal together.
- Put on working clothes again and continue work until evening.
- Evening meal.

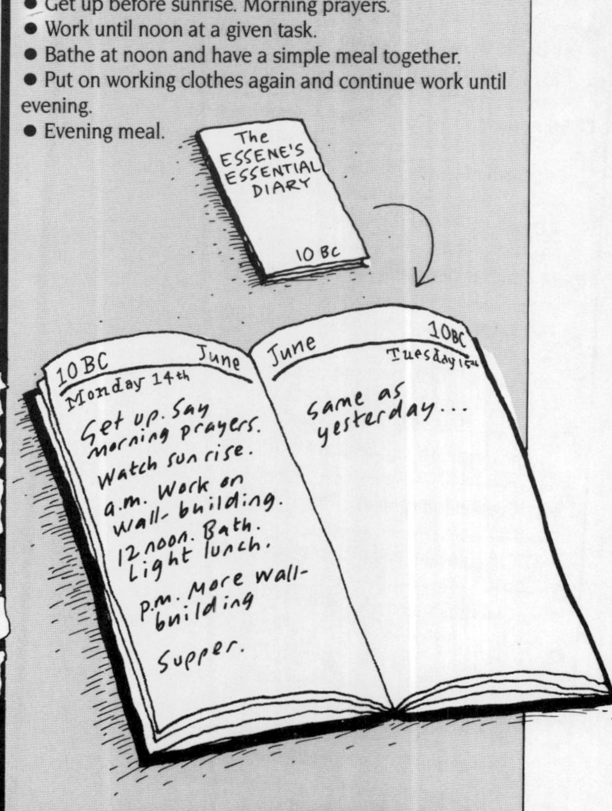

Zealots – the revolutionary party

The Zealots were a group of different revolutionary movements, all totally opposed to Roman rule. They believed that Israel should be free of the Romans, and carried out terrorist attacks on the Roman troops, using all the techniques of guerrilla warfare. Because the Jewish establishment (the Sadducees, the priests and the wealthy) worked with the Romans, the Zealots hated them.

The origins of the Zealots is usually traced back to Judas of Galilee. In AD6 Judas refused to pay tribute to the Roman emperor and caused a Jewish revolt against Rome. The revolt was brutally crushed by the Romans, but the Zealots kept their revolutionary spirit alive for sixty more years. The last Zealot stronghold, the mountain fort of Masada, fell in May AD73. But even after that it was difficult to quench the Zealots' zeal and desire for freedom.

FACT · FILE

EVENTS IN JUDEA UNDER ROMAN RULE
63BC–AD70

- 63BC Roman general Pompey conquers Palestine, enters Jerusalem
- 37 Herod the Great appointed King of the Jews by Roman senate
- 31 Battle of Actium: Antony and Cleopatra defeated: Egypt subject to Rome
- 30 Augustus becomes Roman emperor
- 5(?) Birth of Jesus
- 4 Death of Herod the Great
- 14 Tiberius becomes Roman emperor
- 18 Caiaphas made High Priest in Jerusalem
- 26 Pontius Pilate becomes governor of Judea
  Jesus' ministry begins
- 30 Jesus' death and resurrection
- 33 Conversion of Paul
- 37 Caligula succeeds Tiberius as emperor
- 41 Claudius succeeds Caligula as emperor
- 46–48 Paul's first missionary tour
- 54 Nero becomes emperor
- 64 Rome burns: Nero persecutes the Christians
- 64/66 Deaths of Peter and Paul
- 66–70 Jewish revolt against the Romans
- 70 Romans capture and destroy Jerusalem

Question time

1. What do you know about Roman rule in Palestine after 63BC?

2. Explain what is meant by the term 'Pharisee'.

3. Write a sentence on each of the following:
- the oral (spoken) teachings of the Pharisees
- their Messianic hopes
- how they organized themselves.

4. Complete the following sentences:
- The Essenes have become well known through the discovery of ______________.
- Some Essenes lived in the community at ______________ near the ______________.
- The aim of the community was to ______________
- They believed they were obeying the word of the prophet ______________ which said ______________
- To be an Essene you had to train for ______________ years.
- The Essenes renounced ______________.
- Here is a list of some of the things they did ______________

To do

Write a letter to a first-century newspaper. Imagine you are a Sadducee complaining about the Pharisees and their beliefs and practices. What would you write?

UNIT 2.1

Luke: A Personal Profile

Luke is mentioned three times by name in the New Testament. Each time it happens when Paul, a famous Christian, is writing one of his letters to the early believers:

'Luke, our dear doctor, and Demas send you their greetings.'

Letter to the Christians at Colossae – Colossians 4:14

'Do your best to come to me soon . . . only Luke is with me.'

Letter to Timothy – 2 Timothy 4:9–11

'Epaphras, who is in prison with me for the sake of Christ Jesus, sends his greetings and so do my fellow workers, Mark, Aristarchus, Demas and Luke.'

Letter to Philemon verse 2

From these mentions we know that Luke was a doctor and a good friend of Paul. Outside the New Testament Luke is mentioned by several people. In particular, the Bishop of Lyons, Irenaeus, writing about AD170, said, 'Luke, a companion of Paul, recorded in a book, the Gospel.'

Luke wrote over one quarter of the New Testament, more than any other author. Not only did Luke write his Gospel, but he also continued the story in the *Acts of the Apostles*. Here he writes about what happened in the early church, after the time of Jesus. Luke wrote some of his account in Acts as an eye-witness, because he travelled with Paul the apostle, and saw what happened.

So far we have looked at Luke the writer, the traveller and the friend of Paul. But what about Luke the person? What was he like? Can we know anything about him? We can find out certain things from reading his Gospel.

What was Luke like?

- *Luke's style* He was a clever, educated man. Luke was a Gentile (a non-Jew). All four Gospels were written in Greek, but his very careful use of the language shows he was a first-class communicator. Sometimes he is formal – sometimes he sounds more like a TV commentator reporting action stories first-hand. At other times he shows himself to have sensitive artistic ability, especially when writing personal stories about men and women.

- *Luke cares for people* He writes about people: poor people, outcasts, people who have made a mess of their lives and need to get sorted out (read the story of the Prodigal Son in Luke 15:11–32). As you read his Gospel, notice how he has great sympathy for those in any sort of trouble – especially the sick.

- *Luke likes things to be well-ordered* Not only did he write in good Greek, but Luke's Gospel reflects a Greek approach to life. The Greeks were different from the Jews. They liked precise order and accuracy. Luke places a lot of his stories about Jesus into the framework of a journey to Jerusalem. This is to give the events and teaching Luke writes about a proper place and order that can be followed by his readers. He has a 'tidy' mind.

• *Luke likes history* He writes as a historian. Look at the way he names emperors and kings and cites different specific dates. If you read Luke 3:1–2 you can find seven officials and five territories named in just two verses.

• *Luke enjoys being a Christian* Throughout the twenty-four chapters of Luke's Gospel, there are people who are joyful because of what Jesus does for them. It would be interesting to count how many stories Luke includes where people 'rejoice and praise God'. Certainly at the beginning of the Gospel the angels (in chapter 2) and the disciples at the end of the Gospel (in chapter 24) are full of joy. Luke begins and ends with joy.

The writing of the Gospels

The Gospels were written in the Greek language. Many Greek words have made their way into English (for example, chorus, plastic, photograph). If you look in a dictionary, you will often find that words have a Greek root to them.

Here is the Greek alphabet.

THE GREEK ALPHABET

Α	Β	Γ	Δ	Ε	Ζ
A	B	G	D	E	Z
Η	Θ	Ι	Κ	Λ	Μ
E	TH	I	K	L	M
Ν	Ξ	Ο	Π	Ρ	Σ
N	X	O	P	RH,R	S
Τ	Υ	Φ	Χ	Ψ	Ω
T	U	PH	KH	PS	O

The oldest complete copies of the New Testament are from the fourth century. The most famous is the **Codex Sinaiticus** which was found in St Catherine's monastery on Mount Sinai. You can see it in the British Museum in London. It is copied on *vellum* which is made from the skin of sheep or goats.

Very early copies of the New Testament were written on *papyrus*. Our word 'paper' comes from the word 'papyrus'. Papyrus was made from reed-plants that grew near water. However, papyrus rots much more easily than vellum, so the original copies of the New Testament have not lasted. Very few pieces or fragments have survived the test of time. The oldest discovered fragment of the New Testament is in the John Rylands Library in Manchester. It is a scrap from the Gospel of John and dates back to between AD100 and 150.

One of the Dead Sea Scrolls, a copy of the Psalms, rolled up.

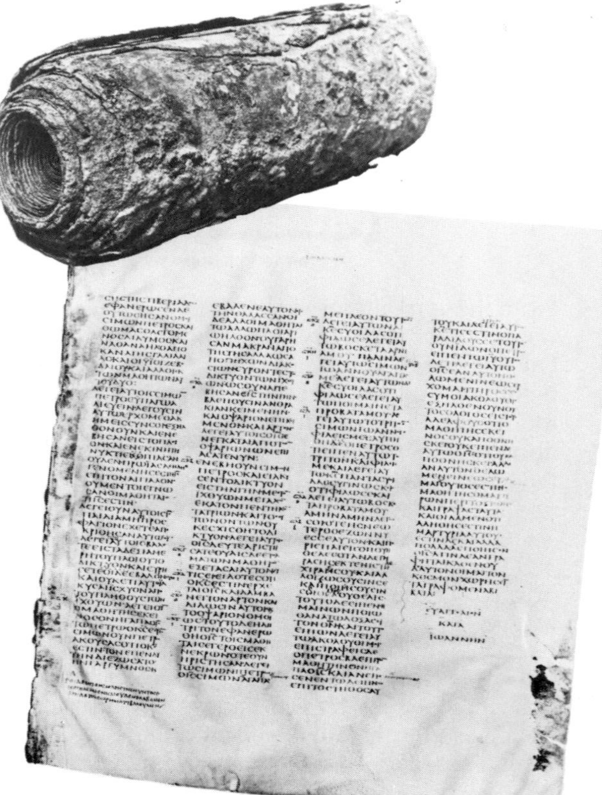

How can we know what the New Testament authors really wrote, when all we have are copies written in the fourth century – long after the events?

Although we have only later manuscripts, portions of the New Testament were copied and recopied with great care right from the start. Christian writers were translated into other languages as well as Greek – e.g. Latin and Syriac.

Syriac is a language similar to Aramaic. Aramaic is the language that Jesus spoke. These translations were made from very early copies which are now lost. So, although what we have now are not original, they were copied very carefully from much older scripts.

It is amazing how some of these fragments have survived almost 2,000 years. Some have been destroyed by those who opposed the Christian faith, but many have been preserved throughout the centuries.

This is chapter 21 of John's Gospel from Codex Sinaiticus, one of the oldest complete copies of the New Testament. Notice that it is written in neat columns and that all the writing is in capital letters. There are no spaces between the words, so it is not easy to translate. The verse and chapter numbers in modern Bibles have all been added by experts in Greek who have translated the text.

FOLLOW UP

Question time

Write in your books the word(s) which best complete each of the following. Write in sentences.

1. Luke is mentioned three times by name in the New Testament. You can find the references in the letters of James/Peter/Paul.

2. From the New Testament we know that Luke was a rabbi/teacher/doctor.

3. Luke did not only write the Gospel, he also wrote ____________.

4. Luke is mentioned outside the New Testament writings by a man called ____________, who was Bishop of Rome/Lyons/Galilee.

5. Luke wrote his Gospel in the Hebrew/Greek/Aramaic language.

6. A Gentile is a Jewish person/a non-Jewish person.

7. What evidence is there in his Gospel to show that Luke was a clever, educated man?

8. How do we know that Luke likes history and writes like a historian?

To do

We know about Luke mainly through what he himself wrote. If someone found your exercise book, diary or a letter, what might it say to them about the sort of person you are?
Would your handwriting be small/large? Sloping/non sloping?
Would you be well-ordered?
What is your personal style?
Look at the way you write things and see if you can become more aware of what comes across in what you write. It could be useful to know more about the messages you send out about yourself, especially when you write for jobs or interviews.

Try your hand at writing Greek. Using the Greek alphabet in this unit, try to write your name using the Greek letters. Then see if you can write and decipher what these mean . . .

ΒΙΒΛΟΣ ΧΡΙΣΤΟΣ ΙΣΡΑΗΛ

Luke's Gospel – the Making

Think for a minute of the different ways in which you can write an essay.

What sources do you use?

- Do you sit down all on your own in complete quiet and write it all out of your own head?
- Do you ask someone else who has useful information on the topic to let you use their material?
- Do you refer to other books in your account, making use of them – but all the time using material in your own way rather than just copying?
- Do you just put on your Sony Walkman and write the first thing that comes into your head on the subject?

There are many different ways to write. Luke, in the introduction (or 'prologue') to his Gospel, tells us something of how his Gospel was originally compiled. Here is what he says:

Dear Theophilus,
Many people have done their best to write a report of the things that have taken place among us. They wrote what we have been told by those who saw these things from the beginning and who proclaimed the message. And so, your Excellency, because I have carefully studied all these matters from their beginning, I thought it would be good to write an orderly account for you. I do this so that you will know the full truth about everything which you have been taught.

Luke, chapter 1, verses 1–4

Who was Theophilus?

- The name *Theophilus* means *lover of God* in Greek. Is it addressed to *any* believer who loves God? Or is this a particular person called Theophilus?
- Some scholars think that Theophilus was an influential Greek, perhaps a convert to Christianity.
- Some think that Theophilus gave Luke money to research and write his Gospel.
- The words *'your Excellency'* may well indicate that Theophilus was an important official.

Luke says that he has produced his Gospel from three sources:

Source 1:
the actual events 'the things that have taken place among us' (verse 1)

Source 2:
the spoken reports 'what we have been told by those who saw these things . . .' (verse 2)

Source 3:
the written reports 'Many people have done their best to write a report of these things . . .' (verse 1)

We are going to look in more detail at source three, the written reports. The first three Gospel writers, Matthew, Mark and Luke, have material in common. That is why they are called **the synoptic Gospels**. The word 'synoptic' means 'looks like'. The written reports used by Luke include material from Mark's Gospel and from elsewhere. But where did the three synoptic writers find their information about Jesus? And when each writer came to write his own Gospel, who used whom? who copied from whom?

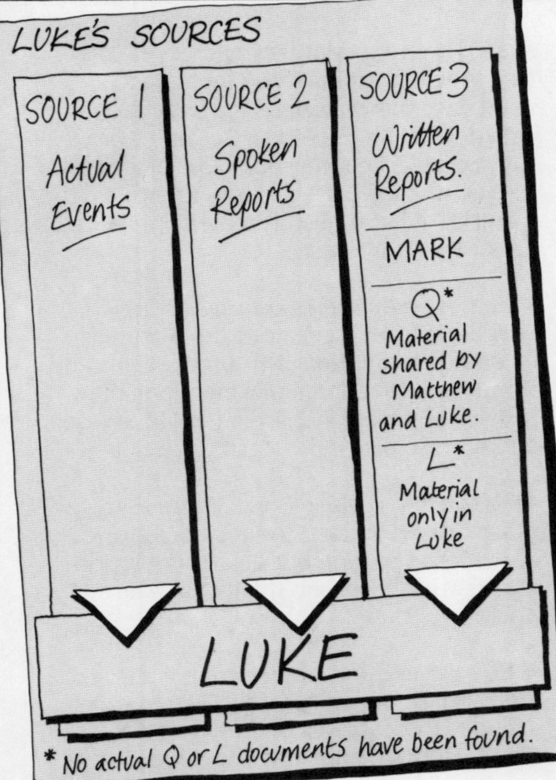

Synoptic sources

The Gospels as we now have them were probably written some forty years after the death of Jesus. However, long before that time, there were stories that had been written down about Jesus. Some of these were probably put together in small collections. These can be called *collections of sayings*.

If you read through Mark's Gospel, you can see how these collections of sayings have been included in the text. Mark usually connects each saying or incident about Jesus by using the Greek word *kai* which means 'and'. The translators have made it easier for us to read, so you do not always have to read 'and' . . . 'and' . . . 'and' . . .

Look at the following example from Mark. Most scholars think that Mark wrote his Gospel first and was used by Matthew and Luke. In just six verses of the same chapter there are three different incidents. See if you can spot them . . .

'Jesus went back again to the shore of Lake Galilee. A crowd came to him, and he started teaching them. As he walked along, he saw a tax collector, Levi son of Alphaeus, sitting in his office. Jesus said to him, "Follow me." Levi got up and followed him.

'Later on Jesus was having a meal in Levi's house. A large number of tax collectors and other outcasts were following Jesus, and many of them joined him and his disciples at the table. Some teachers of the Law, who were Pharisees, saw that Jesus was eating with these outcasts and tax collectors, so they asked his disciples, "Why does he eat with such people?" Jesus heard them and answered, "People who are well do not need a doctor, but only those who are sick. I have not come to call respectable people, but outcasts."

'On one occasion the followers of John the Baptist and the Pharisees were fasting. Some people came to Jesus and asked him, "Why is it that the disciples of John the Baptist and the disciples of the Pharisees fast, but yours do not?" Jesus answered, "Do you expect the guests at a wedding party to go without food? Of course not! As long as the bridegroom is with them, they will not do that. But the day will come when the bridegroom will be taken away from them, and then they will fast . . ."'
Mark 2:13–19

Scholars usually agree that these are quite separate stories which have been brought together as examples of events in Jesus' early ministry. But what happened before they were included in the Gospel? Were they passed on by word of mouth? Often the Jews passed down traditional stories from parents to children in spoken (oral) form without ever writing them down. This is known as the 'oral tradition'. There is a lot of agreement about the sort of stories which are the basic source material for the synoptic Gospels. These stories have been listed under various headings. Here are four different kinds:

- Miracle stories
- Parables and sayings
- Stories about what Jesus did
- Pronouncement stories where Jesus makes a statement.

The verses listed above in Mark's Gospel are examples of the last two types of story. The call of Levi, the tax collector, is typical of the stories about what Jesus did. Whilst the meal at Levi's house is a pronouncement story because it ends with Jesus saying something or pronouncing something quite important – and usually something which is easy to remember.

Two other sources need to be mentioned.

The passion story (Jesus' suffering and crucifixion) It is likely that from very early on after the death of Jesus, the account of his last week and his crucifixion were written down. All four Gospels include it and the story is basically the same. Details in the four accounts of the passion story do differ, however, and this suggests that there may have been more than one written account of events. Look at Mark 14–15. These chapters read as one whole story with no need of 'ands' and 'whens' to connect different sources.

The Old Testament The Jewish scriptures, which Christians call the Old Testament, provided a rich source for the Gospel writers. They frequently quote from it in their writings. Jesus was a Jew and so were his close disciples. The Christian church started among Jewish people who believed that Jesus was their special leader, the promised 'Messiah' foretold and expected in their own scriptures.

Luke's special material

The first three Gospels, Matthew, Mark and Luke, have a lot of material in common. Luke contains 1,150 verses. About 350 of these are in common with Mark's Gospel. So that leaves 800 verses. Of these, another 200 can be traced to be material which is shared between Matthew and Luke – the two writers must have had a common source for this material. This material is called 'Q', from *Quelle*, the German word for 'source'. The remaining 600 verses are unique to Luke. This is always known as 'L' material. What does this material tell us about Luke's interests?

- *He is interested in the supernatural activity of God*. Right from the start of the Gospel to its end there are miracles, angels, signs and wonders. Luke continually mentions the activity of the Holy Spirit in the life of Jesus and his disciples.

- *He cares deeply about the sick*. More than any other Gospel writer, Luke includes stories about Jesus healing the sick. This supports the view of those who think Luke was a doctor.

- *Luke has good news for the outcasts and the poor – they matter*! This is the only Gospel which includes the parables of 'The Lost Son', 'The Lost Coin', and 'The Lost Sheep'.

- *The good news about Jesus is for all people, not just Jews*. Luke includes a lot of material about Gentiles (non-Jews). He includes, for example, the famous story of the Good Samaritan. Luke's Gospel and his second volume, Acts, may be the only two books in the New Testament written by a Gentile.

- *Prayer is important*. Luke continually records Jesus praying in all the important decisions he has to make.

- *Women have rights too*. Throughout Luke's Gospel, special attention is given to what women think and do. Luke is the only Gospel writer who consistently spends much time writing about women.

- *Luke wants the world to know that something joyful has happened*. Luke writes that Jesus' birth will bring joy. Chapter by chapter in the Gospel, where Jesus heals and helps people, his ministry is accompanied by joy and thanksgiving. Even at the very end, after Jesus leaves his followers and is taken back into heaven, they are filled with 'great joy'. These are some of Luke's special themes and from them we can begin to form an idea of what sort of writer he was.

Luke's Gospel

Luke was writing with a purpose. He wanted people to receive the message that was so important to him. He was not just writing a book about Jesus' life, like a biography. He was selecting his special material carefully in order to communicate a particular message to a particular audience.

The word 'Gospel' means 'good news'. The four Gospel writers, Matthew, Mark, Luke and John, wrote because they believed that Jesus was important. They believed that Jesus was the good news. They believed that, in Jesus, God had come close to people, and that when Jesus spoke and did things he was revealing God to them. So the four Gospels are not biographies which observe Jesus' life, they were written by people who had faith and believed in the importance of Jesus as the Son of God and the Saviour of the world.

Throughout this book we will be asking the question, 'what did Luke believe about Jesus?' But before we do that, there are some other questions we need to ask to form a clearer picture of Luke.

FOLLOW UP

Question time

1. Luke's Gospel has an introduction. Another name for it is a ____________.

2. Luke's Gospel is addressed to ____________.

3. In the introduction Luke names three sources he has used. They are ____________.

4. Matthew, Mark and Luke are together called the ____________.

5. The Synoptic Gospels were written about ____________ years after the death of Jesus.

6. What is meant by 'oral tradition'?

7. Why are the first three Gospels called the Synoptic Gospels?

8. Where did the Synoptic writers get their information about Jesus?

9. Name four different kinds of story about Jesus. How do you understand the meaning of one of them?

10. What were Luke's special interests? Make a list of them and then decide whether there is any one particular issue (for example, the sick, women, etc.) that is of importance today in our society. Why do you think this is so?

To do

Compile your own 'gospel'. What good news would you tell the world? What would be your 'special material'? Why did you choose that and leave other things out? Here is an example:

The good news according to Mandy Rudd
I want to tell you the good news about the following three things:
Animal Rights. This is important because ____________.
How to get on with people ____________.
The meaning of life ____________.

Talking-point

When did Luke write his Gospel?
Who was Theophilus? Is it important to know?

Luke's Gospel: The When and the Why

In any great detective book there are essential questions to be asked. They are **the big six**:

We have looked at the first four questions about Luke. Who was he? What were his sources? Where did he find them? How did he use them? There are two more questions to ask before we complete the picture.

When did Luke write his Gospel?
Why did he write it?

When did Luke write his Gospel?

It is worth looking at how scholars try to decide exactly when the Gospels were written. It really is like a detective story. Try to follow the clues and see if you can agree with the conclusions . . .

Clue 1

Luke uses 65 per cent of Mark's Gospel. Some of this material is almost identical, so Luke must have had access to Mark. If Mark is dated AD65 (as most scholars think), Luke must have been written later.

Clue 2

(They get harder as you go on . . .) Luke includes passages in which Jesus predicts that the Jerusalem Temple will be destroyed (see Luke 13:34–5; Luke 19:41–44 and Luke 21:20–24). Some scholars think that these prophecies were not genuine predictions about the future. They therefore say that Luke's Gospel was written after AD70 – the year the Temple was destroyed.

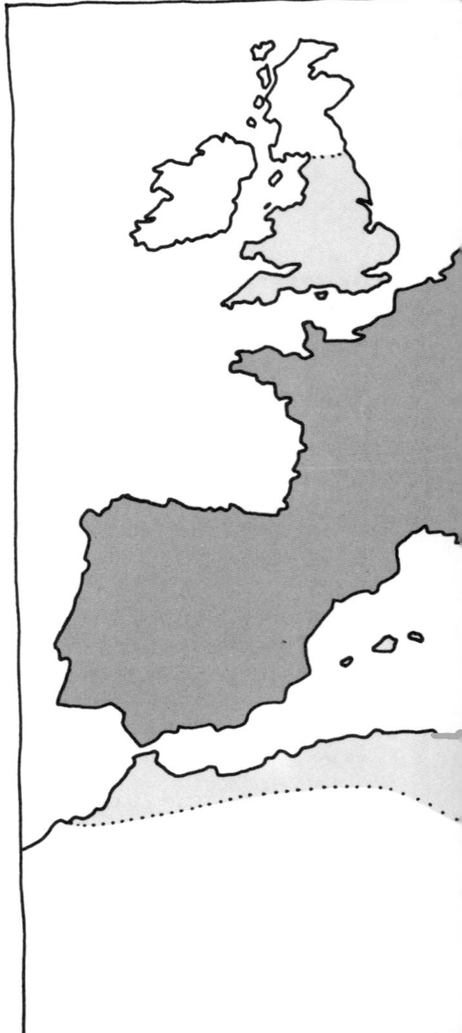

Clue 3

(To be read when you are awake and can think clearly.) Paul's letters tell us that he and Luke were travelling companions. Yet there are differences between Luke's information about Paul (in his second book, Acts) and what Paul writes about himself in his own letters. So it does not appear that Luke knew Paul's letters – otherwise his information would have been more in line with what Paul wrote. This could suggest that Luke's Gospel and his book of Acts were written *before Paul's letters were widely circulated*.

Since Ignatius of Antioch wrote about Paul's letters in AD110, we can assume that Paul's letters were widely circulated by that time and that Luke–Acts was probably written before this date.

Clue 4

(Definitely for detective fanatics or those who have nothing better to do.) The tone of Luke's Gospel tries to convince the Roman rulers of the day that Christianity was not a guerrilla movement set on overthrowing them. Luke is very pro-Roman in his writings. This emphasis of Luke's suggests that Rome had begun to take notice of Christians. Perhaps the Romans had noticed that the Christians were different from the Jews in their beliefs and were worried by this. Stress between Rome and Christianity intensified during the reign of

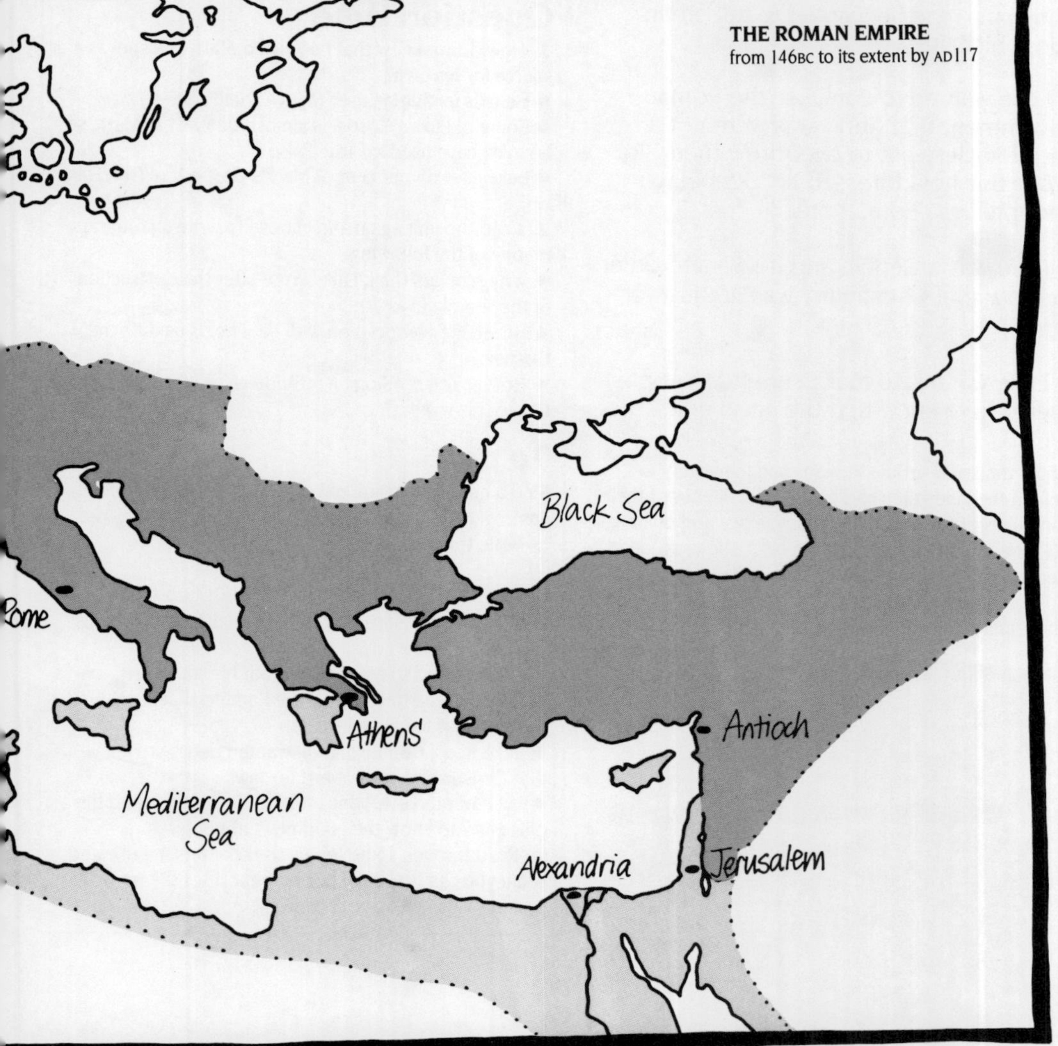

the Emperor Domitian in AD81–96 and it seems likely that Luke–Acts was written around this time.

Why did Luke write his Gospel?

Why should Luke, a Gentile (a non-Jew), go to such lengths to write about a Jewish preacher called Jesus whom he had never met? What caused him to take interest? There are various possible reasons:

- Elsewhere in the New Testament, Luke is always mentioned as being with Mark, so maybe Mark inspired him to write a Gospel as he had heard stories about Jesus.

- Luke became a follower of Jesus – a Christian – and he wanted to tell others about his faith.

- Luke wanted to convince the Roman government that Christians were not a secret society out to overthrow them. To prove this he addressed his Gospel to Theophilus, a Roman official.

- Luke was a Gentile and he wanted others to know that Christianity was not just for Jews.

- Luke wanted to make sure that people everywhere knew that the good news, the Gospel of Christ Jesus, was for the poor and the outcasts of society and not just those who were 'respectable'.

- Luke wanted to set out the full truth about Jesus because there were inaccurate and misleading gospels being published.

Perhaps Luke had just one of these reasons for writing, or perhaps more than one influenced his decision to write. As you read through his Gospel, you may form your own theory.

At the time of Jesus the Romans had constantly to defend the lands they had conquered. Scenes of their conquests ornamented triumphal arches and buildings in Rome. Trajan's column, shown here, shows scenes from the Dacian campaign. Luke may have written his Gospel partly to convince the Roman authorities that Christianity was not a threat to Roman rule.

FOLLOW UP

Question time

1. How do we know that Luke used Mark's Gospel as a source for his own?
- He tells us that he uses Mark True/False
- Some of Luke's Gospel is almost identical to Mark, so he must have used it True/False
- Luke uses 65 per cent of Mark's Gospel True/False

2. Read the unit again and choose to write a paragraph on one of the following:
- Why scholars think Luke wrote after the destruction of the Temple in AD70.
- How Luke's association with Paul helps us date the Gospel.
- How Luke's pro-Roman attitude gives us a clue to the time of his writing.

To do

Find a modern version of Luke's Gospel. Read through some of the chapters and, as you read, think 'Why did he write this Gospel?'

Get into groups of three to six people. Choose one of the following reasons why people think Luke wrote his Gospel:
- Luke wanted to tell others about his faith.
- Luke wanted to convince the Romans that Christians were not out to cause trouble.
- Luke was a Gentile and he wanted people to know that Christianity was not just for Jews.
- Luke wanted everyone – including the poor and the outcasts – to know the good news about Jesus.

Read through some (or all) the chapters in Luke and see if you can find evidence in the text for the particular point of view you have chosen.

John the Baptist

What happened when you were born?

Are there any stories about your birth that your family tell to one another? The race to the hospital? Your midnight arrival? Whatever? In the Bible, and in other stories of the ancient world, the birth of a baby with an important destiny was often accompanied by special signs and events. In Luke's Gospel, Luke begins the story of Jesus' life and ministry with the story of another birth – the prophet John the Baptist.

John is born

READ LUKE 1:5–7, 11–13, 18–20, 39–40, 57–64, 80

John's birth was not like any other child's. There were signs that he was going to grow up to become a great prophet. Luke points these out clearly. He often shows how John was either fulfilling or echoing something already mentioned in the Old Testament. Here are the signs surrounding John's birth.

Sign 1:
The Spirit appears Prophecy had disappeared from Israel about 400 years before John the Baptist was born. The Jews had the written books of the Old Testament prophets, just as we have today, but John's birth saw the beginning of a *new* activity of the Spirit. John's birth was to be the beginning of a new age, accompanied by joy and gladness. In this new age the ability to prophesy was to be given even to ordinary people, like John's mother and father.

Sign 2:
An angel appears to Zechariah and tells him that he will have a son called John. This is a little like the story of the appearance to Manoah before the birth of Samson in the Old Testament.

Sign 3:
'The babe leapt in her womb' (Luke 1:41). This shows that John, even before his birth, recognizes the greatness of Jesus and rejoices.

Sign 4:
Elizabeth is too old to have a baby. Yet the fact that Elizabeth did have a baby was a sure sign that her child came from God and had a special task to do.

Sign 5:
John is likened to Samson and Samuel – two national leaders of the Old Testament. John is also likened to the prophet Jeremiah in that he is possessed by the Holy Spirit even before his birth.

Sign 6:
Luke shows clearly that it is **the task of John to announce Jesus**. John appears to have the power of Elijah, a prophet in the Old Testament. Luke even quotes Malachi 3:1 to make the claim that Elijah will appear again to preach the Messiah. This is Luke's way of setting the stage for Jesus. John is the Elijah who was prophesied. Jesus is to be the Messiah.

FACT · FILE

A gallery of prophets

- *Elijah* was a famous prophet, written about in the Books of Kings. He opposed the evil King Ahab and Queen Jezebel. The Jews believed that he would return again to proclaim the Messiah.
- *Samson* was famous for his great strength. However, he disobeyed God and ended his life by being blinded by his enemies.
- *Jeremiah* was a prophet who prophesied doom and became very unpopular. Once he was even thrown into an underground reservoir because of his preaching. Yet, in the end, events proved him right.

It is clear from Luke's writing that John's birth had all the signs that he would grow up into a great man. In fact, that is just what he did do.

FOLLOW UP

Question time

1. Give the names of John the Baptist's parents.

2. Write a summary of the events surrounding the birth of John the Baptist.

3. Who was Elijah and why is he important in this story of John's birth?

4. Explain how Luke shows that the birth of John the Baptist was an important and special event.

To do

Write or draw the story of the birth of John the Baptist from the time the angel appeared to Zechariah to the point where he regained his speech.

The Ministry of John

Like the prophets of the Old Testament, John had a message for his times. He preached out in the desert by the River Jordan. There he *baptized* people in the water. We will be looking at what John's baptism meant later in this unit. He must have been a striking figure. Matthew's Gospel tells us:

- he ate locusts and wild honey
- he wore clothes made of camel's hair and had a leather belt tied round his waist
- he lived in the desert near the River Jordan.

People came to hear him from miles around. John's message was hard and direct. Repent! Be baptized! He told his listeners to show that their lives had really changed in the following ways:

- by sharing their possessions with people who had less than they had
- by being honest and straightforward in money matters
- by doing their jobs properly and not cheating on others.

The CLAY TABLET

By our Desert Correspondent, Dai O'Thirst

Remember the desert? It used to be a quiet place. But not any more. For the last few weeks crowds have been gathering by the River Jordan to hear John, a new rip-roaring prophet who's jumped out of nowhere. He **claims** to be 'a voice of one crying in the wilderness'. He **sounds** as though he's screaming his head off.

'It's the only way to get them to listen,' explained John, a bearded 30-year-old sporting a camel hair coat. We spoke to him while he was munching a plateful of locusts between turns.

'People have to change,' said John, 'because there are changes coming. They need to be honest and straightforward – there's too much lying and cheating these days.' When asked what changes were coming, John only hinted darkly that they would be **BIG**.

John baptizes people by splashing water on them, a sign that they want to change. We dare say a lot

of them could do with the wash. We wish John all the luck in the desert – keep screaming John – one day they might even hear you in Jerusalem!

In your Clay Tablet today:

- **win** two days at the circus in Rome
- **read** stars with the stars! – this year, will Salome get what she wants on a plate?
- **find out** the results of our exciting spot-the-camel competition

It's all in the Tablet! Keep taking it!

TOMORROW'S SPECIALS in the TABLET...

What was John like?

● *Who was he?* He told the crowds, 'Someone is shouting in the desert, "Get the road ready for the Lord; make a straight path for him."' This was a quote from the prophet Isaiah. John said that he was preparing the way for the coming Messiah. This is also what the angel had said in Luke 1:17.

● *What did he tell them?* He told his listeners that being members of God's chosen people, the children of Israel, was not enough to save them from God's judgment. They had to change their lives. They had to repent.

● *What did he do?* John baptized people. This was a sign that God had forgiven them and taken away their sins. Luke makes it clear that John was offering a new start to Israel – they were to prepare themselves for the coming of the Messiah – Jesus.

We do not have a picture of John growing up. All Luke records about his boyhood is: 'And the child became strong in spirit' (Luke 1:80). These words are like the words used of Samuel in 1 Samuel 2:26 and of Samson in Judges 13:24. Both these men, like John, were dedicated to God from birth.

The word 'repentance' comes from the Greek word *metanoia*, meaning 'to change your mind completely'.

John in the desert

John was not alone in the desert. He had *disciples*. They were the men who lived with him and followed his teaching. It was common practice for a religious leader to have his own disciples in those days.

It is possible that there was a connection between John and his disciples and the strict community of *Essenes* at Qumran by the Dead Sea.

The baptism of John

John baptized people. Jesus did not. But John did baptize Jesus. Ever since then *baptism* has been a *sacrament* of the church. Either as a child or as an adult, the chances are, if you are a Christian, you will have been baptized.

A **sacrament** is an important ceremony. It is to show the world outside that God has done something special within.

Why did John baptize?

It was a **sign of repentance** – baptism showed that you were sorry for all the bad things you had done previously and that you wanted a new start in life.

It was a **sign of forgiveness** – baptism was like being washed clean. It showed that God had forgiven you and that you could make a fresh start.

It was a **sign of change** – once you were baptized you could begin a new life.

It was a **sign to the world** – baptism meant that you showed in public what you felt in private. In being baptized you were showing your family, friends and neighbours that you needed to change and that you wanted to change.

Who did John baptize?

John baptized anyone who wanted to turn away from their sins. Probably most of the people who came to him were Jewish adults.

How did John baptize?

This is a tricky question. No one really knows the answer. The translation of the Greek text in the Bible could mean that John baptized either 'in' or 'with' water.

● Perhaps a person had to go right under the water and then come up again. This could be a sign of dying to the old life, being buried, and then rising to the new one.

● Perhaps the person stood in the river up to the waist and John poured water over that person's head. This could be a sign of God's love and God's Spirit being poured out over the head of the believer.

The original practice, however, is not known to us. All we know is that John baptized in the River Jordan.

Why did John baptize Jesus?

Had Jesus done anything wrong?
Did Jesus need to repent?

Traditionally the Christian church believes that Jesus did not sin. Jesus did not need to repent. Therefore Jesus did not need to be baptized. Baptism for Jesus was not just a new start, it was the beginning of his ministry.

Baptism today

Because Jesus told his disciples to baptize, the Christian church has always baptized its members. But different branches of the church baptize in different ways.

All churches believe in the importance of baptism and in the meaning of baptism. They differ in the *practice* of baptism and still talk about their differences even today.

● In the Roman Catholic Church and the Anglican Church (and some other churches too) **child baptism** is practised.

These churches state that the children of believing parents are welcomed fully into the Christian family. Later, when the child is older, and able to make promises for him or herself, there is a ceremony of *confirmation*.

● In the Baptist Church and other 'Free' churches, **adult baptism** is practised.

Why? These churches state that baptism is only for someone who comes to believe the Christian message personally. Usually these churches practise *full immersion*. The person being baptized is submerged fully in water and then rises again. This can be done in a specially-built water tank in the church, in a river, or even in the sea.

Baptism shows that a person is sorry for past wrong and wants to change. It shows that they are washed clean, ready for a new start. John baptized people who came to him. And Jesus told his disciples to baptize those who wanted to follow him. Today some churches baptize children, others only adults, but all believe in the importance of baptism.

FOLLOW UP

Question time

1. Fill in the following sentences:
John the Baptist ate ____________.
He wore ____________ and lived in ____________.
John told his listeners to change their lives by sharing ____________ being ____________ and doing their jobs properly and not ____________.

2. The word repentance means ____________.

3. Why was baptism important in John's message? Why is it important in the church today?

To do

● Write and produce a news item on John the Baptist for Galilee Television. You will need a group of about six people. Elect an interviewer, spectators (e.g. a priest or a local) and someone being baptized. Your interview should tackle the following:
What John is like.
Why he is attracting the crowd.
Why people are being baptized.
When you have finished, perform it in class.

● Design a survey for your class or school on baptism. Find out who has been baptized. Why? Has it meant anything to them or to others? What did you learn from the survey?

Talking-point

How easy is it to speak up for what you think is right? Is it possible to repent? If so, how?

The End of a Prophet

John the Baptist in the other Gospels

Matthew tells us about John's preaching, appearance and death. See Matthew 3 and Matthew 14:1–12.

Mark opens his Gospel with an account of John. He tells us about John's appearance and death. See Mark 1 and Mark 6:14–29.

John (a different John, remember) shows John the Baptist proclaiming Jesus as the Messiah, 'the Lamb of God'.

All four Gospels show John as announcing the coming of Jesus.

John in danger

Prophets in the Bible always had a hard time. What they said often made them unpopular and they were beaten, imprisoned or even killed. John the Baptist was no exception to this. He spoke out against the ruler, Herod, because he had divorced his wife to marry Herodias, his brother's wife. Such a marriage was against Jewish Law and John said that it was wrong.

John had already criticized Herod for many of the other evil things that he had done. But this was the last straw. John was put in prison.

Matthew 14 and Mark 6 tell us about John's death. Luke does not.

- On Herod's birthday his niece, Salome, danced at the party.
- Herod was so pleased with her that he promised to give the girl whatever she asked.
- Encouraged by her mother, Salome asked for the head of John the Baptist on a dish.
- Herod did not want to kill John. Yet he had given his promise to Salome and so he gave orders for John to be beheaded.
- John's head was given to Salome on a dish and she gave it to her mother.
- John's disciples came, took his body, and buried it. Then they went and told Jesus.

In this sad way, John the Baptist ended his life.

The work of prophets

In the Bible, the prophets had two tasks. They had to speak out against evil and injustice *in the present*. And they also warned what would happen *in the future* if people refused to listen to what God was saying through them. We usually think of prophets as people who predict the future. But a true prophet (in the Bible's sense) wants to see the world changed for the better today and tomorrow.

This was exactly what John the Baptist did. He told people to repent and change their ways. And he predicted what would happen to them if they refused to do so. There are some individuals and organizations who work in this prophetic way in our own times.

Oxfam works in many developing countries and speaks out against hunger, disease and exploitation.

Greenpeace warns of the dangers of pollution and the damage caused by bad use of the earth's resources.

Amnesty International speaks out for prisoners all over the world who have been jailed for their beliefs.

In the Bible, prophecy is something more than all this. It is a *spiritual* activity, calling people to God. It is not just political, economic or environmental. Prophets were often unpopular because their message was hard-hitting, and many of them had to pay for their beliefs with their lives.

Modern prophets

Oscar Romero

was a Roman Catholic priest. In the 1970s he was appointed Archbishop of El Salvador, a country ruled by a violent, military regime. The government thought that Romero would be too quiet to speak out against them and their cruelty — but they were wrong. In 1977 a peaceful protest in San Salvador was brutally broken up by the police when they fired directly into the crowd.

Oscar Romero changed suddenly. He began to speak out strongly for the country's poor. Once he asked, 'What good are beautiful highways, and airports, beautiful buildings full of spacious apartments, if they are only put together with the blood of the poor?'

On 24 March 1980 Romero was shot dead as he celebrated mass in the cathedral. But he and his words have not been forgotten.

Dietrich Bonhoeffer

was a German theologian with a strong social conscience. When Hitler came to power in Germany in 1933, the Nazis quickly began to impose control. They forbade public meetings, limited the freedom of the press, and sent many people to prison. Bonhoeffer spoke out against this, but in 1934 the church was forbidden to criticize the government.

Soon Hitler began his terrible persecution of the Jews and in 1939 the Second World War broke out. Bonhoeffer worked with the German resistance and helped the small groups of Jews fleeing from the Nazis to escape over the border into Switzerland. He also plotted to overthrow Hitler. In 1943 he was arrested as an enemy to Hitler and his Reich and was put in prison.

Then, in 1944, a bomb exploded, wounding, but not killing Hitler. Hundreds of people were arrested after this and Bonhoeffer's part in the plot was discovered. On 9 April 1945, less than a month before the war ended, Bonhoeffer was put on trial, condemned, and hanged.

Are there prophets today? Organizations like Greenpeace warn of the dangers of pollution.

We have seen how the birth of John the Baptist was the beginning of a *new age*. Although this is true, it is also true that for Christians John the Baptist's life and ministry marked the end of the *old age* – the age of the Old Testament. Luke shows that John the Baptist is like Elijah. He is the last great prophet in line with the prophets found in the Old Testament. Luke makes it clear that John's task was to announce the coming of the Messiah – Jesus.

So, John was the end of the old – Jesus was the beginning of the new.

Individuals also speak out against those who exploit people. Desmond Tutu is one of those who speak for the oppressed, reminding us that God values every person equally, regardless of race, colour, wealth or status.

FOLLOW UP

Question time

1. What have you learned about John the Baptist from Gospels other than Luke?

2. How does the Old Testament illustrate Christian belief about John the Baptist?

3. What is prophecy in the Bible? What is its purpose?

4. How important is it for Christians to be prophets in the world today?

To do

Here are some views people have about baptism. Which of these is most popular with your class and why?

- Everyone who belongs to the Christian faith should be baptized when they are a baby.
- No one who is not a Christian should be allowed to be baptized.
- It's everyone's right to be baptized, whether they belong to the church or not.
- It's not right to baptize children. They should be baptized only when they are old enough to decide for themselves that they are believers.

Now arrange an interview with your local vicar/priest/pastor or church leader. Ask him/her to comment on the list and to tell you why they think as they do.

The Birth of a King

What happens when a royal baby is born?

- Crowds gather outside the hospital.
- Cameras record the first news.
- Newspapers are full of the event.
- Everyone wants to know the name.

In the first two chapters of his Gospel Luke tells us about Jesus' birth.

Luke was a historian. He was writing about real events and real people. But he was also trying to show that God was active in history. For Luke, therefore, the birth of Jesus had a special *meaning*.

The stories about Jesus' birth and boyhood are found in the first two chapters of Luke.

What is Luke trying to show in his first two chapters?

He says that Jesus was foretold by the prophets of the Old Testament. What had been promised and written about centuries before was finally going to happen!

- Luke emphasizes *continuity*. He says that the New Testament follows directly on from the Old. *The old covenant* was the relationship God formed with the Children of Israel through Abraham. *The new covenant* was to be the new relationship that God formed with the church through Jesus.
- Luke also emphasizes *promise* and *fulfilment*. By constantly quoting the Old Testament, Luke pictures Jesus as the Messiah.

Luke was probably a Gentile, a non-Jew. His Gospel has a strong *Greek* interest, but Luke 1 and 2 are very *Hebraic* in style. The two chapters are written in the style of a Jewish legend or poem. Perhaps they came from a written Hebrew source and were later translated into Greek.

The birth of Jesus foretold

READ LUKE 1:26–38

The mother of Jesus and the father of John

There are some striking similarities between the birth of Jesus and the birth of John.

- Mary is **troubled** (Luke 1:29), like Zechariah (1:12).
- The angel **reassures** Mary (Luke 1:30), just as he reassures Zechariah (Luke 1:13).
- The angel **prophesies** to Mary about Jesus' birth and destiny (Luke 1:31–33). These are like the words that the angel uses to Zechariah about John the Baptist (Luke 1:13–17).
- Mary asks how she can have a child, being still a virgin (Luke 1:34). This is similar to Zechariah's question about how Elizabeth, his wife, can have a child as she is so old (Luke 1:18).

Mary was a *virgin*. This meant that she was going to give birth to Jesus without first having had sexual intercourse. Mary is presented as a virgin in fulfilment of the prophecy in Isaiah 7:14. Luke mentions Mary's virginity but does not quote the prophecy (see Matthew 1:21). Matthew adds that Joseph planned to divorce Mary quietly – but then an angel appeared to him in a dream and told him not to (Matthew 1:19–21).

Mary is presented as a virgin in Matthew and Luke. Mark and John do not mention this. In fact, the Gospel writers tell us very little about Mary. They do not mention her age, her appearance, her birth or her death. Yet Luke obviously thought the virgin birth was important. It was important in order to understand Jesus' person, nature and ministry.

What could Luke's reasons for this have been?

- *The virgin birth is true.* It is historical. Luke wrote down the events just as they happened. This means that he had reliable documents *or* he checked the story with eyewitnesses – perhaps even with Mary herself.

Jesus was born in the small hill-town of Bethlehem, just a few miles south of Jerusalem.

● *The virgin birth is a story* that grew up about Jesus after his death.

Either way, the virgin birth is controversial, but several *theological* reasons have been put forward as to why Luke wished to present Jesus as being born of a virgin.

The theology of the virgin birth

● Luke's writing has a strong Greek interest. He also seems to be pro-Roman. Luke's Gospel may well have been for Gentile, non-Jewish readers. The Greeks and Romans had many stories about great heroes who were *literally* thought to be children of the gods. Often such children had an earthly mother and a heavenly father. Hercules is an example of this. The Egyptian king, the pharaoh, was also believed to be the son of the sun-god. He, too, had an earthly mother and a heavenly father. Many rulers and important figures in the ancient world, therefore, were thought to be in some way divine. It could be that in order to present Jesus as an extraordinary person, Luke wrote about Jesus as having a 'heavenly' birth from a virgin.

● In the Old Testament, the Spirit of God came upon prophets to inspire them. Then the Spirit left them again. *But Jesus was born in the Spirit.* He did not have to acquire the Spirit – he had it right from conception. Luke uses this point to emphasize Jesus' extraordinary nature.

● Jesus is the beginning of a *new kind of humanity*. He is a new kind of human being. His birth marks the fulfilment and end of the old age and the beginning of the new.

If you look at the two genealogies (family trees) of Jesus, in Matthew 1:1–16 and Luke 3:23–38, you can see that they are different. Matthew places his genealogy at the beginning of the birth story; Luke places his at the beginning of Jesus' ministry. If you compare Luke with Matthew, Jesus is not only the heir of David and the seed of Abraham. He is also the second or *eschatological* Adam and the Son of God. (The word *eschatological* is used to describe something that has to do with *the end of the world*.)

In the first century AD, about 5–600,000 Jews lived in Palestine. Three and a half million were scattered in other countries. Many of the Jews who lived in these other countries spoke Greek. They had their own version of the Old Testament in Greek, called the *Septuagint*. In Hebrew the prophecy of Isaiah 7:14 says a *young girl* will give birth. The Hebrew word was translated into Greek as *virgin*. Perhaps Luke understood the word in this context – i.e. that Mary was a virgin.

Or did Luke include this story because it fulfilled the prophecy he found in Isaiah?

Whatever view we take about whether Mary was *actually* a virgin, Luke makes it plain that God was about to do something new for the world with the birth of Jesus.

Artists down the ages have pictured the virgin and child. This is a twelfth-century portrait from Istanbul.

Mary in the Gospels

For all the importance that she has gained in the tradition of the church, Mary is not mentioned very often in the Gospels. In John's Gospel she is not even mentioned by name.

1. She is mentioned at the birth of Jesus – Luke 1 and 2; Matthew 1 and 2.
2. She looks for the boy Jesus at the Temple – Luke 2:41–52. (Here, and at the wedding feast at Cana are the only times we have on record when Jesus and Mary speak to each other.)
3. She arrives when Jesus is preaching – Mark 3:31.
4. She is mentioned when Jesus preaches

at Nazareth – Mark 6:3 (not in Luke).
5. She is present at the wedding in Cana – John 2:1–11.
6. She is at the foot of the cross – John 19:25.
7. In Luke's Gospel Mary speaks four times – in Matthew she is silent.
8. Mary is with the disciples as they pray in the upper room – Acts 1:14.
9. Paul mentions in his letter to the Galatians that Christ was 'born of a woman' (Galatians 4:4). It would have been unusual to mention this and perhaps it shows that Mary was already becoming important to the early church. (The letter to the Galatians is one of the earliest New Testament documents. It was probably written around AD57.)

Mary today

Mary is a very important figure in the Roman Catholic church. Protestant Christians, however, have never given her very much significance. If you go into a Roman Catholic church (and some Anglican churches) you will find a statue of Mary as well as a statue of Jesus. Mary is a mother – she is human. Because she is the mother of Jesus, and because she understands what it is to be human, many Roman Catholics ask Mary to pray for them. They divide her story into four parts, each with a special title:

- *Annunciation* – this is when the angel comes to tell Mary she will have a baby.
- *Visitation* – this is when Mary goes to see her cousin Elizabeth.
- *Nativity* – this is the story of the birth of Jesus at Bethlehem.
- *Purification* – this is the account of Jesus' circumcision eight days after he was born.

Roman Catholics also have four beliefs about Mary. These beliefs have grown up in the tradition of the church over hundreds of years. They are called *dogmas.*

- *Divine Motherhood* – Mary is the mother of God.
- *Virgin* – Mary was a virgin when she gave birth to Jesus *and remained a virgin always.* Jesus' brothers, mentioned in Luke 8:19 and Mark 3:31, were cousins, or Joseph's children by a previous marriage.
- *Immaculate Conception* – Mary had no sin like other human beings. In order to give birth to Jesus, who was perfect, in some way she had to be perfect herself.
- *Assumption* – Mary did not die like other people, but was taken directly into heaven.

Some dates

- 1854 – the dogma of Immaculate Conception declared.
- 1954 – Mary declared Queen of Heaven.
- 1950 – the Assumption is made an article of faith by Pope Pius XII.

FOLLOW UP

Question time

1. Explain what is meant by the old covenant and the new covenant.

2. How important is it for Christians to believe in the virgin birth?
- It is very important for Christians to believe in the virgin birth, because ______________ and if they do not believe it means ______________.
- It really doesn't matter if Christians believe in the virgin birth or not, because ______________.
- It is very difficult to believe in the virgin birth, because if you do you have to ______________.

3. How would a belief in the virgin birth help Christian believers today?

4. What theological reasons may Luke have had for including the story of the virgin birth?

5. How important is Mary in the church today?

To do

- Design a Christmas card based on one aspect of the birth story from Luke's Gospel.
- Using both Matthew and Luke, imagine that Joseph kept a personal diary. What kinds of things might he have written when he discovered Mary was pregnant?
  Now do the same for Mary. What might she have felt and thought at this time?

The Birth of Jesus

In western countries Christmas Day must be the best-known day of the whole year. Families come together. It is the time of peace and goodwill. People give presents, eat turkey and watch television. They hang decorations and put up a tree. Christmas is the time of tinsel, bright lights, Santa Claus and Rudolph the red-nosed reindeer.

But 25 December is also the day when the Christian church celebrates Jesus Christ's birth. It is a time for a different kind of rejoicing. Christians believe that in the person of Jesus, God became a human being. Christmas Day, therefore, is a very special date in the Christian calendar.

Was Jesus really born on 25 December?

We do not know the *date* when Jesus was born – and not all Christians celebrate Christmas on 25 December. The Russian and Greek Orthodox Churches have their Christmas on 6 January. That is when most other parts of the Christian church celebrate *epiphany* – the time when the wise men brought gifts of gold, frankincense and myrrh to the baby Jesus.

If we do not know the exact date when Jesus was born, why do we celebrate Christmas on 25 December? There are at least two explanations:

25 December is close to 21 December. That is the date of the *winter solstice*, the shortest day of the year. It is exactly the middle of winter. It is when pagan northern peoples used to light fires to celebrate the return of the sun. Light overcoming darkness is an idea strongly associated with Jesus.

The Romans used to have a festival called *Saturnalia* which took place towards the end of December. This was a time for throwing parties and giving presents – just like some aspects of Christmas today. In the early days of Christianity, Christians decided to try to 'Christianize' this pagan festival by celebrating the birth of Jesus at the same time.

Do we know the year of Jesus' birth?

Christian countries have two ways of counting the years. They are:

BC=Before Christ.

AD=Anno Domini (this is Latin, meaning 'In the year of our Lord').

We know certain facts from the Bible that we can check with other writers. We know:
- when Herod the Great ruled (he died in 4BC)
- when Quirinius was governor of Syria (from AD6–9)
- when Augustus was emperor of Rome (from 31BC to AD14).

Jesus was probably born between 6BC and AD6. But this is only a guess, based on the dates above. Scholars have tried to fit the story in the Bible with what we know of history at the time, and there are problems in discovering the exact year of Jesus' birth.

Almost everyone knows the Christmas story. The popular version goes like this: Mary and Joseph went to Bethlehem (Mary on a donkey). When they arrived there was no room at the inn. Mary gave birth to Jesus in a stable and laid him in a manger. Afterwards, with the ox and the ass looking on, shepherds, wise men and angels gathered around to sing, rejoice and worship.

But wait a minute! The Christmas story, as told each Christmas, is a *mixture* of the accounts in Matthew and Luke. On top of that, centuries of tradition have added extra details – including some of the best-known ones. If you study Luke's account of Jesus' birth, it is amazing how short it is.

Jesus is born

READ LUKE 2:1–7

This passage shows us three things about how Luke sees Jesus' birth.

Luke stresses history
Luke places the birth of Jesus in history by mentioning real people like Caesar Augustus and Quirinius. Notice how Luke gives Jesus' birth a *world setting*. He does not do this for the birth of John the Baptist. Luke shows how God works even through the Roman Empire to bring about his ends.

Luke stresses prophecy
Micah 5:2 prophesied that the Messiah would come from Bethlehem. David, Israel's greatest king, was born there and Joseph is a descendant of David. It is important, therefore, that Luke shows the Messiah as being born in Bethlehem.

Luke stresses symbolism
– There is the symbol of Bethlehem – Jesus is the Messiah.
– There is the symbol of the manger – Jesus has a humble birth.
– There is the symbol of the shepherds (in Luke 2:8–20) – they represent the poor and the outcast whom God wants to welcome into his Kingdom.
– There is the symbol of the angels (in Luke 2:13–14) – they show God at work and the rejoicing in heaven at Jesus' birth.

Shepherds and angels

READ LUKE 2:8–20

The shepherds were humble people. They were looked down on because their work kept them from joining in all the Jewish feasts and ceremonies. They appear in the story as the people God wishes to bring into his Kingdom. There are many others in Luke's Gospel. The shepherds also show *wonder*. This is something Luke mentions again and again. There are many wonders to come.

The birth of Jesus: two writers

This is how **Matthew** records the birth of Jesus:
- Visit of the wise men and appearance of the star (Matthew 2:1–12). Matthew does not say that the wise men were kings or that there were only three of them.

● There is much more about Herod in Matthew's account.
● Matthew's account includes the escape to Egypt (Matthew 2:13–18). It also includes the slaughter of the innocents. This was when Herod killed all the boys under two years of age in and around Bethlehem (Matthew 2:16).
● Matthew has very little about Jesus' actual birth. There is no census, no inn, and no manger.

Luke's account has the following elements:
● Luke has the census (Luke 2:1).
● Luke has the inn and the manger (Luke 2:7).
● Luke has the story of the shepherds (Luke 2:8–20).
● Luke includes the account of the angels' appearance (Luke 2:9–14).

Luke's account of Jesus' birth may be short, but there can be no doubt that Luke treats these events as being very important. Jesus' birth, after all, was the beginning of a new era of God's activity in the world. But how is this expressed?

The Spirit appears

The Holy Spirit appears in power. This was the same Spirit, active in the Old Testament, who spoke through the Old Testament prophets. In the first two chapters of Luke (the chapters that deal with the birth of Jesus) the Holy Spirit is mentioned no less than *six* times (Luke 1:15, 1:41, 1:67, 2:25, 2:26, 2:27).

Angels appear

These messengers from God are signs of his extraordinary activity and they speak for God.
● *Luke* 1:11 An angel appears to Zechariah to announce the birth of John the Baptist.
● *Luke* 1:26 Gabriel, the angel, appears to Mary, the mother of Jesus. He tells her that she will have a son.
● *Luke* 2:9–14 Angels appear to the shepherds. An angel tells the shepherds that Jesus has been born at Bethlehem. These lowly men are the first people to know about the birth of the Messiah.

FACT FILE

Angels

Angels sometimes appear in the Old Testament story. They were messengers from God. Sometimes they looked like ordinary people, and sometimes they took other forms. In the Bible they usually appear when something important is going to happen. The three most important angels were called **archangels**. Their names were:
- **Gabriel** who appeared to Mary and Zechariah
- **Raphael** and
- **Michael**.

The church today – songs of gladness

The birth of Jesus is accompanied by joy and gladness. There are many references to this. When they realize what is happening, Mary, Zechariah and Simeon (an old priest – see the next Unit), sing songs of joy. These songs are still used in many churches today. Together they are called *canticles* and each one has a special name:

● Mary's song is called the *Magnificat* (Luke 1:46–55). It is based on the Song of Hannah (mother of the prophet Samuel) in 1 Samuel 2:1–10. It is also like Miriam's song of praise after the defeat of the Egyptians in Exodus 15:20–21). It shows how Mary is like the *remnant of Israel*. In the Old Testament the remnant refers to the few people who have kept faithful to God's Law.

● Zechariah's song is called the *Benedictus* (Luke 1:68–79).

● The angels' song is called the *Gloria in Excelsis* (Luke 2:14).

● Simeon's song is called the *Nunc Dimittis* (Luke 2:29–32).

FACT FILE

- **Jesus** means 'God saves'.
- **Christ** means 'anointed one' – the kings of Israel were anointed to show they had been chosen by God. 'Christ' is the Greek translation of the Hebrew word 'Messiah'.
- **Immanuel** (from the prophecy in Isaiah 7:14) means 'God with us'.
- 'Jesus' is the Greek form of the Jewish name *Joshua*. In the Old Testament, Joshua led God's people into the Promised Land (Joshua 3). Jesus' full name would have been *Joshua ben Joseph* (*ben* meaning 'son of'). Luke presents Jesus as **Saviour**, **Christ** and **Lord**.

Who was this baby?

Luke presents the baby Jesus as:

- the Son of God
- the promised Messiah. The Messiah was to be a great king. He was to rule over Israel and save the country from its enemies. He was also to save the people from their sins. The Messiah's rule was to be *kingly* and *godly*.

The first people to be told about the birth of Jesus were some shepherds, out on the hills around Bethlehem, minding their sheep. They were rough, poor and uneducated – not the sort of people we might expect to receive a deputation of angels!

FOLLOW UP

Question time

1. What have you learned about the date of Jesus' birth?

2. Why do we celebrate Christmas on 25 December?

3. What symbolism lies behind:
Bethlehem
The manger
The shepherds
The angels?

4. How does Luke express Christian belief about the baby Jesus?

To do

● Do you know the difference between Matthew's story of the birth of Jesus and Luke's? Attempt this quiz, then check your answers against the accounts in Matthew and Luke.
Visit of wise men and star   Matthew or Luke?
Mention of inn and manger   Matthew or Luke?
The story of the shepherds   Matthew or Luke?
There is much more about Herod in   Matthew or Luke?
Mary and Joseph flee into Egypt   Matthew or Luke?
The angels appear   Matthew or Luke?
The census   Matthew or Luke?

● Is the Christmas story important for people? It is not unusual for some people to say that Christmas has lost its meaning and that it is commercialized. Find out if the community in your area think there is a religious side to Christmas. Design a questionnaire and include the following questions:

What three things on this list are most important to you at Christmas?
- the family get together
- Christmas dinner: turkey and plum pudding
- good television
- presents – giving and receiving
- seeing the children enjoy themselves
- the religious meaning
- carols
- spirit of good will
- mistletoe and decorations
- parties

Christmas has no meaning for you – why?

Add some of your own questions to the survey. Test it out on people and then come together with your class or group and discuss the result.
Write up your findings in your file.

● Interview the local priest/vicar/minister. Ask him or her what Christmas means to them in terms of their religious faith.

● Read the following verses from well-known carols and identify the Christian beliefs about Jesus which are expressed in them.

He came down to earth from heaven
Who is God and Lord of all,
And His shelter was a stable,
And His cradle was a stall;
With the poor and mean and lowly
Lived on earth our Saviour holy.

Christ, by highest heaven adored;
Christ, the everlasting Lord;
Late in time behold Him come,
Offspring of a virgin's womb:
Veiled in flesh the Godhead see;
Hail the incarnate Deity,
Pleased as Man with man to dwell,
Jesus our Emmanuel!
Hark the herald angels sing
Glory to the new-born King.

Hail the heaven-born Prince of peace,
Hail the Sun of righteousness;
Light and life to all He brings,
Risen with healing in His wings.
Mild, he lays His glory by,
Born that man no more may die,
Born to raise the sons of earth,
Born to give them second birth.

UNIT 4.3

Jesus in the Temple

When you were a baby you may have been *christened* or *baptized*. Water was poured over your head in church. This was a sign that you had become part of God's family, the church. Many churches baptize babies, although some baptize only adult believers.

The Jews did not baptize babies. But they did *circumcise* baby boys. Circumcision is the removal of the foreskin of a boy's penis. Other nations apart from the Jews practise circumcision. But, in Judaism, circumcision has a special *religious significance*. Circumcision was part of God's 'covenant' (or agreement) with Abraham, the father of the Jews (see Genesis 17:10–14).

READ LUKE 2:21–24

Like all other Jewish boys, Jesus was circumcised when he was eight days old. This was part of the Jewish Law. Luke stresses very strongly that everything connected with Jesus' birth was carried out according to Jewish Law. He notes this no less than *five* times in Luke 2, verses 22, 23, 24, 27 and 39.

Mary and Joseph took Jesus to the Temple in Jerusalem, where:

- Jesus was circumcised (Luke 2:21)
- Jesus was consecrated to God (Luke 2:22 – see Exodus 13:2, 12)
- A sacrifice was offered to God (Luke 2:24 – see Leviticus 12:8)

Simeon and Anna

READ LUKE 2:25–40

In this passage, Anna and Simeon act as *representative figures*. They show certain truths about Israel which Luke wishes to write about.

Simeon is 'righteous and devout' (Luke 2:25). He is waiting for the *consolation of Israel*. That is, he is waiting for God to come and comfort Israel.

Anna is also very faithful. She worships, fasts and prays (Luke 2:37). She is waiting for the *redemption of Israel*. That is, she is waiting for God to come and save Israel for himself.

Both Anna and Simeon are very old. They are part of the Old Testament era that has come to an end with the birth of Jesus. Simeon has been promised that he will not die until he has seen the Messiah (Luke 2:26). Simeon says that Jesus will be a *saviour* for the Gentiles and for Israel. Jesus therefore is to be the Messiah for the whole world.

Luke 2:35. The sword that will pierce Mary's soul is a reference to Jesus' death.

Jesus goes missing

READ LUKE 2:41–52

This is a very human story. Mary and Joseph lose Jesus. They go back to Jerusalem to find him. They discover him after three days in the Temple. Mary is worried, but Jesus answers her by saying,

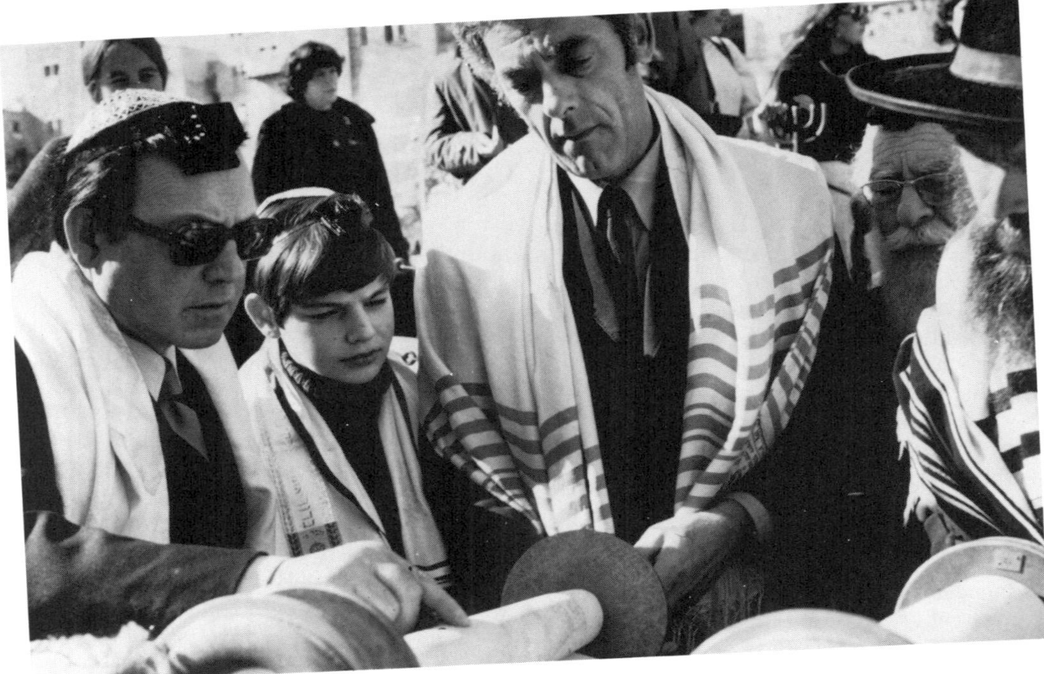

A Jewish boy has his bar mitzvah (today normally at the age of thirteen) at the Western Wall in Jerusalem.

'Didn't you know I had to be in my father's house?'

This might seem a strange answer to give to your mother!

Look at this story closely once more:

- Mary and Joseph do not realize that Jesus has stayed behind in Jerusalem.
- They find him only after three days (three is always a special number in the Bible).
- He is in the Temple – the Jews' holiest place, and God's house.
- He is with the teachers of the Law.
- They are amazed at what the boy Jesus knows about God and the Law.
- Jesus answers his mother's worried question in a strange way.
- He goes back to Nazareth and is *obedient* to them. He does what his parents tell him.
- Mary is pleased and finds a special meaning in Jesus' behaviour.
- Luke 2:52 echoes and increases the words of Luke 2:40.

This was not just an incident in Jesus' daily life. It is a story with a special meaning.

The account of Jesus' circumcision shows Jesus becoming part of the people of God, like all Jewish boys. He was recognized as the Messiah only by Anna and Simeon.

The account of Jesus' boyhood and his visit to the Temple has a similar meaning. The Passover was the most important Jewish festival. It celebrated God's freeing of Israel from slavery in the land of Egypt. Many Jews went to the Temple in Jerusalem to celebrate this feast.

The passage tells us that Jesus was twelve (Luke 2:42). This was the age when a Jewish boy became an *adult*. The Jews have a special ceremony to mark this called *bar mitzvah*. The bar mitzvah is when a boy stops being a boy and becomes a man.

So this story shows Jesus becoming an adult. Jesus makes a break with his earthly parents by leaving them for the Temple. Instead he wishes to become closer to his heavenly Father. This is the reason for his strange answer to Mary in Luke 2:49.

From now on Jesus is more aware of himself as the Son of God.

The end of the beginning

Luke is the only Gospel writer to tell us anything at length about the boyhood of Jesus. His account includes the three most important events in any Jewish boy's life:

- his birth
- his circumcision – the sign that he is part of the people of God
- his bar mitzvah – when he is twelve and becomes an adult

Through an account using history, prophecy and symbolism, Luke has set the scene for the main part of Jesus' life. He is to be the Messiah who will save the whole world. His life will be lived in the power of the Spirit in signs, prophecies, miracles, prayer, joy and gladness. Jesus' ministry is about to begin.

FOLLOW UP

Question time

1. What is circumcision and what is its religious significance?

2. On what day are Jewish boys circumcised?

3. What do you know about Simeon? What was he waiting for?

4. Who was Anna and what was she waiting for?

5. Luke is the only Gospel to tell us anything at length about the boyhood of Jesus. Read the story again. What important thing is Luke showing us about Jesus in this passage?

To do

- Write a short play about Mary and Joseph losing Jesus in Jerusalem. Include Mary and Joseph and Jesus as main characters and any others you may need. Stay as close to the actual story as you can but expand it to produce a life-like episode of what might have been said and done.

- Find out about Jewish bar mitzvah. Write about it and illustrate your account.

- Design a poster of HAVE YOU SEEN THIS BOY? In it, describe Jesus, his age, characteristics and where he was last seen. Offer a reward for information leading to his discovery.

Jesus the Son of God

Think for a minute how people describe you to others. Sometimes you hear yourself called many different names . . . take Geoff, for instance.

These sort of comments tell us what different people think about Geoff. The Gospel writers, Matthew, Mark, Luke and John, do the same thing. They tell us who they think Jesus is by using various titles for him. The first one we are going to look at is the title **Son of God**.

Background to the term 'Son of God'

The term 'Son of God' is mentioned in different ways:

- **The Messianic Son of God in Judaism**

The idea of a Messiah who is Son of God goes back to God's promise to King David in the Old Testament. God promised David that his descendants would succeed him on the throne of Israel and that one of them would be the Son of God. Passages in the Old Testament to look up are: 2 Samuel 7:14, Psalm 89 and Psalm 2:7.

Psalm 2 declares that the coming ruler will be called the King and God's Son. While there is an Old Testament background for the title, the expression 'Son of God' never became a popular way of describing the Messiah among the Jews.

- **The idea of the divine man in Greek thought**

Another possible background to 'Son of God' is in the Greek idea of *divine men*. The Greeks believed in men who were thought to possess divine power and the ability to work miracles.

- **The Son of God in the Gospels**

Right at the beginning of his Gospel, Mark (in Mark 1:1) makes it clear that he understands Christ to be the Son of God. Matthew also says that the disciple Peter realized that Jesus is both the expected Messiah and the Son of God (Matthew 16:16). He showed this in Peter's declaration at Caesarea Philippi.

One thing is very important: in the synoptic Gospels Jesus never uses the title 'Son of God' to describe himself. But he does frequently refer to himself as 'the Son'.

Luke and 'Son of God'

There are some important passages in Luke's Gospel where Jesus is referred to as the Son of God . . .

At his baptism

'And a voice came from heaven, "You are my own dear Son. I am pleased with you"' (Luke 3:22).

How are we to understand this? A voice comes from heaven and says that Jesus is God's Son and has pleased God.

- Is Jesus realizing at his baptism that he loves God as a son loves a good father?
- Or is God appointing Jesus at his baptism to be his Son in the world?
- Or was Jesus God's only Son before his baptism and is God confirming what was already true?

At his temptation

'The Devil said to him, "If you are God's Son, order this stone to become bread"' (Luke 4:3).

The Devil realizes that Jesus, as the Son of God, could call upon God's supernatural power to help him. The Gospel writers believed in this kind of power (see Mark 1:24 where Jesus, at the start of his ministry, is recognized by demons).

At his trial by the Council

'They all said, "Are you then, the Son of God?"' (Luke 22:70).

In Luke's Gospel, Jesus does not deny this; neither does he *claim* that he is God's Son. He replies, 'You say that I am.' The Council take this as an admission that Jesus is claiming to be the Son of God: now they can accuse him of blasphemy.

Why was this? What did the title 'Son of God' mean to people in Jesus' day? Why were the Jewish religious leaders so furious when the title was applied to Jesus?

The meaning of the term 'Son of God'

Scholars point out that 'Son of God' can be used in at least *four* different ways:

A human being may be called a son of God because God created him or her.

A person may be a son of God because he/she loves and obeys God and calls him a heavenly Father.

The title 'Son of God' was given to the kings of Israel who thought of themselves as special representatives of God. They believed that God had chosen them to rule for him.

In the New Testament, and in later Christian thought, 'Son of God' is given a higher meaning. Jesus is the Son of God because **he is God** and shares the divine nature of God (see especially John's Gospel).

An important passage for studying how Jesus is understood in the synoptic Gospels is: Matthew 11:25–27/Luke 10:21–22. This passage uses material common to Matthew and Luke only.

READ LUKE 10:21–22 

Notice what the passage says:

- *God has hidden the truth from the wise.* The Kingdom of God was not acknowledged by everyone.
- *God the Father has given Jesus all things.* Christ has been trusted with God's truth to communicate to others. It is because Jesus is God's Son that he has been trusted with this.
- *No one knows who the Father is except the Son.* Jesus knows God the Father in the same

way that the Father knows the Son. The knowledge that Jesus has of the Father is unique, and his relationship as Son of the Father is unique.

This passage says that because of the relationship between Jesus and God, his Father, he has been given a message from God. The passage does not simply talk about Jesus being conscious of God as a believer, it speaks about the mutual relationship between Father and Son.

The big question is: who was Jesus? Was he merely a son of God by being religious and obeying God? Was he Son of God because God chose him as a human being among many to represent him to the people? Or was Jesus really God walking on earth? Did he actually share God's nature?

FOLLOW UP

Question time

1. Fill in the following sentences with the correct words: The idea of a Messiah who is Son of God goes back to the promise God made to ____________ that his descendants would ____________ and one of them would be ____________. Another possible background for the title can be found in Greek thought and the belief in ____________.

2. Name three occasions in Jesus' life when he is referred to as 'The Son' or 'The Son of God'.

3. What do you know from scholars about the meaning of the title 'Son of God'?

To do

Find out what people believe about Jesus. Design your own BELIEFS POLL, e.g.

Q1. Do you believe Jesus . . .?

- existed – why?
- didn't exist – why?
- don't know – why?

Q2. Do you believe Jesus was . . .?

- a special person – why?
- a prophet – why?
- an ordinary person – why?
- God's Son – why?

What are the most popular views? Do people have good reasons for holding them?

Which one is true? Is there any way of finding out the truth? Does truth exist? Can we find it? Or is truth more a matter of personal opinion?

UNIT 5.2

Jesus the Son of Man

How would you like to be known? Think of some of the titles you admire:

- Anna, the brainy one
- Dave, the he-man
- Sharna, the most popular in the class
- Paul, the friend of everyone
- Tim, the laugh-a-minute
- Lucy, the lovely
- Ahmed, the best footballer.

What would be your favourite title?

In the Gospels, the *Son of Man* was Jesus' favourite way of describing himself. In fact, it is the only title he freely used. And yet 'Son of Man' is never used by anyone else to describe Jesus – even the early Christians. So, what does the title 'Son of Man' mean to Jesus and what would the people of his day have understood by it?

How 'Son of Man' is used

The title 'Son of Man' is used in Jewish literature and in the four Gospels.

In the prophecies of Ezekiel it means simply 'a human being'. 'Son of Man' is a phrase used to describe a normal everyday person.

In Psalm 8 'Son of Man' refers to the nation of Israel, which has been made strong by God.

In the visions of the prophet Daniel
The Book of Daniel uses symbolic language. The prophet has four visions of different beasts and these symbolize the cruel empires that have conquered Israel. Then, into the vision comes a human figure: 'one like the Son of Man'. This figure symbolizes 'the people of the Supreme God'. God is going to give his people power and greatness (Daniel 7:13, 22).

In the 'Similitudes of Enoch' (a Jewish book written between the time of the Old Testament and the New Testament) the figure of the Son of Man occurs again. This time he is less of a symbol and more of an individual person.

So why did Jesus call himself the 'Son of Man'? As we have seen, the title has its roots in Jewish literature, and therefore represents certain ideas:

- Is Jesus saying that he identifies himself with ordinary people, especially the weak and humble?
- Is Jesus saying that he has a special role from God who has given him power and authority to establish God's Kingdom?
- Is Jesus simply using the title as another way of saying 'I'?

Jesus may be using the title in different ways at different times. No one really knows the exact meaning of 'Son of Man' as Jesus used it. Perhaps Jesus even intended the title to be a mystery. Perhaps he wanted people to think about why he called himself the Son of Man – and not just have an easy answer.

Daniel's Son of Man

'During this vision in the night, I saw what looked like a human being. He was approaching me, surrounded by clouds, and he went to the one who had been living for ever and was presented to him. He was given authority, honour, and royal power, so that the people of all nations, races and languages would serve him. His authority would last for ever, and his kingdom would never end.'

The 'Son of Man' in Luke's Gospel

Here are some passages where Jesus uses the title 'Son of Man'. Look them up and read them. How do you think Jesus is using the title? In what situation or context?

Luke 5:23–24
'Is it easier to say, "Your sins are forgiven you," or to say, "Get up and walk?" I will prove to you then, that the Son of Man has authority on earth to forgive sins.'

Luke 6:5
'And Jesus concluded, "The Son of Man is Lord of the Sabbath."'

Luke 9:22
'He also said to them, "The Son of Man must suffer much and be rejected by the elders, the chief priests, and the teachers of the Law. He will be put to death, but three days later he will be raised to life."'

Luke 12:8
'I assure you that whoever declares publicly that he belongs to me, the Son of Man will do the same for him before the angels of God. But whoever rejects me publicly, the Son of Man will also reject him before the angels of God.'

Luke 12:40
'And you, too, must be ready, because the Son of Man will come at an hour when you are not expecting him.'

Luke 21:27
'Then the Son of Man will appear, coming in a cloud with great power and glory.'

Luke 22:69
'But from now on the Son of Man will be seated on the right of Almighty God.'

FOLLOW UP

Question time

1. What do you know from scholars about the meaning of the title 'Son of Man'?

2. In what ways can the title 'Son of Man' be understood when used by Jesus of himself?

3. Look up the verses suggested in the chapter. How do you think Jesus is using the title 'Son of Man' to apply to himself? Give reasons for your answer.

To do

- Design a chart on THE SON OF MAN. You can use it for revision later on in the course. Make it colourful, bold and simple – like this:

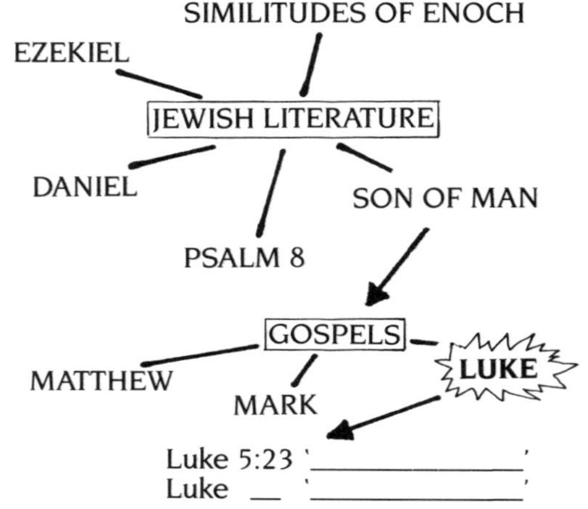

- Read the prophet Daniel (chapter 7:13, 14 and 22, 23) and represent this apocalyptic vision in picture form.

Jesus as Messiah and Lord

Jesus the Christ, Jesus the Messiah

The word 'Messiah' means the *anointed one*, the one chosen by God for a special task. 'Messiah' is Hebrew, but the word 'Christ' is Greek and means the same. In the Old Testament the title is given to the kings of Israel, so it is a royal term. When kingship ceased, the title came to be applied to a future king who would restore Israel's power and who would bring peace and prosperity to all the world.

'Christ' is not Jesus' surname, although we have become so familiar with the name 'Jesus Christ' that it sounds like it. It is actually a title: Jesus, the Christ.

The New Testament writers thought Jesus was the . . .

one anointed by God

the royal king who had been promised

the one who would restore Israel to glory

the one who would bring peace to the whole world

What they had experienced of Jesus inspired them to speak of him in these terms.

But the New Testament does not say that Jesus ever claimed these titles for himself. In fact, at times he resisted being identified with them (Luke 9:21; Matthew 9:30).

Jesus is Lord

The early Christians gave the title 'Lord' to Jesus. Luke often used this title in his Gospel, more frequently than the other Gospel writers. But what did it mean?

The Greek word for 'Lord' is *kyrios*. This word has different meanings.

- Kyrios can simply mean 'sir'.
- Kyrios can be a term of respect to anyone in authority.
- Kyrios can even be used to translate the Old Testament name of God, *Yahweh* or *Jehovah*.

'Jesus is Lord' became a profession of faith among Christians after the resurrection. Here are some passages from the Gospels that use this title:

The angel said:
'This very day in David's town your Saviour was born – Christ the Lord!' (Luke 2:11)

Peter said:
'Go away from me, Lord! I am a sinful man!' (Luke 5:8)

Luke said:
'After this the Lord chose another seventy-two men and sent them out two by two . . .' (Luke 10:1)

The disciples said:
'Lord, teach us to pray . . .' (Luke 11:1)

Luke said:
'Very early on Sunday morning the women went to the tomb . . . they found the stone rolled away from the entrance, so they went in; but they did not find the body of the Lord Jesus.' (Luke 24:1–3)

Messiah and Christ in Luke's Gospel

Here are some passages in Luke to look up.
Read them in context. Who is speaking?
What is the situation in the narrative?

Luke 3:15
'People's hopes began to rise, and they began to wonder whether John might perhaps be the Messiah.'

Luke 2:25
'At that time there was a man named Simeon living in Jerusalem. He was a good, God-fearing man and was waiting for Israel to be saved. The Holy Spirit was with him and had assured him that he would not die before he had seen the Lord's promised Messiah . . .'

Luke 9:18–20
'One day when Jesus was praying alone, the disciples came to him. "Who do the crowds say I am?" he asked them . . . "What about you?" he asked them. "Who do you say I am?" Peter answered, "You are God's Messiah." '

Luke 24:26
'Was it not necessary for the Messiah to suffer these things and then to enter his glory?'

FOLLOW UP

Question time

1. The Jewish word 'Messiah' means ____________.

2. The Greek word for Messiah is ____________.

3. In the Old Testament the title Messiah is given to ____________.

4. Look at and learn the Bible passages from Luke quoted in this chapter: Luke 3:15; Luke 2:25; Luke 9:18, 19; Luke 24:26.
Who is speaking? What is the situation in the narrative?

5. Jesus is Lord. The title 'Lord' is used especially by Luke to describe Jesus. The Greek word for Lord is ____________

6. Explain the different meanings associated with the title 'Lord'.

To do

- Write or record/broadcast a radio programme entitled: 'AN ENQUIRY INTO JESUS OF NAZARETH – Was he the Messiah?'

  The programme should include:
  – *an introduction* to listeners about the Jewish hope of a Messiah
  – *information* about how Luke presents Jesus as Messiah
  – *any problems* with this way of seeing Jesus
  – *a challenge* to listeners to make their own assessment.

- Design a SPEECHOGRAM: i.e. quotes from Luke's Gospel about Jesus as the Messiah.

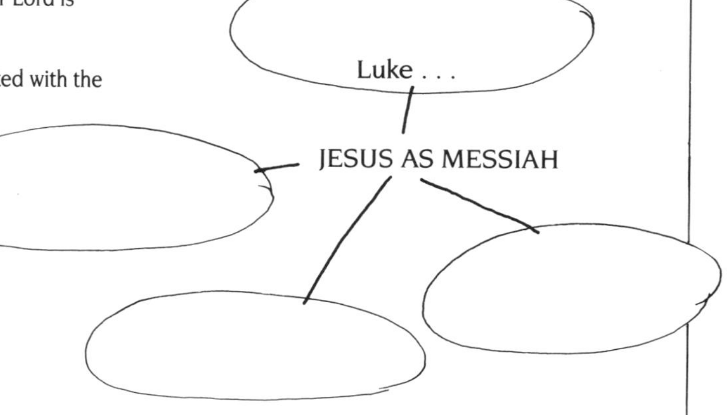

UNIT 6.1

Jesus is Tempted

We are tempted to do all sorts of things. Here is a list of temptations which was recently drawn up by a group of fourth-year pupils:

'I'm tempted to forget my homework and then tempted to copy my friends' so I don't get into trouble.'

'I've been tempted to cheat in exams.'

'We are all tempted to go out of school without a pass.'

'I am always tempted to lie in bed rather than be on time for school.'

'I am often tempted to tell lies, it's easier than telling the truth.'

'I was once tempted to steal some jeans – "they won't miss one pair", I said to myself.'

Jesus began his work for God when he was about thirty years old (Luke 3:23). Before he did anything publicly, he went to the desert to be alone with God. Luke writes that during this period, Jesus was tempted. Here is the story in Luke's Gospel:

READ LUKE 4:1–13, & MARK 1:12–13

Notice that Jesus was tempted to do three things:

Temptation 1

Jesus was tempted to use his power for himself.

Stones to bread.
Devil 'If you are God's Son, order this stone to turn into bread.'
Jesus 'The scripture says, "Man cannot live on bread alone."'

The story tells us that Jesus had gone for forty days without food. Here he was tempted to use the power that God had given him for himself. After all, if he was going to help others, surely he should help himself first?

Jesus said that people need more than food to keep them alive. He quoted from the Jewish Law and the full quote is: '. . . man must not depend on bread alone to sustain him, but on everything that the Lord says' (Deuteronomy 8:3). In other words, people need to listen to God to keep themselves fully alive. Jesus overcame the temptation to settle for personal comfort – instead his life was to be for God and others.

Temptation 2

Jesus was tempted to build his own empire, not God's.

Worship the Devil – worship wealth.
Devil 'I will give you all this power and all this wealth . . . if you worship me.'
Jesus 'The scripture says, "Worship the Lord your God and serve only him."'

Jesus was tempted to become politically and financially powerful. It must have been a difficult temptation to resist. Israel had been overrun many times by foreign leaders and the Jewish people were looking for a special leader, a Messiah, who would free them from their enemies. Why not help them and become wealthy and powerful at the same time?

Jesus overcame the temptation to build his own empire. He would not worship the Devil, money or power. Only God is to be worshipped. Again Jesus quoted from the Old Testament Law (Deuteronomy 6:13).

Temptation 3

Jesus was tempted to use his power to impress the world.

Throw yourself down! Prove yourself!
Devil 'If you are God's Son, throw yourself down from here . . .'
Jesus 'The scripture says, "Do not put the Lord your God to the test." '

This was a difficult temptation to overcome. This time the Devil quoted scripture at Jesus. The temptation went like this: if Jesus really was God's Son, then surely God would protect him from pain? If he survived the 450 foot drop from the Royal Tower of the Jerusalem Temple to the Kidron Valley this would have proved to everyone that he was special. People were expecting the Messiah to come 'surrounded by clouds' (Daniel 7:13). The world would fall at Jesus' feet and follow him.

But Jesus refused. He overcame the temptation to impress the world with marvellous acts of power. He would not test God to show his power (Deuteronomy 6:16), but he would trust God for the power to overcome temptation and the Devil.

Luke tells us that the Devil departed from Jesus for a while, but that these temptations occurred again in his ministry. At the end of his life, Jesus was tempted again, three times. Once by soldiers, once by a criminal, and once by the ordinary people. They all told him to use his power to save himself from death (Luke 23:35–37, 39). But Jesus used God's power not to save himself but to triumph over evil and to bring in the Kingdom of God (Luke 11:20).

Luke is using the 'Q' source in this story and he is reflecting on the Old Testament account of God's people wandering in the wilderness. *The 'Q' source* is the material

FACT FILE

• **Fasting/Lent** Jesus fasted for forty days and forty nights. Fasting is when someone deliberately goes without food. Religious people fast for special reasons. Sometimes it is to show their sincerity in giving up their lives of comfort for God – or it can be to discipline the mind and body so that they are controlled. Perhaps the believer wants to be more aware of spiritual things rather than material things. In the Christian church today, Jesus' time in the desert is remembered by the season of **Lent**. It begins with Ash Wednesday and lasts for forty days (not including Sundays) until Easter. Traditionally, Christians have practised some form of self-discipline during Lent.

• **The devil/devils** In the New Testament the word(s) 'devil' and 'devils' refer to spiritual beings which are hostile to God and to people. In Luke's Gospel there are references to people possessed by devils or demons – in some cases it was believed that this caused sickness, e.g. dumbness (Luke 11:14) or abnormal behaviour such as living among tombs (Luke 8:27).

For many modern people the mention of the devil appears to be a legend or an imagined figure out of fairy stories.

For others, the New Testament stories are myth. Myth is not the same as fairy story. Myth is a special way of communicating difficult truths in picture or story form. For example, the evil that people experience in the world could be presented as an imagined figure – e.g. the devil.

• **Is the devil imagined – or is he real?** It is often said that devil-possession was simply the way that first-century people talked about what we would now call sickness or madness.

However, the Gospel writers show a difference between sickness and possession by devils. In Matthew 4:24 it says, '. . . people brought to him (Jesus) all those who were sick, suffering from all kinds of diseases and disorders: people with demons, and epileptics, and paralytics – and Jesus healed them all.' So Matthew is aware of the differences between all these conditions – *he does not say that everyone who was sick had demons.*

Some Christians today believe that the devil is real – a spiritual being who exists to tempt and to bring evil to the world. The Church of England and the Roman Catholic Church still have written prayers to say against the Devil and demons.

which is found in both Matthew and Luke, but not in Mark. If you read Mark's account of Jesus' temptations, it is only two verses long. The account of Jesus' temptations in Matthew is similar to that in Luke.

The Old Testament. This story about Jesus is like the Old Testament story about Moses (Exodus 34:28). They both were in the desert and they both fasted 'forty days and forty nights'. The phrase 'forty days and forty nights' may mean literally forty days and nights, or it may be a way of saying 'a long time'.

Names for the Devil in the Bible

- **Satan**=accuser
- **Beelzebub**=Lord of the Flies
- **Lucifer**=Bearer of Light
- The Greek word in the New Testament for devil is *diabolos*, which also means 'accuser'.

FOLLOW UP

Question time

1. Where was Jesus when he was tempted?

2. About how old was he at the time?

3. What were the temptations he faced? List them.

4. How did he answer the temptations of the devil?

5. What is fasting?

6. What is the connection between Jesus' temptation and the Christian season of Lent?

7. Luke is using two sources in his story about the temptations – what are they?

To do

What is temptation? Temptation may mean different things to different people. Get a large sheet of paper and begin to pass it round the class. Each person writes a sentence which begins: TEMPTATION IS WHEN ____________ When the sheet is complete discuss different ways people deal with these situations.

Talking-point

- Is the Devil real or imagined?
- Is evil: real and powerful?

– Is it found in people or outside them?
– Is it good gone wrong?
– Or is it people's bad deeds?
– Is it only what is done or can it be something not done?

Jesus is Rejected

Have you ever thought about the saying that those who know you best understand you least? It *seems* to make more sense to say that those who know you best (your friends, your family, your neighbours) should understand you better. But often that is not the case . . .

'My parents haven't a clue about what I am like. I'm not the university type, I just want to leave school and get a job.'

'I've been going out with him for six months and he doesn't know the first thing about me or he would never have said what he did.'

'When will they understand that I don't like going to discos! I'd rather stay at home and read a book.'

Why is it that we are misunderstood?

Perhaps it is because other people have expectations of us. They think that if we are intelligent we should go to university. If we are young and good-looking we should want to go to discos. Also, it is easy for adults who have known us for a long time to have a set picture of what we are like. They remember us when we were six but they do not recognize us when we are sixteen because we have changed.

When people try to change, their friends

either try to accept what is happening, or try to put them down. Rejection happens when you or your opinions are not acceptable.

Almost all we know about Jesus up to the age of about thirty is that he was a carpenter's son from Nazareth in Galilee. One day he got up to teach in the local synagogue and shocked the congregation. They were expecting an ordinary local boy to speak and instead they were amazed at his ability. Their expectations were upset . . .

Jesus is rejected at Nazareth

READ LUKE 4:16–28

Luke gives an account of how Jesus was rejected at the beginning of his ministry. He was rejected by his own people – and even by his family and friends. If you look at Matthew's and Mark's versions of this story (Matthew 13:53–58; Mark 6:1–6) you will see that theirs is a shorter account – so Luke has added some details which he thought were important. He did this for two reasons:

● *Luke believes that Jesus is the Servant of the Lord prophesied by Isaiah.* Luke is quoting the Old Testament prophet Isaiah. Hundreds of years before Christ was born, Isaiah spoke of a special person, the Servant of the Lord, who would be empowered by God to do certain things. He would . . .

– **bring good news** to the poor
– **proclaim liberty** to the captives
– **and recovery of sight** to the blind
– **set free** the oppressed
– **and announce** that the time had come when the Lord would save his people.

In this chapter of Luke's Gospel, Jesus reads the passage from the scroll, gives it back to the attendant, sits down, and everyone's eyes are on him as he says: 'This passage of scripture has come true today, as you heard it being read.'

In other words, Luke emphasizes that Jesus is the expected Servant of the Lord, promised centuries ago by Isaiah. The prophecy comes true as Jesus reads the scroll. Luke understands the Servant of the Lord and the Messiah to be the same person. Jesus is about to deliver the oppressed and the poor.

● *Luke shows that Jesus' ministry is for everyone, not just the Jews.* At first everyone was impressed with Jesus' sermon. They had to ask themselves: 'Isn't he the son of Joseph?' They had seen a different side to the carpenter's son. But, as his sermon went on, they became very angry. Jesus said that during the ministry of the famous prophet Elijah God had sent him to help a foreign widow rather than any of his fellow-Jews. And, during the ministry of the prophet Elisha, God had sent the prophet to heal a foreigner called Naaman and not any of his fellow-Jews.

The gospel of Jesus, according to Luke, is a message of good news not just for Nazareth or for the Jews. The Jews are no more important than the Gentiles. The

FACT·FILE

● **The Sabbath** This was the seventh day of the week (Saturday). It had to be kept separate from the rest of the week because it was 'holy'. It was a day of rest. The Jews were not allowed to do any work on this day.

● **The synagogue** was a place of worship and education. It was at the centre of Jewish religious life. There was no ordained minister and any male who had some religious education could be invited to take part in the services.

The Sabbath service began with the attendant sounding a trumpet three times (the Chazzan). Then there was a prayer which included the Shema (a reading from Deuteronomy 6:4–9). The Shema was followed by two different kinds of readings. The first reading was taken from the Torah, the Jewish Law, and this was followed by a free reading from the Prophets.

These readings were followed by a sermon (everyone sat down for this) and the blessing. So, when Jesus was invited to preach at Nazareth, he chose the free reading from the Prophets which was the text for the sermon he gave. In this case he chose Isaiah 61:1–2 and Isaiah 58:6.

gospel is **universal** – it is for the whole world.

The people in Nazareth rejected this message. Their response was violent – they dragged Jesus out of the synagogue to a hill at the edge of town and would have thrown him over a cliff if he had not managed somehow to escape. How dare he say that God cared as much for foreigners as he did for 'his chosen people' – the Jews. It was blasphemy.

Jesus did not heal anybody in Nazareth. He said that a prophet is never welcomed in his home town.

Later in his Gospel, Luke pictures Jesus being rejected – not just as a prophet, but as the Messiah, the Saviour of the world. This takes place on another hill in another city – Jerusalem. Once again, Jesus was dragged out of the town, this time to be crucified.

Question time

1. What happened in a synagogue?

2. Why did Jesus stand to read and sit to speak?

3. What is the Shema?

4. How does Luke show that Jesus' ministry is for everyone in the telling of the rejection at Nazareth?

To do

Jesus was rejected in his home town. *What is rejection?* Get into groups of five or six. One person is elected to be the writer and has a felt-tip pen. Take a large sheet of paper and write in bold letters in the middle of the page WHAT IS REJECTION? Members of the group speak sentences one by one and the scribe writes them on the page. For example: 'Rejection is when your friends don't speak to you.'

Show your list to the rest of the class. Discuss the issues raised.

Talking-point

Are there ways of coping with rejection? What sorts of things can we do to help ourselves?

UNIT 6.3

Jesus Calls the First Disciples

What are your best friends like? Are they all very much alike or are they completely different? Did they choose you, or did you choose them? Maybe you are part of a group who go around a lot together. Can you remember how and when you first met?

In chapter five of his Gospel, Luke records how Jesus called his first disciples. They were his close friends, but the word 'disciple' means more than just a friend, it means 'a learner' – someone who follows closely. The disciple follows the teacher closely. Here is the story as told by Luke, and the story from Mark.

Jesus calls his disciples

READ LUKE 5:1–11 & MARK 1:16–20

You will see that there are differences between these two accounts:

- **Mark** suggests Jesus was alone on the shores of Galilee.
Luke mentions 'the crowd'.

- **Luke** tells of how Jesus got into Simon's boat and taught from there.
Mark does not mention this.

- **Luke** tells us that they fished all night and then with Jesus' help caught a huge catch of fish.
Mark does not include this part of the story.

- **Mark** talks about four disciples including Andrew.
Luke mentions only three by name.

Why do the two accounts of the story differ?

There may have been two different occasions when Jesus first met and went fishing with the disciples. Perhaps the first occasion is only part of the story and so Luke completed it with the full details.

Other scholars think that this story about Jesus happened much later in his life. There is a similar story in John's Gospel (21:1–19). These scholars say that Luke confused a later incident with his first appearance to Simon, James and John and that this explains the differences between Luke's account and Mark's account.

But if you look, you will see that the two stories are more different than they are alike. It looks as if they are separate events.

Note: Matthew follows Mark's account fairly closely.

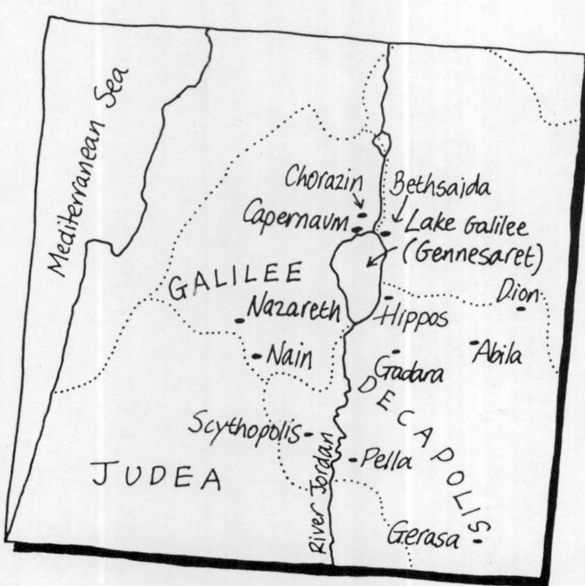

Whatever the solution, the story is a remarkable one.

Jesus and Simon

Picture yourself sitting with the crowd: it's a hot day and the waters are gently lapping round the shores of Lake Gennesaret (another name for Galilee). Jesus is in Simon's boat, a few metres from the shore. Everyone knows Simon locally. He's a tough fisherman with plenty of muscle and a lot of talk.

Jesus is talking about God and everyone is listening. He finishes speaking and turns to Simon: 'Push the boat out further to the deep water, and you and your partners let down your nets for a catch.'

Simon protests. He knows how to fish; Jesus does not. Some days you just have to accept that there are no fish around – it's a bad day, or, in this case, a bad night. It's useless to try again, at least so soon. So why did he decide to follow Jesus' instructions? What made him go against all his fisherman's sense and take this advice? Was it a hunch? Or a risk? Or just something to do?

It's interesting to note what Simon actually says to Jesus: '. . . we worked hard all night and caught nothing. But *if you say so*, I will let down the nets.'

Jesus has had an effect on Simon. Because Jesus says it is worth doing, Simon does it.

Fishermen still take their boats out on Lake Galilee, as they did in Jesus' day. We know that four of Jesus' disciples – Peter and his brother Andrew, James and his brother John – earned their living by fishing the Lake.

. . . and there were fish, and more fish, and yet more fish. It takes a lot of fish to stretch the nets to breaking-point.

It was more than just this extraordinary event that had impressed Simon. Simon could have said: 'What a genius!' or 'What an incredible fisherman!' But he did not. Instead the effect on Simon was a moral one. He said he was a sinful man.

What had happened showed Simon something about himself. Why? Perhaps he was overwhelmed by what he had caught. Perhaps he said to himself, 'Why should this sort of thing happen to me? I don't deserve it.'

The story ends with Jesus saying, 'Don't be afraid; from now on you will be catching men.' And Simon, with his partners James and John, left everything and followed Jesus.

Understanding the story

Christians understand this story in different ways.

- *It can be taken at face value.* It is a story about a miraculous haul of fish. Luke wants his readers to know that Jesus is showing supernatural insight and control over natural forces. So he is someone special and Simon Peter recognizes Jesus' powerful presence. This causes him to fall on his knees in worship and leave everything to follow Jesus.

- *It can be seen as symbolic.* At the time Luke was writing, the early Christians were continuing their mission after Jesus' ascension. This is a story used by Luke to symbolize success. The 'large number of fish' breaking the nets was a symbol of the successful mission by Peter and the early disciples in 'catching men', or making converts. So the story is not simply about a miraculous haul of fish. Instead, Luke's purpose is to reflect the experience of the early church in catching a miraculous haul of converts.

The twelve disciples (or apostles)

Luke tells how Jesus went up a hill and spent the whole night praying before he chose the twelve disciples (Luke 6:12–16). Here is the list – some of the information we have comes from outside Luke's Gospel.

Simon
(whom Jesus named 'Peter' – from the Greek meaning 'rock'). He was a man of action, a leader. He often acted before he thought. He recognized Jesus as the Messiah and swore to follow him for ever. Yet, at the time when Jesus was on trial, Peter denied even knowing of him. Even so, after the resurrection, Jesus gave Peter special responsibility for looking after his followers.

James and John
(nicknamed by Jesus 'Sons of Thunder'). These two brothers were fishermen. They were known for their hasty tempers and their desire to be powerful and great. Peter, James and John were the three disciples who were closest to Jesus.

Andrew
was the brother of Simon Peter. He brought his brother to meet Jesus.

Matthew
(also known as Levi). He was a tax collector when Jesus called him. He is thought by many to be the author of the first Gospel.

Simon the Zealot
was the revolutionary of the group. The Zealots aimed to overthrow the Romans and free the country from their power.

Philip
came from the same town as Simon Peter and Andrew – Bethsaida in Galilee. Philip told Bartholomew that he had found the Messiah.

Thomas
(over the years called 'doubting Thomas'). Thomas was unconvinced about Jesus' resurrection unless he could personally see him and touch him. Eventually he did.

Bartholomew, James (the Son of Alphaeus), Judas (the son of James) We know nothing for certain about these three.

Judas Iscariot
kept the finances of the group. He also betrayed Jesus by telling Jesus' enemies where he could be found. He sold this information for thirty pieces of silver. Matthew records that Judas later hanged himself (Matthew 27:1–10). Judas is always named last in the lists of the disciples.

The sign of the fish

The fish became an important symbol for the early Christians. It represented Jesus' presence with them. The Greek word for 'fish' is *ichthus*. These letters were used as a secret code in the days when it was dangerous to be a Christian:

I = *Iesus* meaning **Jesus**
C = *Christos* meaning **Christ**
Th = *Theou* meaning **of God**
U = *Uios* meaning **Son**
S = *Soter* meaning **Saviour**.
Jesus Christ, Son of God, Saviour.

Question time

1. What is a disciple?

2. What are the differences between Mark and Luke in narrating the story of the call of the first disciples?

3. How do you account for these differences?

4. Write an account of the call of the first disciples according to Luke.

5. How do Christians understand the story?

6. What do you think a Christian disciple should be like?

To do

- Draw a **portrait gallery**.

Select one, two or even three of the disciples and 'paint' – i.e. sketch – their portrait. Underneath the outline of each face print the name. Try to 'say' something about the disciple's character or actions in the picture rather than in words. For example, Matthew was a tax collector. Can you represent this symbolically?

- Design a poster to show the importance of the **sign of the fish**. Use a large sheet of plain paper. Draw the Christian symbol of the fish and show what the word ICTHUS represents.

- WORD SQUARE

H	V	U	U	R	S	U	R	X	E	N	N	K	A	J
V	B	P	B	X	Y	E	O	P	N	Z	T	S	P	S
T	Y	C	Q	H	S	C	U	E	T	E	J	W	R	C
O	A	P	T	W	G	S	M	C	H	T	N	W	Q	J
I	R	G	O	X	H	S	D	W	Z	C	E	F	Z	L
R	I	M	J	R	N	R	A	K	E	H	W	J	E	H
A	R	V	E	O	E	N	F	M	T	R	A	Q	O	B
C	M	H	M	T	H	X	U	T	O	D	D	Y	X	Y
S	A	I	E	O	B	E	A	S	S	H	W	N	W	I
I	S	P	J	W	E	M	O	L	O	H	T	R	A	B
J	W	H	A	U	V	R	C	R	S	Z	K	J	G	W
F	C	I	M	N	D	G	S	P	P	T	P	Z	D	H
Y	R	L	E	Q	V	A	W	X	W	A	L	G	I	X
D	N	I	S	G	A	K	S	P	M	L	F	P	T	I
X	I	P	G	P	V	V	R	U	I	K	P	R	S	H

Read Luke 6 to find the disciples in this Wordsquare. There are 16 hidden words, some horizontal, some vertical, some diagonal. They may read from right to left; up or down. Can you find them?

The Coming of the Kingdom

How many times have you seen signs like this? Our lives are full of signs. Every day we see signs telling us to **stop** and **go**. We see signs telling us to **wait**, **cross the road**, **turn left** or **turn right**. In fact, there are thousands of signs all around us. Often we do exactly what they tell us to do, without thinking.

Road signs are rules. They tell us what to do. Often the reasons for the signs are easy to understand. If we did not obey some signs, there would be car crashes, accidents or chaos.

Every country has a set of rules. Together these are called the *law*. Some countries also have a monarchy. Britain, for example, is a *kingdom* ruled by the queen. Nowadays, however, she does not have much real power. In the past, the situation was different. The king or queen had real power and *ruled absolutely*. Their *word* was *law*. There was nothing anyone could do about it. In some countries of the world this is still true today.

When Jesus began to travel and teach in Galilee, he talked about a Kingdom. He talked about the *Kingdom of God*. In fact, the Kingdom of God was at the centre of the message that Jesus preached. It was a new kind of rule. But what was this Kingdom? And what did Jesus mean by it?

What did the Jews believe about the Kingdom of God?

The Jews in Jesus' time knew what they meant by the *Kingdom of God*. It was not a new idea to them. In fact, the Jews were waiting for two different kinds of kingdom:

- *They thought about the Messiah* who they believed would be a descendant of King David. He would come and rescue the Jews from their enemies (especially the Romans), and make Israel an important country again. By the time Jesus was born, the Jews had lost their kings. This made them long for a special and important king – the Messiah – to come to save them.

- *They thought about the 'Day of the Lord'*. The Jews also hoped that God himself would come and rule over them. The day when he would appear to do this was known as *the Day of the Lord*. God would remove all the evil from the world. He would defeat Israel's enemies and gather together all the people of Israel who were living in different countries. The prophets in the Old Testament wrote about the Day of the Lord. Many Jews who had lost hope in an earthly Messiah looked forward to God acting with power. This second view was popular in Jesus' time. It is *apocalyptic*.

Apocalyptic describes when God shows himself in great supernatural power and breaks into history. Apocalyptic writing usually focused on the end of the world.

The Jews had had their own kings in the past. But they were sure of one thing. God was their *real* king. In the psalms and the books of the prophets, God was written about as King over *Israel* and King over the *whole earth*. The Jews believed that God was their *real* King, even though they were ruled by the Roman emperor. But some time in the future, God would show himself king openly, overthrowing all earthly rulers.

For the Jews, the Kingdom of God was made up of those people who followed the Jewish Law. That was where God's rule could be seen – in the lives of the people who followed God.

But, when Jesus came, he preached a different kind of Kingdom.

The arrival of the Kingdom

What did the Gospel writers think? They were in no doubt that the Kingdom of God (that is, the rule of God) was seen in Jesus' life – in the things he said and did.

Luke shows that the Kingdom of God did not come with an army of soldiers. The Kingdom of God did not come with fire from the sky. Instead, it came with one man and his twelve followers. The Kingdom came into history, but it did not change history in the way that the Jews had expected.

Jesus did not start a political movement or a revolution. He did not preach the violent overthrow of the Roman Empire. The Kingdom that Jesus preached was not a country or a state. Instead, Jesus talked about the *rule of God* in people's lives. Where God rules is where his Kingdom is to be found. This idea was right at the heart of Jesus' message.

Palestine at the time of Jesus was occupied by the Roman army, and most of those who were waiting for God to send his Messiah thought of him as a great general who would set them free from Roman rule.

FOLLOW UP

Question time

1. What do you know about the Kingdom of God as it was understood by the Jews in Jesus' day? Complete the following sentences:

The Jews were waiting for the Messiah. He was a descendant of ____________.

His task would be to ____________.

They also believed in the Day of the Lord. This was a special day when ____________.

The word 'apocalyptic' means ____________.

The Jews thought that ____________ was King.

For the Jews the Kingdom of God was those people who ____________.

2. In what ways does Luke show that the Kingdom of God has come in Jesus?

UNIT 7.2

Works of Power

We have already examined the temptations of Jesus in the desert. We have also read about his baptism, and his rejection in the synagogue at his home town of Nazareth. Try to recall these events as we look at Jesus beginning to preach about the Kingdom of God.

Jesus goes to Galilee

READ MARK 1:14–15; MATTHEW 4:23 & LUKE 4:14–15

After Jesus' rejection at Nazareth, he went to Capernaum. This was the beginning of Jesus' travels. He went about Galilee preaching, healing and casting out demons. These were signs that the Kingdom of God had come. Luke emphasizes that Jesus was not offering people new rules to live by – he was offering them new lives.

Sign 1★★★ The Kingdom defeats evil

READ LUKE 4:31–37

Immediately after his rejection at Nazareth, Jesus went to Capernaum where he cast out a demon. This was an important sign that the Kingdom of God was defeating the Kingdom of Satan. (Remember how Jesus defeated the temptations of the Devil in the desert.) The demon knew who Jesus was, but Jesus told it to be quiet (Luke 4:34).

It is interesting to note that, in the Old Testament, the enemies of the Jews were *other nations*.

In the Gospels, the enemies of God are *evil spiritual forces*.

The casting out of demons was an important part of Jesus' ministry (this must not be confused with healing people). Luke shows how Satan is being defeated. Matthew 25:41 makes it clear that the Kingdom of God will come with the destruction of the Devil and all his angels.

Sign 2★★★ The Kingdom defeats prejudice

READ LUKE 4:38–39

It is important that the first healing that Luke writes about is the healing of a *woman*. Women were thought of as second-class citizens in the society of that time. Here Luke is making an important point. What Jesus has to offer, the Kingdom of God, is also for *women*.

The Jews of that time would certainly not have thought about the Kingdom of God in this way.

Two important sayings of Jesus:

- **Luke 11:20**
'But if I drive out demons by the finger of God, then the kingdom of God has come to you.'

- **Luke 10:18**
'I saw Satan fall like lightning from heaven.'

These two sayings show the *power* of Jesus in defeating Satan and how important that was to bring about the Kingdom of God.

Sign 3★★★
The Kingdom encourages faith

READ LUKE 4:40–44

In sharp contrast to the people of Nazareth, the people of Capernaum brought many sick people to Jesus to heal. Instead of trying to kill him, they ask him to stay. Jesus, however, says that he must preach 'the good news of the Kingdom' and goes on his way.

READ LUKE 10:11

Sign 4 ★★★
The Kingdom affects people powerfully

The signs of the Kingdom of God were present in Jesus. But Jesus also gave power to his disciples.

● *Luke* 9:1–6 Jesus sent his twelve disciples out and gave them power to cast out demons and to cure diseases. They were to take nothing with them. They were to have faith and preach the Kingdom of God.

● *Luke* 10:1–4, 17 Jesus sent out seventy other disciples (in some versions, seventy-two) in exactly the same way he sent out the twelve. They too were to take nothing with them, but to have faith and preach the Kingdom of God.

Twelve and **seventy** were special numbers for the Jews.

● There were **twelve** tribes of Israel.
● The Jews believed that there were **seventy** nations in the whole world.
● The Jews also believed that the Law, the Torah, had originally been given in **seventy** different languages.
● The sending out of the **twelve** is symbolic of the Gospel going out to Israel.
● The sending out of the **seventy** is symbolic of the Gospel going out to the whole world.

Jewish people would have understood the meaning of both these different numbers quite well.

FACT

The Pharisees had disciples, as Jesus did. They asked their disciples to follow the Jewish Law. Jesus asked his disciples to follow him. This was a big difference between Jesus and other Jewish religious leaders.

Who is the Kingdom of God for?

The Kingdom of God is for the people whom the respectable Jewish religious leaders would not accept. These included women, tax collectors, sinners, prostitutes and Gentiles (non-Jews). In one way, the Kingdom is for everybody. The Kingdom is for the *whole world*.

● *The Kingdom of God is for the lost.* The three stories in Luke 15 are all about this. They are: the lost sheep, the lost coin, and the lost son. God is shown bringing his Kingdom to the lost and outcast. Here, God is fulfilling the promise that he made in Ezekiel 34:16, 22. Jesus didn't just talk about this. On many occasions he was criticized for eating with criminals, prostitutes and the much-hated tax collectors (Luke 15:1–2).

READ LUKE 9:48 & LUKE 18:16–17

● *The Kingdom of God is for the childlike.* Jesus said that the Kingdom of God is for people who have the trust and simplicity of little children.

READ LUKE 18:24–25

● *It is hard for the rich to enter the Kingdom of God*. The Jews believed strongly that, if you were good, God would reward you. Jesus, however, said that the Kingdom of God is a *gift*. Good things come to people who believe *now*, despite their lack of wealth or importance. That is why the signs of the kingdom include the lame walking, the deaf hearing, the blind seeing and the dumb speaking. But the way is narrow (Luke 13:24). Money and importance can be serious obstacles to becoming part of God's Kingdom. Instead of accepting God's importance, people are too busy worrying about their own.

READ LUKE 17:20–21

● *Where is the Kingdom of God*? Jesus makes it plain here that the Kingdom of God is *not* a place. The Kingdom of God is in people and can be found among them.

● *The Kingdom is to come.* Just as the Jews believed in God's final rule to come at the end of time, so Jesus preached about the future reign of God. The signs of the Kingdom of God that were seen in the life and ministry of Jesus were only the first taste of the life of the age to come. In fact, the age that began with the birth of Jesus will only end with the end of the world. That is when the final rule of God will come.

This rule will mean:

– The defeat of Satan and his angels (Matthew 25:41)

– A society without any evil (Matthew 13:36–43)

– A great feast of rejoicing (Luke 13:29)

Luke even says that people will be different. There will no longer be any men or women – just people. They will live together for ever. There will be no marriage and they will be like angels (Luke 20:35–36).

So the Kingdom of God is both *present* and *future*. Jesus proclaimed that God *does* reign and that God *will* reign.

FOLLOW UP

Question time

1. According to Luke, who is the Kingdom of God for? Answer this question by writing a short account with quotations from Luke to support your points.

2. What do you understand by Jesus' saying; 'How hard it is for a rich person to enter the Kingdom of God'? Choose one of the following; say why you chose that answer and what you mean by it:
● It is hard for a rich person, because God does not love the rich – only the poor.
● It is hard for a rich person, because they have so much money they can do what they like, and they don't have time for God.
● It is hard for a rich person, because having money makes them feel as important as God.
● It is hard for a rich person, because they have to spend so much time worrying about their wealth, and looking after it all, that they miss looking for God.
● It is hard for a rich person, because ____________ (your own reason).

3. According to Luke, where is the Kingdom of God? Which of the following is true?
● The Kingdom of God is a special place that we cannot see. True/False
● The Kingdom of God is only in the future when people go to heaven. True/False
● The Kingdom of God was in the past when there were holy people in the Bible. True/False
● The Kingdom of God is in the people who let God rule their lives. True/False

To do

Write or draw your own parable. One of Luke's famous parables is the prodigal (or lost) son. Write or draw your own version of this story but use modern characters and features instead of first-century ones.

The Teaching of the Kingdom

These are things Jesus said about the Kingdom of God:

READ LUKE 9:48

Jesus welcomes people into his Kingdom who will be like little children.

READ LUKE 9:60 & LUKE 18:29–30

To enter the Kingdom of God you must want to do so more than anything else. The Kingdom of God must be more important even than your own family.

READ LUKE 12:29–31

The Kingdom of God is more important than food, drink or money. If you are part of the Kingdom, you should not worry about these things. God, your Father in heaven, will provide you with everything you need.

READ LUKE 10:11

The Kingdom is near.

READ LUKE 11:20

The Kingdom is powerful.

READ LUKE 16:16

The Kingdom is coming, even now, and is entered with force.

READ LUKE 17:20–21

The Kingdom of God is among you. Jesus' sayings show that the Kingdom of God is not just a new set of rules. Entry to the Kingdom depends on how a person *responds* to Jesus. If a person accepts Jesus and his teaching then they become a part of his Kingdom. This was a very new idea for the Jews. In Luke's Gospel the Kingdom, the Spirit of God and prayer always go together.

What did Jesus say about the Kingdom?

'After this, Jesus travelled about from one town and village to another, proclaiming the good news of the Kingdom of God' (Luke 8:1–3). Jesus did not travel alone, however. He went with his twelve disciples and with a party of women who helped look after him.

The old way of sowing seed was for the farmer to scatter it by hand from a bag slung across his shoulders. This is the picture in Jesus' parable of the sower.

What is the Kingdom of God like?

Jesus taught stories called parables (see Unit 8.3) to show what the Kingdom of God is like. Some of these parables are very well known.

The parable of the banquet (Luke 14:15–23).
Here Jesus said that the Kingdom of God is like a banquet. It is a celebration. In this story the invited guests do not come. Instead, the person throwing the party goes out to look for people who *will* come. This story shows God saving the lost, the outcast and the unlikely (see Luke 19:10). There is also the idea that Jesus will be like a *bridegroom* and the Kingdom of God will be like a wedding feast – a time of freedom and celebration.

The parable of the sower (Luke 8:5–15).
In this story, the people who hear the word of God are like seeds falling in different kinds of *soil*. One patch of soil encourages growth – but the others kill the seed. The parable graphically shows how people respond to Jesus' message.

The parable of the mustard seed (Luke 13:18–19).
This story shows how a small seed can become a large tree. A tree like this was used in the Old Testament as a picture of Israel giving shelter to the nations of the world. Here Jesus is saying that it is not Israel, but the Kingdom of God that will give the shelter. Just as Israel has rejected Jesus – and so rejected the Kingdom others, not from Israel, will come into the Kingdom.

The parable of the yeast (Luke 13:20–21).
This story shows how only a small piece of yeast is needed to affect the whole loaf. Jesus said that the Kingdom of God may start small, but one day it will change the whole world.

Is the Kingdom of God the same as the church?

Christians believe that:

- The followers of Jesus belong to the Kingdom of God, but they are *not* the Kingdom of God.
- The church is *part* of the Kingdom of God, but it is *not* the Kingdom of God.
- The Kingdom of God is the rule of God. The church is a society of men and women who have accepted God's rule in their lives.

The end of the world – and the Kingdom

READ LUKE 17:20–37

This passage is *apocalyptic*. Jesus is talking about the end of the world and the final coming of God's Kingdom. This was a *future* event which Jesus preached. It would be like the 'Day of the Lord' that the Jewish prophets had hoped for. God's Kingdom would finally break into the everyday world, history would end, and the people of the Kingdom would reign with Jesus for ever.

FOLLOW UP

Question time

1. According to Luke's Gospel, what is the Kingdom of God like? Illustrate your answer from one of the parables.

2. What did Jesus say about the Kingdom of God? Refer to the sayings of Jesus in your answer: Luke 9:48; Luke 9:60; Luke 18:29; Luke 12:30; Luke 10:11; Luke 11:20; Luke 16:16.

3. What is Jesus' teaching about the Kingdom of God in the parable of the mustard seed?

To do

Read and illustrate the parable of the sower (Luke 8:5–15). Divide your page into sections and use pictures to symbolize the parable. What do you understand this parable to mean?

UNIT 8.1

Teaching on How to Live

Jesus was a teacher. He did not teach in a school, however, and he was not paid a wage. Sometimes he taught inside the synagogues or in somebody's house. At other times he taught in the open air in the middle of a town, in the country, or on the shores of Lake Galilee. In this story he is teaching on a plain (a level place). This was not the kind of teaching you would receive in school – Jesus taught about how to live in the Kingdom of God.

The sermon on the plain

READ LUKE 6:17–49

If you were to move from your house, your town and your country, you would need to learn important new things. You would probably need a new language and a new way of doing things. It is no good driving on the left in America if everyone else is driving on the right.

Jesus said that people who are under God's rule, in the Kingdom of God, are under a different form of government. As well as living as citizens of their own country, they are living as citizens of the Kingdom of God and that means that they have to be like God (Luke 6:36) in their actions towards others.

In his 'Sermon on the Level Place' Jesus taught a number of things about being in the Kingdom:

- how to be happy (Luke 6:20–23)
- how to respond to people who hate you (Luke 6:27–37)
- how to give criticism (Luke 6:37–42)
- how to tell the difference between people: good and bad (Luke 6:43–45)
- how to build a foundation for life (Luke 6:46–49)

Jesus' teaching on happiness and sorrow

READ LUKE 6:20–26

What did Jesus mean when he said, 'Happy are you poor; the Kingdom of God is yours'? Why should the poor be happy? A number of Jesus' other sayings are also puzzling: 'Happy are you who are hungry now; you will be filled.' 'Happy are you who weep now; you will laugh.'

Did he mean that only poor people, hungry people and miserable people in this world will enter the Kingdom of God? Or only those who have been unpopular? Jesus was not saying that poverty and suffering are good in themselves. Rather, those who know they are poor and hungry and sorrowful and rejected are better off than those who think they have got everything.

In God's Kingdom, true happiness does not come through having an easy, trouble-free life with plenty of money, food and drink. Jesus gave his blessing and approval to those who realized that there is more to life than just having a good time. People who know they are poor and have problems that cannot simply be met by wealth, possessions and popularity are happy in the Kingdom because their needs can be met by God.

So the happiness to be found in the Kingdom of God is the result of being a certain kind of person. Such a person can look forward to God helping them because he/she experiences God's generosity now. Think how different this is from most of what is said about being happy today – on TV, in the papers, and among our friends.

Jesus' teaching on loving enemies

READ LUKE 6:27–36

Jesus' teaching on loving enemies is famous because it is so very different from what is normally expected in society. Think about it:

– If you get picked on for a fight, you are expected to fight back.

– If someone threatens you, you threaten them.

– If someone talks about you behind your back, you give them as good as you get.

Instead of all this, Jesus told his disciples to *love* their enemies. What did he mean?

● *It's a special kind of love.* In the Greek language there are different words for our one word 'love'. The word *eros* means passionate love – we get the word 'erotic' from it. The word *philia* means warm affection – the sort of love we have for close friends, brothers or sisters. Jesus did not use either of these words here. He did not say that his followers had to fall in love with their enemies, or love them like best friends.

Instead, Jesus used the Greek word *agape*, which is the sort of love that comes from God, and is based on God's nature. A*gape* is when a person has a genuine concern and interest for the welfare of other people – even when they 'curse', 'ill-treat' (verse 28) and 'hit you' (verse 29).

'Love your enemies,' Jesus said, 'and pray for those who ill-treat you. If anyone hits you on one cheek, let him hit the other one too.' He turned normal human attitudes upside-down.

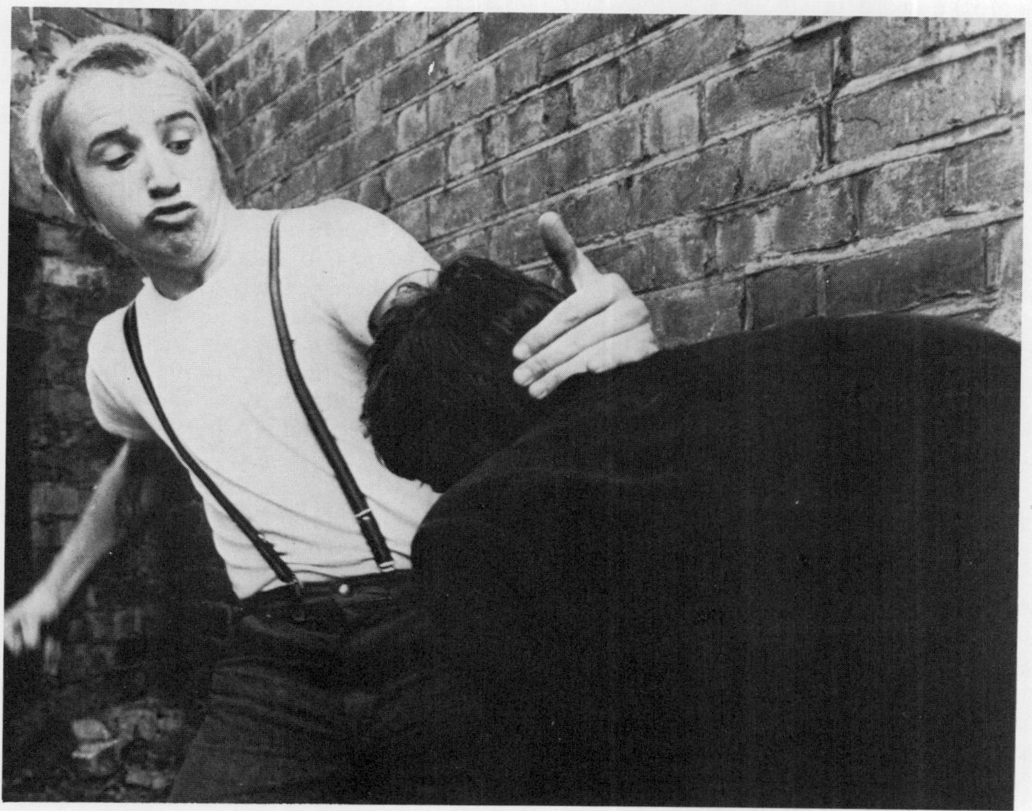

● *It goes further than doing good things.* Jesus was not saying that his followers should just do their duty as good neighbours. His followers were to love others, even when nothing was expected in return. The rule was not to give to others what they give to you but to do for others just what you want them to do for you (verse 31) – even when this meant lending somebody something and not getting it back (verse 35).

If a disciple showed this sort of love, it demonstrated that he or she was part of God's family and God's Kingdom.

When you treat people much better than they deserve, you show *mercy* to them. God is good to the ungrateful and the wicked (verse 35). Followers of God should be *merciful* just like their Father in heaven.

Think what would happen in your school or family if people were treated much better than they deserved, if people refused to fight back, or if every time someone swore they received a kind word.

Jesus' teaching on judging others

READ LUKE 6:37–42

This passage can easily be misunderstood. If you read it without much thought it appears to be saying, 'Never pass an opinion on everything, never criticize the behaviour of others.' But that is not the point Jesus was making. Neither was he saying that judges or law courts should be abolished. He was saying **do not live dishonestly with double standards**. In other words, it is not fair to demand something of someone else when we do not expect it of ourselves.

Jesus then made fun of the situation of one person criticizing someone else for a fault that they both had. (Jesus had a good sense of humour.) He told his listeners first to take the log out of their own eyes before trying to take a tiny speck out of other people's eyes. He did not say it was wrong to take the speck out of other people's eyes to help them see clearly, but the only people who can do that are those who have got their own vision clear first.

Jesus' teaching on identifying good people

READ LUKE 6:43–45

This is a very simple picture but a profound one. If you went to a thorn bush and discovered figs growing on it, you would say something was wrong. If you went to a blackberry bush and discovered grapes, you would wonder what was happening. It is obvious. A tree can only produce its own fruit. The *external* is an expression of the *internal*. And the same is true of people. What comes out of their mouths, the things they say, as well as the things they do, express what is in their hearts – good things or bad things.

Jesus' teaching on building a foundation for life

READ LUKE 6:46–49

Luke ends the sermon on the plain with a parable. The parable could even be from Jesus' own experience. He may have seen a house which had collapsed because of insecure land or faulty foundations. Perhaps he had seen someone who had built a house near to a river which was dry in summer but flooded in winter. This is a common situation in Israel. There are two men contrasted in this story:

The man who dug deep and laid the foundation of his house on rock.

The man who laid no foundation for his house.

When everything is fine you can see no difference between the houses, but when the flood comes you know the difference. Without a foundation the whole structure collapses.

Jesus said that people are like that.

Those who stand on a strong foundation are the ones who come to him, listen to his words and obey him (verse 47). Those who hear his words but do not obey them are on dangerous ground. The one has a foundation for life, the other does not.

A house built without foundations is bound to collapse. Jesus said that to hear his words and do nothing about them is like building with no foundations.

FOLLOW UP

Question time

1. Give examples of how Jesus' teaching on loving enemies might be applied in practice by Christians today (Luke 6:27–36).

2. What did Jesus mean when he told his followers not to judge others? Select your answer and give reasons for it.

Jesus meant:

- Never pass an opinion on anything or criticize others.
- Judges and law courts should be abolished.
- Do not live dishonestly with double standards.

3. What answer would you give to someone who insisted that only poor people will enter the Kingdom of God, according to the teaching of Jesus in his 'Sermon on the Level Place'?

To do

- Illustrate Jesus' teaching on judging others in picture form (Luke 6:37–42).

- Make a **Happiness Chart**.

Do a class survey on what makes people happy. Everyone can choose six things to record, but you must put them under these headings:

– things you want
– people you like/love
– spiritual or personal

You can list all six under one heading if you want. When you have collected all the responses pin them up and look at what makes your class happy. The results show what people value most. Discuss your findings. What might Jesus' list have looked like?

UNIT 8.2

Teaching on How to Pray

When you were little you were taught many things. You were taught how to speak, how to eat with a knife and fork (or chopsticks, or with your hands). Someone taught you to fasten your shirt, write your name and cross the road. Later on you learned how to hold a conversation, how to do sums, how to make coffee or cook a meal. But did anyone teach you how to pray?

Some people reading this book might say 'yes'. Many others will say 'no'. We do not all come from religious families and not every school teaches its pupils to pray.

Jesus taught his disciples how to pray. In chapter 11 of Luke's Gospel there are three things that tell us about Christian prayer:

- the Lord's Prayer
- the story of the friend at midnight
- a comparison of good fathers – earthly and heavenly.

The Lord's Prayer

READ LUKE 11:2–4 & MATTHEW 6:7–13

Throughout the centuries Christians have said this prayer when they meet together. Yet it is easy simply to repeat it without understanding what it means. Here we look into it in more depth . . .

'Father' If Jews used the term 'Father' for God they would say *Abinu*, a formal word. But when Jesus prayed, he used the word *Abba*. *Abba* is the word a Jewish child uses when he or she speaks to his or her 'dad'. Jesus said that when you pray to God he is not far away – he is as close to you as a loving father. In this prayer Jesus approached God as his Father and taught his disciples to do the same.

'May your holy name be honoured; may your kingdom come' Before Jesus came to the subject of personal needs, he prayed for God's name to be honoured. God comes first. This is a prayer to God to act and show himself. But it is also an act of *dedication*. When the disciples pray, they dedicate themselves to honouring God's name.

'Give us day by day the food we need' This is not just physical food like bread, but a prayer for basic human needs to be met day by day. Some translators say it means 'the bread necessary for existence'. The food which God provides meets both physical and spiritual needs.

'Forgive us our sins, for we forgive everyone who does us wrong' The disciple needs to forgive other people. No hard attitude of unforgiveness should prevent God from answering his prayer and forgiving him his sins.

'And do not bring us to hard testing' This hard testing refers to the inward temptations and struggles that God's followers experience. The prayer is not blaming God for testing and asking him to remove it, for God does not test people in this way. Rather it is a plea for God to act for his people and bring them out of the evil they experience.

The story of the friend at midnight

READ LUKE 11:5–8

This is a parable found only in Luke. It is clearly meant to be about prayer. This story shows how even when people are bad neighbours they will still respond to someone in need. There are two possible lessons in this parable:

• *God's character is very different from the unwilling friend.* You will not find evidence for this in the story itself, but if you look up Luke 18:1–8 there is a parallel parable about an unjust judge (and in Luke 11:9–13 the comparison between fathers). This judge is contrasted with the willingness of God to act for his people.

• *Go on praying even if you do not receive immediate answers.* This also fits in with the parable of the unjust judge in Luke 18:1–8.

A comparison of good fathers – earthly and heavenly

READ LUKE 11:9–13

These four verses complete Jesus' teaching on prayer. Jesus said several things in this passage:

• *Ask, and you will receive.* Prayer is asking. The disciple can be confident that he or she will receive an answer from God.

The cutaway drawing shows a typical small house in first-century Palestine. The walls were of mud-brick, and the flat roof of brushwood over rough beams, plastered over with mud. The animals were housed downstairs, below the kitchen area, which was raised a little. The family lived and slept upstairs, with the roof as an extra room or workspace. A house like this is the setting in Jesus' story of the friend at midnight.

'Lord, it wasn't my fault - honest. Well, it was a little bit ...'

'Hello, it's me again, I'm really up to my neck in it this time.'

'Dear God my life is in ruins. Is it wrong to like him so much?'

'I gotta thank you. It's only right innit? After all what you done. I think you're ace.'

'Dear God, I've got lost. Show me the way home.'

● *Seek, and you will find.* Prayer is also seeking. This thought is found in the Old Testament where people call out to God, but do not know if God is there. Jesus said that those who actively search for God will have their search rewarded.

● *Knock, and the door will be opened to you.* Prayer is gaining entry. The picture here is of a person knocking at a closed door in order to go in. In other words, prayer is active. It requires effort and investigation because there are things to be found and opened. And these things will be good . . .

● *The good father.* 'Would any of you who are fathers give your son a snake when he asks for a fish?' (Or a scorpion when he asks for an egg?) Both snakes and scorpions can be harmful. Good fathers do not give evil gifts. Even imperfect fathers know how to give good gifts to their children. How much more does God give good gifts? This is another picture of comparison. The good gift in Luke's Gospel is the Holy Spirit whom God gives to those who ask.

What Jesus said about prayer . . .

- **To the merchants in the Temple** 'It is written in the scriptures that God said, "My Temple will be called a house of prayer", but you have made it a hideout for thieves' (Luke 19:45–47).

- **To Simon his disciple** '. . . I have prayed for you, Simon, that your faith will not fail' (Luke 22:31–32).

- **To his disciples just before his death** 'Pray that you will not fall into temptation' (Luke 22:40).

- **To God** 'Father, if you will, take this cup of suffering away from me. Not my will however, but your will be done' (Luke 22:42).

- **To God while he was dying in extreme pain** 'Father in your hands I place my spirit' (Luke 23:46).

- **To some disciples** 'Be alert and pray always that you will have the strength to go safely through all those things that will happen . . . ' (Luke 21:36).

When Jesus prayed

Throughout Luke's Gospel Jesus prays at different times and in different places. Luke often records him praying before an important decision or during difficulty.

Jesus prayed . . .

- when he was baptized (Luke 3:21–22)
- in lonely places away from the crowds (Luke 5:16)
- all night before he chose his disciples (Luke 6:12)
- on the mountain at his transfiguration (Luke 9:28–29)
- the Lord's Prayer, to teach his disciples (Luke 11:1–5)
- for strength to do God's will (Luke 22:39–44)
- as he died, for God to receive his spirit (Luke 23:46)

Jesus told two parables about prayer in Luke's Gospel:

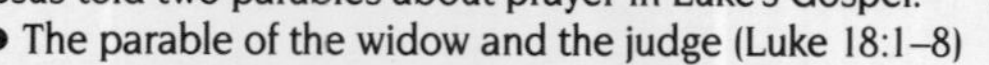

- The parable of the widow and the judge (Luke 18:1–8)
- The parable of the tax collector and the Pharisee (Luke 18:9–14)

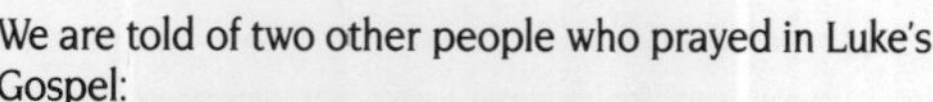

We are told of two other people who prayed in Luke's Gospel:

- **Zechariah** saw an angel when he was praying (Luke 1:8–20)
- **Anna** the prophetess prayed night and day (Luke 2:36–38)

FOLLOW UP

Question time

1. List times in Jesus' life when he prayed.

2. Outline a parable in Luke's Gospel which is about prayer.

3. What do we learn about prayer from Jesus in the parable of the friend at midnight?

4. What have you learned about the Lord's Prayer?

To do

Conduct a **Prayer Poll** in your class or in your school. Ask people to fill in the following chart, and then collect the information.

Do you ever pray?
I pray when I'm depressed.
I've never prayed.
I prayed once when I was in trouble.
I pray from time to time.
I pray every day.

What do you think prayer is?
Asking God's help for yourself?
Asking God's help for other people less fortunate than you?
Getting to know God better by talking to him?
Thinking about God.
Thinking about the good things in life?
Concentrating on yourself?
Or is it a combination of some of these things?
Or something else?

Were you surprised by your findings?
Did many people pray? Why?

Talking-point

Are there many people in the group who believe that prayer has been heard or answered? Or do you know of anyone who would claim such a thing?

UNIT 8.3

Teaching by Parables

Jesus taught in parables. Some of these are very famous – for example, the parable of the good Samaritan and the prodigal (or lost) son.

It is important to understand what parables are, and what they are not, because they form such an important part of Jesus' teaching. About one third of his recorded teaching was in parables. Even people who don't really know about them often quote them in everyday speech. Have you heard any of these phrases?

'He's not using his talents.'

'She's hiding her lamp under a bushel.'

'Help came at the eleventh hour.'

'I'd count the cost before you take that job.'

'He won't let me off till I've paid the last farthing.'

All of them come from parables that Jesus told.

What is a parable?

Children are often taught that a parable is 'an earthly story with a heavenly meaning'. It is a good explanation for children, but if we want to understand parables we have to know more than that. The word 'parable' comes from the Greek word *parabole*, and means a comparison or an analogy. So some of Jesus' parables are comparisons. They compare what is known and familiar here on earth with the Kingdom of God which is spiritual and less familiar . . .

'The Kingdom of God is like . . . a woman who takes some yeast' (Luke 13:20).

'The Kingdom of God is like . . . a man who takes a mustard seed' (Luke 13:18–19).

To understand the parable you have to go to the end of the story to find out what happened when the man took the mustard seed or the woman took the yeast.

Although the word 'parable' is Greek, Jesus was Jewish, not Greek, and his parables reflect Jewish traditions. The Hebrew word for parable is *mashal* and it can mean sayings, or proverbs, or allegories, or similes. A proverb is a common saying in everyday use.

- A *saying* For example, 'The measure you use for others is the one God will use for you' (Luke 6:38). Sayings can be similes or proverbs, but they are also powerful sentences which catch the listener's attention and can be easily remembered.

- A *symbol* For example, 'The mustard seed grows into a tree' (Luke 13:18–19) is a symbol of the Kingdom of God. A symbol stands for something beyond itself. A symbol points to another order of reality.

All of these different elements can be included in what the Bible means by parables. But there is another important thing to note. Parables are *not* the same as allegories.

The difference between a parable and an allegory

In an allegory, each detail of the story has an equivalent, other meaning when the story is explained. Later on in this book we will be looking at the parable of the lost son. It is a simple story that Jesus told about a son who left his father, taking his inherited money – and then got into trouble. Tertullian, an early church leader (AD160–220) used allegory to explain this story. For Tertullian, the elder son in the story represents the *Jew*; the younger (or lost) son is the *Christian*. The money the younger son claimed is the knowledge of God which a person has as his right as a human being. The man whom the younger son had to work for when he ran out of money was the Devil, and so on.

Everyone loves a story, not just children. Jesus used stories – some humorous, some shocking – as a simple way of getting across a serious message about God's Kingdom.

In the earliest days, the parables therefore had *two* settings. There was their **original setting** in the ministry of Jesus, and their **later setting** in the life of the early church.

We can summarize the difference between parables and allegories like this:

A parable usually has *one point to it*. An allegory has many.

A parable is *life-like*; it involves real pictures of everyday life. An allegory does not have to be true to life. For example, in the parable of the lost son, the money the young man took is real money and not spiritual knowledge.

Although allegories and parables are different, on a few occasions Jesus mixed both together. An example of this is the parable of the tenants in the vineyard (Luke 20:9–18). The best-known allegorical parable is the parable of the sower (Luke 8:4–8 and Luke 8:11–15). In all three

synoptic Gospels, Jesus gives a detailed explanation of what the parable means.

Scholars argue whether Jesus used allegory in this way or not. If he did, it was not often. Some say that this explanation of the parable of the sower is not really Jesus speaking, but that the first Christians added the explanation to teach the early church why its preaching sometimes worked and why it sometimes failed.

Is this the only explanation? Is there any reason why Jesus should not have used allegory? After all, the word *mashal* (as we have seen) can refer to different types of saying. Perhaps Jesus decided to give his disciples some personal tuition on parables!

Here are some of the parables Jesus taught. The first three appear only in Luke's Gospel. Read them. What is your response to them? What do you think they mean? Why?

- The parable of the rich fool (Luke 12:13–21)
- The parable of the Pharisee and the tax collector (Luke 18:9–14)
- The parable of the lowest place (Luke 14:7–11)
- The parable of the yeast (Luke 13:20)

How did Jesus use parables in his teaching?

- Jesus used parables as a form of *good storytelling*. Think for a minute – what makes a good story? There is a build-up in the story. People or things are contrasted – good and bad, silly and wise. Different characters are presented to the listener – for example, the vicar, the builder, or the Prime Minister. Then there is the punch line at the end. Jesus used all these storytelling skills. Read the parables and find them.

- Jesus used parables *to force people to think*. The parables were meant to call for a response from those who heard them. The listener is given the opportunity to make a judgment about what the parable means in everyday life. But the parable is also concerned with the Kingdom of God.

Jesus said: 'He who has ears to hear, let him hear.' In other words, go and work it out for yourselves.

● Jesus used parables *to answer those who confronted him*. Different people were in conflict with Jesus – especially the religious people of the day. Jesus sometimes answered them with a story (see Luke 15:1–7).

Why did Jesus teach in parables?

READ LUKE 8:9–10

According to this explanation (which is a quotation from the Old Testament, Isaiah 6:9–10) the purpose of the parable is to *hide the truth rather than to show it*. Many people reject this idea and say that it is more likely that the parables had two levels: the obvious meaning and the hidden meaning. People who listened carelessly would only see the surface meaning, while those who wanted to follow Jesus would come to understand the deeper meaning.

Parables and sayings only in Luke

About the Kingdom of God

– The new wine (Luke 5:37) *Jesus' message is new*
– The good Samaritan (Luke 10:30) *Outcasts*
– The friend at midnight (Luke 11:5) *Persistence/what God is not like*
– The persistent widow (Luke 18:1) *Persistence/what God is like*
– The lowest place (Luke 14:7) *Being humble*
– The poor guests (Luke 14:12–13) *Outcasts/the poor*
– The man who built a tower (Luke 14:28) *Counting the cost of being a disciple*
– The king going to war (Luke 14:31) *Giving up everything for the Kingdom*
– The lost coin (Luke 15:8) *Finding the Kingdom*
– The lost son (Luke 15:11) *The love of the Father*
– The shrewd manager (Luke 16:1) *Being faithful in small things*

About those who are not ready for the Kingdom

– The rich fool (Luke 12:16) *Trusting in wealth and not God*
– The unfruitful fig-tree (Luke 13:6) *Unfruitful lives*
– The locked door (Luke 13:23) *God will receive unlikely people*
– The rich man and Lazarus (Luke 16:19) *God will receive unlikely people*
– The Pharisee and the tax collector (Luke 18:9) *Sinners will be heard*
– The tenants in the vineyard (Luke 20:9) *Jesus will be rejected*

FOLLOW UP

Question time

1. What is a parable? Complete the following sentences:
● The word 'parable' is Greek and means ____________.
● Some of Jesus' parables are similes. A simile is ____________.
● Some of Jesus' parables are symbols. A symbol is ____________.
● Some of Jesus' parables are comparisons. They compare ____________.
● The difference between parables and allegories is that ____________.

2. Why did Jesus teach in parables? Was it:
● to hide the truth rather than to show it?
● to reveal the Kingdom of God?
● to create mystery, so that people would think for themselves?
● or for some other reason?
What do you think? Discuss the issue. You may want to choose more than one of these reasons.

To do

Drama. Get into groups of three or four and write a drama script for one of the following:
● the parable of the rich fool (Luke 12:13–21)
● the Parable of the Pharisee and the tax collector (Luke 18:9–14)
● the parable of the lowest place (Luke 14:7–11)
You may need a narrator to introduce the play and keep it going with explanations. Act it out in front of your class.

UNIT 9.1

Miracles – Who Needs Them?

Jesus was a miracle worker. He healed people and cast demons out of them – and stranger things besides. These miracles showed Jesus' power. Many people believe that Jesus' miracles happened just as they were written about in the Bible – others are not so sure. But one thing is sure. Before we start talking about whether Jesus' miracles happened or not, we have to be sure about what a miracle is.

A miracle is:

1. Sharon Bentwhistle agreeing to go out with Kevin Krackit.
2. Being let off homework.
3. Walsall F.C. winning a game – oops!
4. Being allowed to lie in on a Saturday morning without being screamed at.
5. Not having to do the washing up.
6. Passing my exams

What is a miracle?

Is it . . .

- the birth of a baby?
- going to the moon?
- spring, when the flowers come out?
- television?
- heart operations?
- electricity?

People often say that *nature* is full of miracles. After all, no one can make a tree or a flower.

People also say that *inventions* or *developments in science* are miracles. Some things that were impossible a few years ago are now part of our everyday lives. These things cause us to *wonder* and they are *unexpected* – just like miracles.

However, these aren't true miracles at all. They just appear so because we can't fully understand them. Those who *do* understand them don't see them as miracles. To a heart surgeon a heart op is just a heart op!

So what is a real miracle? Here are some possible miracles:

- Someone who has been 'brain dead' for 24 hours suddenly gets up and carries on a normal life.
- You discover one morning that you can float in air without any effort.
- 'Spot', your pet mongrel, suddenly begins to recite the Top Ten charts from 1960 to the present day.

In the fifteenth century a parachute jump would have been regarded as magical or miraculous. People then did not understand the laws of nature as we do now. Some things seem miraculous, but aren't. A real miracle is something that happens in a different way from the regular laws of nature.

The Bible and miracles

In the Bible miracles are *signs of power.*

The Jews believed in miracles

The Jews believed that God had delivered them from slavery in the land of Egypt. In their escape, God had parted the Red Sea for the people of Israel to cross (Exodus 14). At the heart of Jewish belief, therefore, was a belief in the mighty miracles of God.

The Old Testament also contains many stories about miracles, especially in the stories of the prophets Elijah and Elisha.

Jesus performed miracles

Jesus lived at a time when everyone believed in miracles. The people who lived then had no problem in believing that there were forces of good and evil in the world that could either help them or harm them.

In fact, Jesus was not alone in working miracles. There were many other people in his day who claimed amazing powers for themselves. The difference between Jesus and the other miracle workers was in the *meaning* and the *effect* of Jesus' miracles.

The Jews in Jesus' time had *apocalyptic* beliefs. Perhaps they had begun to adopt these when they were in exile in Babylon. They began to believe more in demons and angels – in supernatural powers and in the end of the world. These beliefs are more like *Babylonian* beliefs and are not found in any developed way in the Old Testament.

Why did Jesus need to perform miracles?

Luke believes that Jesus came to offer salvation – he came to give freedom from sickness and oppression. The miracles were **signs of God's salvation** (see Unit 9.2 for more about this). They showed God breaking into history and saving the lost and the outcast.

Did Jesus really perform miracles?

Different people have different answers to this question. Many people agree on the *meaning* of the miracle stories, but they disagree on whether the miracles actually happened or not. Here is a range of opinions on this question:

Yes, the miracles happened just as Luke recorded them. Jesus was the Son of God and could work with God's power.

No, the miracles are only legends. They are stories of power to show that Jesus was a powerful person. They were added to the story of Jesus' life only later.

Some miracles happened; others did not. It is possible, they say, that Jesus healed people. It is not possible, however, that Jesus walked on the water or fed 5,000 people with five loaves and two fish.

The miracles happened, and the stories have been chosen carefully by Luke to show something about the power and character of Jesus and what he had come to preach – namely, the Kingdom of God.

The miracles did not happen. They are only special stories to show something of the power and character of Jesus and what he had come to preach – namely, the Kingdom of God.

Whatever we think of the miracles, they were important to Luke. In his Gospel, even Jesus' birth was miraculous. Mary was a virgin and an angel told her that she would have a son without an earthly father. So Jesus was surrounded by the supernatural right from the start of the Gospel. Luke believed that the real miracle of Jesus was to change people's lives and bring them into the Kingdom of God. Jesus' other miracles are there to show the *power* of this Kingdom and to give people a taste of what the Kingdom of God is like.

Through the miracles Luke shows that Jesus is:

- the Messiah
- the Son of God
- the fulfilment of the Old Testament promises

He also shows what Jesus does:

- he brings salvation to the whole world
- he preaches and teaches about God
- he announces the Kingdom of God
- he attacks the influence of the Devil

A miracle is a 'marvellous event due to some supposed supernatural agency'. (*Oxford English Dictionary*)

How are we to understand miracles?

Either the miracles happened or they did not. They are factual events or they are legendary stories.

Perhaps events, like the healings, did happen and the people thought they were miracles. If Jesus did the same things today we would have another explanation for them.

The miracles did happen – but our beliefs about what is possible and not possible have changed.

Maybe, instead of asking whether the miracles happened or not, it is better to ask: *what stops people today believing in miracles?*

'Science has disproved miracles.'

People think this because science has explained so much of how the world works. The world is governed by rational laws. If it contains *only* things that we can see, touch, taste, smell and hear, there is no room for miracles – and we feel disturbed at the thought of any of these rules being broken.

But although science explains *how* things work, it does not explain *why* things are there, or what their meaning is. In any case, a miracle is an event that *breaks* the normal 'scientific' laws – or seems to.

It is not science that says miracles are impossible, it is *what we believe about science.* Miracles are outside our experience. People say:

'Miracles don't happen in our society, therefore they do not exist.'

But that is not quite true. Many so-called miracles do still happen. Some churches still claim that miracles of healing and the casting out of demons happen even today.

'If many people *do not* believe something, it is hard to believe that it is true.'

Our beliefs are affected by what other people believe, but that doesn't mean we're right.

'In our society it is hard to believe in supernatural miracles.'

True, but that does not mean that they cannot happen.

Remember, a miracle is more than just a *show of power* – it involves *a way of seeing the world.*

To enter God's Kingdom, the people whom Jesus taught and helped had to see God working.

Does it matter whether the miracles happened or not?

There are different answers to this question.

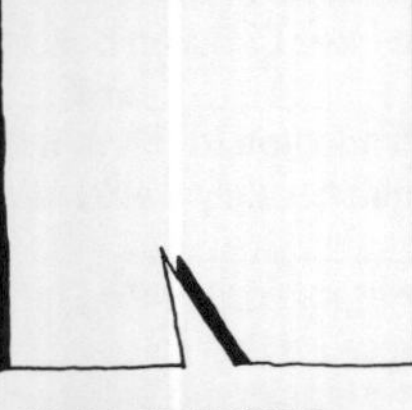

NO, IT DOESN'T

- Some people look at the *theological* meaning of the miracles – what do the miracles tell us about God? They do not worry if they actually happened or not.
- Some people believe that Jesus' teaching and life are what is important. The stories of the miracles count only as illustrations of Jesus' character.

YES, IT DOES

- Some people believe that the miracles showed who Jesus really was. They believe that Jesus' life, words and power have to go together to convince people that he is really the Son of God.

In the end, no one can actually *prove* whether the miracles happened or not. But there can be no doubt that the miracle stories are important for Luke. They help to explain the significance of Jesus. The miracles, therefore, have a *theological* meaning.

But what about us? Do Jesus' miracles have any importance today? Did they really happen? And, more than that, does it really matter if they happened or not?

In Jesus' time everyone believed in miracles. Today that is not the case. What do you think?

Question time

1. What is a miracle? Explain your view.

2. Why did Jesus perform miracles? What explanation might Christians give in answer to this question?

3. How important is it for Christians to believe in miracles?

- It is very important for Christians to believe in miracles, because otherwise it is difficult to believe in basic Christian beliefs about Jesus, such as ____________ and ____________. In addition to this is, if Christians cannot believe in miracles they would have problems believing ____________.
- It is possible for Christians to believe in miracles because they ____________.
- Miracles are unimportant for the Christian because they only ____________. What is really important is not whether the miracles actually happened but rather ____________.

To do

- *Debate* the issue: 'This class believes that miracles can and do happen.' The class selects speakers for and against the motion. Then, after each has given his or her views publicly, vote on the issue.
- *Class survey*

Get a large sheet of cardboard or paper. Draw two lines on the page so that it is divided into three columns. Write the headings

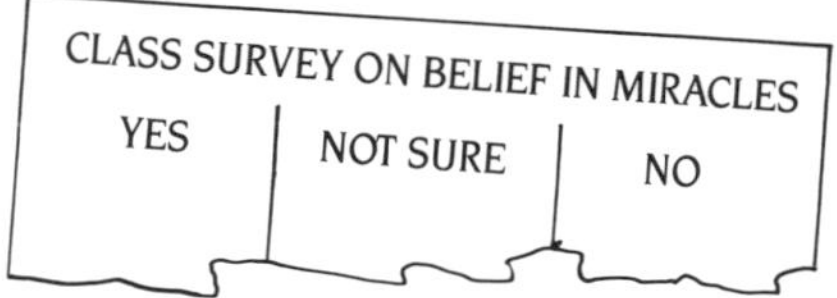

Pass the card round the class for each person to put a tick in the appropriate column and then write a sentence to explain their choice on another piece of paper. Discuss the differences of opinion.

Talking-point

Is seeing believing? Look at the photo and information from Lourdes. What do people believe about what they saw? Why do you think their interpretations of the event differed? What is true in this event?

UNIT 9.2

Jesus and his Miracles

Luke must have thought that Jesus' miracles were important and had a meaning – otherwise he would not have written about them.

Miracles in the Gospels

In the four Gospels there are about thirty-five different occasions when Jesus performed a miracle. These miracles fall roughly into *four* groups:

When Jesus healed the sick, including blindness, deafness and dumbness.

When Jesus raised people from the dead There are three examples of this in the Gospels – the widow of Nain's son, Jairus' daughter, and Lazarus.

When Jesus cast out demons People believed that these demons were evil forces or spirits of the Devil that often caused illnesses and mental disorders.

When Jesus showed his power over nature Jesus walked on water, fed 5,000 people with five loaves and two fishes, and calmed a fierce storm.

Miracles as evidence of the Kingdom

When Jesus spoke in the synagogue at Nazareth right at the beginning of his ministry, he quoted from Isaiah 61:1–2. He said that

- the poor would hear good news
- people in prison would be set free
- the blind would see
- the oppressed would no longer have to suffer
- God was about to save his people.

These were to be evidence that the Kingdom of God was at work.

- *When Jesus healed the sick* he showed the love of God reaching to people who were suffering.
- *When Jesus raised people from the dead* he showed that the power of God was stronger than death and nothing could stand in God's way.
- *When Jesus cast out demons* he showed that the Kingdom of God was stronger than the kingdom of Satan – and that Satan was being defeated.
- *When Jesus showed his power over nature* he showed God's power breaking into the world. God could do marvellous things for his people that were unexpected and seemed impossible.

The miracles in Luke

Luke records examples of all four kinds of miracles in his Gospel. They are as follows:

Jesus heals the sick

– Man with a skin disease (Luke 5:12–13)
– The centurion's servant (Luke 7:1–10)
– Peter's mother-in-law (Luke 4:38–39)
– The paralyzed man (Luke 5:18–25)
– The woman with a haemorrhage (Luke 8:43–48)
– Man with a paralyzed arm (Luke 6:6–10)
– The blind beggar (Luke 18:35–43)
– The man with swollen limbs (Luke 14:1–4)
– The ten men with a skin disease (Luke 17:11–19)
– Healing the ear of the High Priest's slave (Luke 22:50–51)

Jesus raises people from the dead

– Jairus' daughter (Luke 8:41–42, 49–56)
– The widow's son at Nain (Luke 7:11–15)

Jesus casts out demons
– The man with demons at Gadara (Luke 8:27–35)
– Dumb man with a demon (Luke 11:14)
– Boy with epilepsy and a demon (Luke 9:38–43)
– Man with an evil spirit at the synagogue (Luke 4:33–35)
– Crippled woman with an evil spirit (Luke 13:11–13)

Jesus shows his power over nature
– Jesus calms the storm (Luke 8:22–25)
– Jesus feeds the 5,000 (Luke 9:12–17)
– The marvellous catch of fish (Luke 5:1–11)

Luke records that Jesus calmed a fierce storm on Lake Galilee, showing his complete command over the forces of nature.

Where did Luke get his miracles?

Altogether, Luke records twenty miracles of Jesus. Of these twenty:

- fourteen are also in Mark
- two are 'Q' material – only in Matthew and Luke.

These are:
– The centurion's servant (Luke 7:1–10)
– The dumb man with a demon (Luke 11:14)

- Four miracles are found only in Luke:

– The crippled woman with an evil spirit (Luke 13:11–13)
– The man with swollen limbs (Luke 14:1–4)
– The ten men with a skin disease (Luke 17:11–19)
– Healing the ear of the High Priest's slave (Luke 22:50–51)

The purpose of miracles

In the synoptic Gospels, the Greek word used for 'miracles' is *dunameis* – a word meaning 'acts of power'. John's Gospel, however, uses the word *semeia*, 'signs' to describe Jesus' miracles. The miracles have a meaning beyond what can be seen with the eyes. For the synoptic writers in particular, Jesus' miracles show . . .

- *the power of God* Jesus tells the paralyzed man (Luke 5:18–25) that his sins are forgiven. The Jews believed that only God could forgive sins. But the man's healing is more than simply physical, it is a healing of his relationship with God. The miracle of this man's healing brings him into the Kingdom of God.

- *the power of faith in God* When Jesus healed the centurion's servant (Luke 7:1–10) he said, 'I tell you, I have never found faith like this, not even in Israel.' The centurion's faith became part of Jesus' miracle. It was not just the healing that was important. It was important that the centurion saw that Jesus' power to heal came from God. Jesus' miracles, therefore, helped people to have faith in God and bring them into God's Kingdom.

- *the depth of God's love* When Jesus saw the widow at Nain (Luke 7:11–15) he told her not to cry. He went over and touched the coffin of her son and brought him back to life. Jesus' miracles were not just a *show of power* – they were *acts of love*. Jesus' miracles helped people, touching and changing their lives. They showed people something of the power of God and how much God cared for them.

There is no doubt that Luke thought Jesus' miracles were important. They were signs of God's power and God's Kingdom. They showed who Jesus was. They showed he was not just a man of words – he was the Son of God.

FOLLOW UP

Question time

1. Jesus' miracles in the Gospels fall into four groups – what are they?

2. Give an example of Jesus healing the sick. Outline the story and say where it is found in Luke's Gospel.

3. What do the miracles show about Jesus?

To do

Imagine that you are a spectator in the crowd at the healing of the woman with a haemorrhage (Luke 8:43–48).

After the event the local newspaper wants an eye-witness report of what happened. Use the Gospel account to help you reconstruct what it must have been like. Use the first person ('I') and include the following in your account:
– the location of the event
– the atmosphere in the crowd after this had happened
– what people were saying
– what Jesus said

What sort of conversation might have gone on in the crowd? Would everyone have seen it as a miracle?

UNIT 9.3

The Meaning of the Miracles

The stories that Luke writes in his Gospel about Jesus always have a meaning. They are there, not simply to tell a story, but to tell Luke's readers something about Jesus' life, person and ministry. They help to explain *the meaning of Jesus.*

The miracle stories in Luke are often found in a special *context*. If you read what comes before and after the miracle, you often see that the miracle shows more than just Jesus' power. It might show Jesus' attitude to the Gentiles, for example, or perhaps to the Jewish Law.

In their own way, the miracles give Luke's readers a strong idea of what Jesus was like.

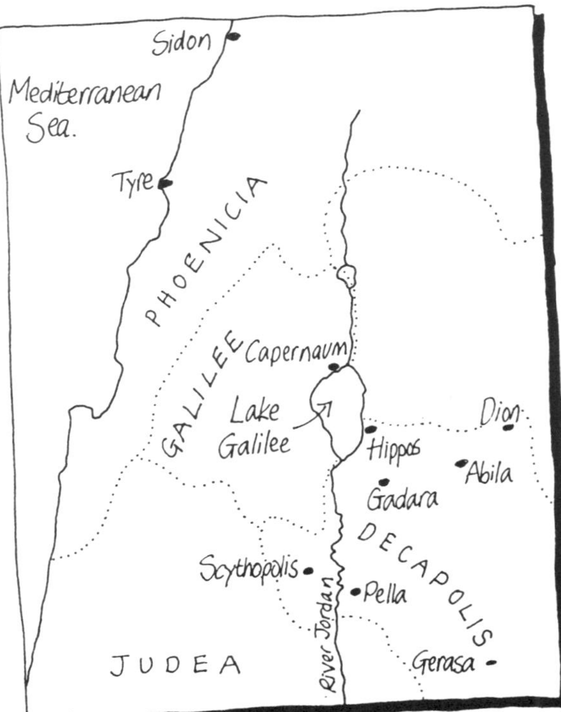

The miracles show the coming of the Kingdom of God. And they show the power of the Holy Spirit working through Jesus (Luke 4:14; 24:49).

In this unit, we will investigate four different miracles that Jesus peformed. Each miracle story is an example of the four types of miracle that we looked at in the last unit. Luke puts these four miracles together in a group (Luke 8:22–56). These stories also appear in Mark, though Luke changes them slightly. Luke usually shortens Mark's stories to fit them into his own longer Gospel.

In these stories, Luke adds 'acts of power' to Jesus' words to make people question who he really was.

Jesus calms the storm 1

READ LUKE 8:22–25

This story of Jesus' power over nature tells us some important things about Jesus. It shows:

- *Jesus was powerful.* The storm calmed down when Jesus told it to.
- *Jesus was mysterious.* Jesus' disciples were amazed and afraid at what Jesus had done. They already knew that he was a teacher and a prophet, but this miracle showed that he was more than that.
- *Jesus responded to people.* Jesus calmed the storm because his disciples had asked him to. It was not his idea. He must have been very tired from his teaching and travelling to have slept through such bad weather.
- *Jesus had faith.* Jesus had no doubt that the storm would die down because he had told it to. He had faith. This was the same faith that he wanted his disciples to have.

Another way of looking at this miracle is to say that Luke is giving a special message to the early church.

- The stormy sea is not a real sea – it is a picture of the troubles and problems of life. The early church suffered dreadful persecution and the stormy sea is a picture of the church's situation.
- The boat is symbolic of the church.
- The disciples are the Christians crying out to Jesus to save them. The boat is filling with water.
- Even in a time of very bad trouble and hardship Jesus hears the cries of his followers and comes to save them.

This is an *allegorical* or *figurative* ▶▶▶

Lourdes works its miracle

JOSEPH Charp
face beams a
as he walks
li
rs in a

The newspaper headline below this picture read: 'Lourdes works its miracle.' Joseph Charpentier (59) had been wheelchair-bound for 19 years when he came to the grotto at Lourdes to pray for a cure. During the healing service he was anointed with oil, and ten minutes later, to quote his own words: 'I felt a great warmth rise from my feet to my heart.' The picture shows him standing for the first time. And he returned to his village pushing his wheelchair. The villagers were amazed, but not all were convinced.

'I won't say it's a miracle, but it's certainly extraordinary,' said the priest.

A Paris physiotherapist said, 'This recovery was too spectacularly quick to be plausible.' Wasted leg muscles can be revived only slowly.

A rheumatologist suggested Charpentier might have been suffering from a psychic disorder: Lourdes produced a psychological shock which broke the syndrome of unconsciously simulated illness.

interpretation of the story. This view of the miracle says that the miracle was not historically true, but nevertheless it had a meaning for the lives of Christians in the early church – the very people Luke was writing for. Many Christians have accepted both the historical accuracy of the story *and* its deeper significance.

The Bible said that humankind was to be the Lord of Nature (see Genesis 1:26; Psalm 8). But men and women lost this position by becoming separated from God by their disobedience. Jesus was not separated from God and was able to show what it was like to be Lord over nature.

Jesus and the man with demons at Gadara

After calming a stormy sea, Jesus goes on to calm a stormy mind. Luke probably put these two stories together to show that Jesus had authority over chaos in nature, and over chaos in people. The miracle shows his power over demons. Note that in crossing the Sea of Galilee, Jesus was moving from territory lived in by the Jews to territory lived in by Gentiles.

- The man was alone and mad, living among the tombs.
- He was occupied by an army of demons – called 'legion'. (Israel was occupied by an army of Romans divided into *legions*. A legion included 6,000 men.)
- The demons knew who Jesus was and came out at his command.
- The demons were 'unclean' things and went into 'unclean' animals – a herd of pigs. (According to Jewish law, pigs were 'unclean' – they could not be eaten.) Perhaps Jesus sent the demons into the pigs, which then drowned, to show the man that they had really left him and would never return.
- The local people were afraid, but the man was cured. By meeting Jesus the man had been freed from the demons and changed completely. Once more, the Kingdom of God had defeated the rule of Satan in people's lives.

Jesus had shown that it was Satan's army and not the Roman army that he wanted to defeat.

Another way of looking at this miracle is to say:

- The man was mentally disturbed. Perhaps the disruption that the Roman army had caused in his life some time in the past had deranged him. This may be why the demons are called 'legion'.
- Instead of meeting brutality (from the Romans) or rejection (from the local people) the man is *accepted* by Jesus. It is Jesus' acceptance that causes the man's healing.

Jesus and Jairus' daughter

READ LUKE 8:40–42, 49–56 **3**

This miracle shows Jesus' power over death. Jesus returned to Galilee where a great crowd was waiting for him.

- Jairus was a Jewish leader, and an elder of the synagogue. It must have taken courage for him to come forward and ask Jesus for help. Many other Jewish leaders were against Jesus.
- Luke, unlike Mark, makes the girl Jairus' only daughter. It is clear that this miracle is not just a show of power – it is an act of love. Jesus wants to help Jairus and give him back his daughter.
- Jesus goes to Jairus' house. The people there laugh at Jesus. But Jesus ignores them and raises the girl from death. This story shows how God can do the impossible. He can give back what seems to have been lost for ever.

There are two other examples in the Gospels of Jesus raising someone from the dead. They are:

- the widow of Nain's son (Luke 7:11–17)
- Lazarus (John 11:38–44)

Some believe that these stories are not historically true; others disagree. Another view is that these stories *preview* Jesus' own death and resurrection. In bringing the dead to life, Jesus is prophesying what will happen to him and showing how those who have faith in him will share in the life to come.

Jesus and the woman with a haemorrhage

READ LUKE 8:43–48

This fourth miracle shows Jesus' power over illness.

- The story of Jairus' daughter is interrupted by the appearance of a woman with a haemorrhage. The woman had an illness which made her bleed without stopping.
- According to Jewish Law, the woman's bleeding (which was menstrual) meant that she could not join in the Jewish religious ceremonies. The Jews believed that even if she touched another person then she passed her uncleanness on to them. It is not surprising that she tried to touch Jesus without letting him know that she had done so.
- Jesus felt the woman's touch.
- Jesus felt healing power go out of him.
- Jesus made the woman tell the crowd what she had done.

Jesus did not want to embarrass the woman. But he did want her to know that it was not just his power, but her faith that had made her well.

Some scholars see the woman's faith as the most important point in the story. They would say that it is a story about the faith that a follower of Jesus should have, more than a story about the healing power of Jesus. Obviously, Luke could have intended it to be *both* a healing story and a story about faith.

FOLLOW UP

Question time

1. Outline the miracle of the storm on the lake (Luke 8:22–25).
How is Luke using this story?
What does the miracle show about Jesus?
How has this story been understood by different people?

2. Fill in the following sentences (about Jesus and the man with demons at Gadara: Luke 8:26–29):
The man was alone and mad and he lived ____________.
He was occupied by an army of demons called ____________.
Jesus commanded the demons to ____________.
They left the man and entered ____________.
The people in the area were ____________.

Why do you think Luke has included this miracle? What does it show about the Kingdom of God?

To do

Front page headline (see Luke 8:40–42, 49–56). You are the chief reporter on the *Galilee News.* Design a front page report including headline on the healing of Jairus' daughter.

Talking-point

Do people still believe in demons today? Who does? Why do they?

Jesus, Friend to Outcasts

How many times have you heard these words or thought them? Maybe there are people in your school who think some of these things about you. Maybe there are people in your school that no one wants to know.

An *outcast* is somebody whom no one wants to know. This might be because of age, disease, belief, anti-social behaviour, colour of skin, gender, race, or simply because someone is in some way 'different'. Whatever the reason, an outcast is shut out of normal society.

In ancient Israel there were many such people. The Jewish people believed that they had been chosen by God and had a special relationship with God. The Gentiles (non-Jewish peoples) did not have this relationship with God.

As in any society, there were people who were not liked, and who were treated as outcasts.

- *The Romans* The Romans had conquered Israel and were hated as any occupying army is hated.
- *The Samaritans* The Samaritans held some Jewish beliefs and were racially related to the Jews. There were many religious and cultural disagreements between the Jews and the Samaritans. Both sides distrusted and feared each other.
- *The lepers* People in Jesus' time were afraid of catching the terrible disease of leprosy. Lepers were isolated from society, so to catch leprosy meant giving up your work and your family. No one would touch a leper. The Jews saw this disease as a punishment from God.

Jesus and outcasts

One of the remarkable features of Jesus' ministry is that he helped and welcomed outcasts. This aspect of Jesus' ministry was foretold by Mary in the *Magnificat*, a prophetic song recorded in Luke 1:46–55. When Jesus began his ministry in his home town of Nazareth (Luke 4:18–19), he quoted Isaiah 61:1–2, showing how God would change the destiny of all outcasts.

Jesus travelled around the countryside preaching, teaching and healing. Luke makes special mention of Jesus' dealing with certain outcasts and tells their story.

Here are three outcasts whom Jesus met on his journey.

The centurion (read Luke 7:1–10) The centurion was a Roman officer. He was a man whom the Jews would have hated, but Jesus praised him for his faith. He said that he had not seen such great faith as this centurion's in the whole of Israel. Instead of turning away from him, Jesus answered his request and healed his slave.

The man with leprosy (read Luke 5:12–14) Jesus not only healed this leper, he *touched* him. This is something that no one ever dared to do. They would normally have been too afraid of catching the disease.

It is also interesting to look at Luke 17:11–19 and the story of the ten lepers whom Jesus healed. In this story, the only one who came back to thank him was a *Samaritan*. Jesus' Jewish listeners may well have been shocked by the ending of this story.

The tax collector (read Luke 19:1–10) The story of Zacchaeus is funny and well known. Jesus welcomed Zacchaeus and invited himself to his home. Tax collectors were despised by ordinary Jewish people because they worked for the Romans and made money out of the poor. Many people would have disapproved of Jesus making friends with this man, especially as Jesus was a religious figure.

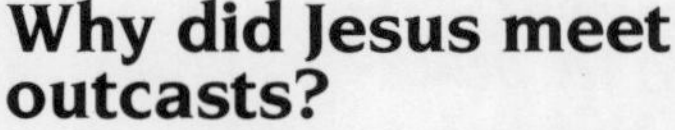

Why did Jesus meet outcasts?

Jesus came to proclaim a Kingdom – the Kingdom of God. This Kingdom was not to be a political state, like the country of Israel, but the rule of God in people's lives.

In his Gospel, Luke shows:

- that the Kingdom of God is also for *Gentiles*. This is an important point in the story of the healing of the centurion's slave in Luke 7.

- that the Kingdom of God is *universal*. The Gospel of Jesus is to be for the whole world. This is made very clear in Luke 24:47 where it is emphasized that the Gospel is to be preached to all nations.

- that though the Gospel is for the whole world, Jesus is still a *Jewish* Messiah. Luke emphasizes this. One example is that Jerusalem, the Jewish capital, is given much greater importance than in the other Gospels.

It is a feature of Luke's Gospel that the religious people – those who should have known most about God – rejected Jesus. At the same time, many outcasts, those who had themselves been rejected, became part of the Kingdom of God.

What did Jesus do for outcasts?

- *He healed them*. The centurion's slave and the leper were both healed.
- *He welcomed them*. Jesus did not turn away from the centurion, the leper or the tax collector, even though other people did not approve of them.
- *He forgave them*. Jesus often went to the parties of those who were looked down on. His explanation to those who criticized him for this was that these were the very people he had come to help. Jesus also told the outcasts that their sins had been forgiven. This made him unpopular, as the Jews believed that only God had the right to forgive sins. In their opinion Jesus was, after all, only a man.

Other outcasts whom Jesus healed

- **Man with an evil spirit** (Luke 4:31–36) Jesus drove out an evil spirit. People who had evil spirits in them often acted strangely and became outcasts. Luke 8:26–39 tells a long story about such a man and how Jesus healed him.
- **Tax collector** (Luke 5:27–32) Jesus called Levi, a tax collector who must have been despised by the local community.
- **'Sinful woman'** (Luke 7:36–50) Jesus was anointed with oil by a 'sinful woman'. This woman was probably a prostitute.
- **Woman with a haemorrhage** (Luke 8:43–48) Jesus healed a woman who had been bleeding for a long time. According to Jewish Law, the woman's bleeding would have made her *unclean*. She too was probably an outcast.

What did Jesus say to the outcasts?

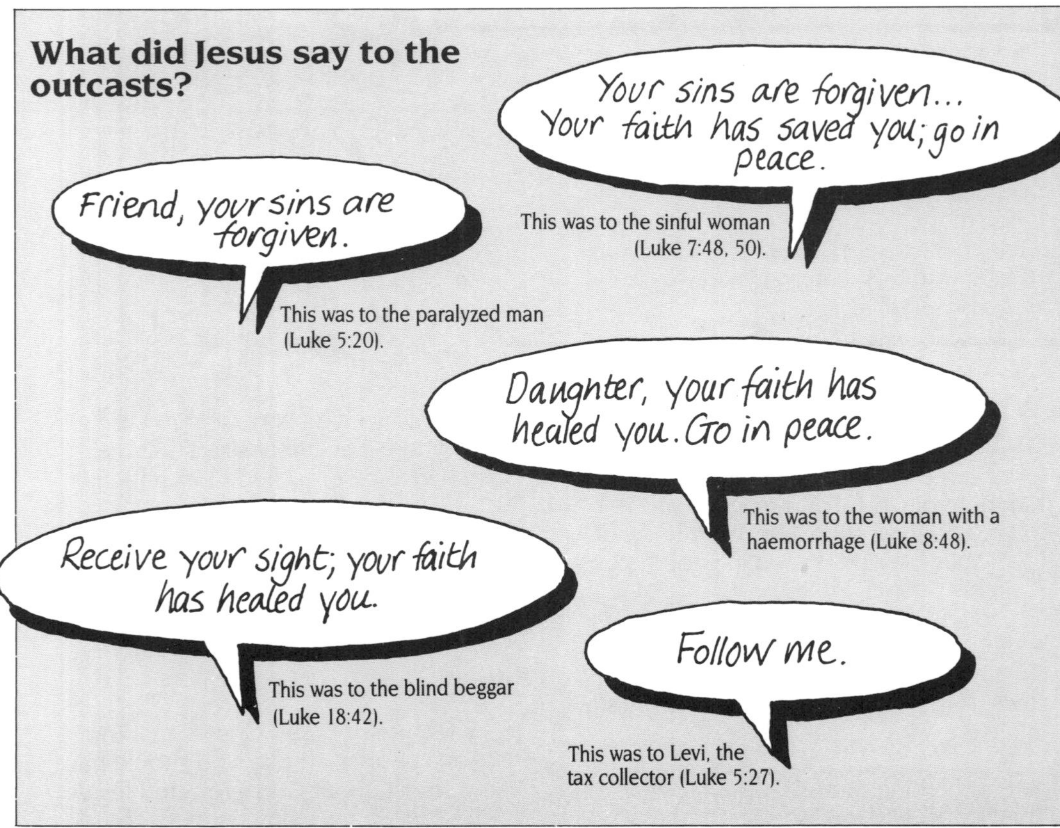

This was to the sinful woman (Luke 7:48, 50).

This was to the paralyzed man (Luke 5:20).

This was to the woman with a haemorrhage (Luke 8:48).

This was to the blind beggar (Luke 18:42).

This was to Levi, the tax collector (Luke 5:27).

FOLLOW UP

Question time

1. What is an outcast?

2. Why were Samaritans treated as outcasts?

3. What do we learn about the Kingdom of God from what Luke records about how Jesus treated outcasts?

4. What did Jesus do for outcasts?

To do

Draw a *speechogram* like the one below. Then fill the speech bubbles with what Jesus said to the outcasts of his day.

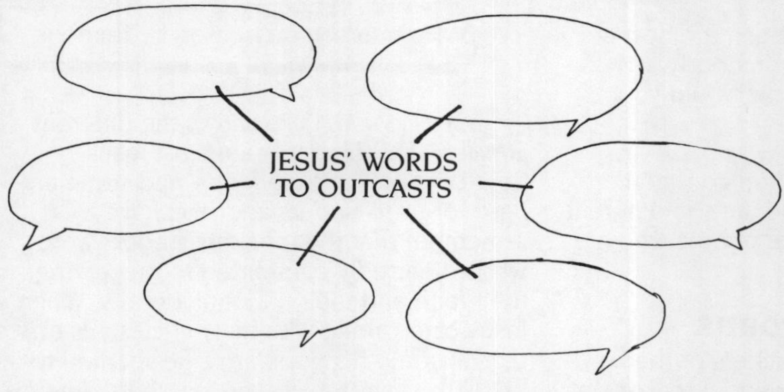

Talking-point

Who are the outcasts in our society today? Choose from this list (or add to it and explain your choice):

Gypsies
The poor
Unemployed people
Single parents
Prisoners
Tramps
The elderly
The disabled
Ethnic minorities
Drug addicts
Aids sufferers

UNIT 10.2

Jesus, the Outcast

- Imagine you have been top of the class for a year and somebody arrives who is better than you. How would you feel?

- Imagine you have been the ace footballer in the team for eighteen months and someone arrives who is better than you. How would you feel?

- Imagine that you have been the best at drama in your class and somebody arrives who is better than you. How would you feel?

Jealousy, fear and *prejudice* often go together. We do not like people who are too different from us and we do not like people who are much better than us.

Grumbles and groans

The Pharisees and the teachers of the Law did not like Jesus for a variety of reasons. Here are some of the things they said about him:

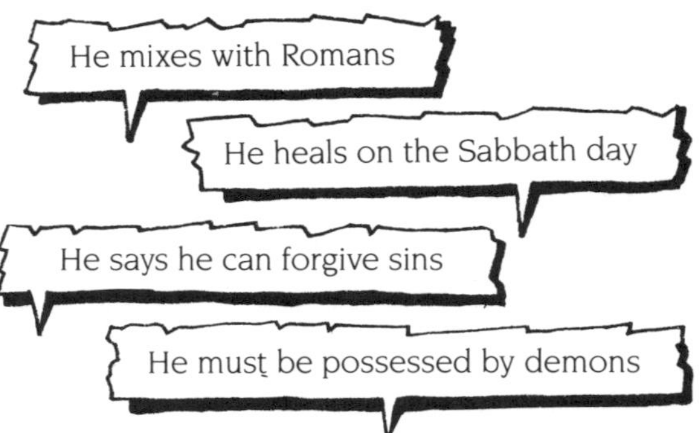

In his Gospel, Luke shows the different *prejudices* that there were against Jesus. Some of these are obvious – and some are hard for us to understand. You have to remember that the religious leaders were whole-heartedly committed to preserving their faith and their national identity. When Jesus came along with his miracles, his new teaching and his popularity, he seemed to break the Jewish Law. The Jewish leaders did not like this. They saw Jesus as a *threat*. They wanted him stopped.

Why were the religious leaders so prejudiced against Jesus?

There were many reasons for their hostility to Jesus:

- *Jesus healed on the Sabbath* (Luke 6:6–10). For the Jews, the Sabbath day was holy. It was the day of rest and the Jews were commanded to do no work (see Exodus 20:8). But Jesus healed on the Sabbath. According to the Pharisees' interpretation of the Law, this counted as work and so they said that Jesus was breaking the Law. If he was breaking the Law, he could not properly love God. But Jesus rejected their interpretation of the Law. He said it was lawful to show God's love and forgiveness on the Sabbath.

• *Jesus forgave sins.* For the Jewish faith, forgiving sins was something that only God could do. Jesus caused shock and offence by telling people that their sins were forgiven.

• *Jesus' disciples broke the rules* (Luke 6:1–5). In this story the Pharisees criticized Jesus' disciples for picking and eating grains of corn on the Sabbath. In the Pharisees' eyes this counted as work. Jesus answered them by saying, 'The Son of Man is Lord of the Sabbath.' He said that he had authority over the Law. This was going too far for the Pharisees.

• *Jesus criticized the religious leaders of his day* (see Luke 11:37–54). The Pharisees did not like Jesus because he spoke out against some of them. Jesus criticized the Pharisees who:

The scroll contains the Torah, honoured in Judaism as God's sacred Law. The Pharisees regarded themselves as entrusted with keeping and teaching God's Law: when Jesus appeared to break it they were outraged.

– followed the Jewish laws, but were 'full of greed and wickedness' (Luke 11:39).
– seemed to practise the Law, but neglected the love and justice of God (Luke 11:42).
– loved the most important seats in the synagogue and being greeted as important people in the market-place (Luke 11:43).
– loaded people down by giving them unnecessary rules to follow. They did not really help people (Luke 11:46).
– people like them killed the prophets in olden times (Luke 11:48).
– hindered people from coming close to God (Luke 11:52).

Naturally the Pharisees and the experts in the Law objected to Jesus' words. They began to look for ways to remove him.

• *He mixed with outcasts.* This made him 'unclean' in the eyes of the Jewish leaders. If you were clean you were acceptable to God. If you were not clean you were not acceptable to God. You became clean and stayed that way by following the Jewish Law very closely. This included not mixing with criminals and people who had suspect morals.

• *Jesus made great claims for himself.* He was the son of a carpenter and had no special religious training. When he preached at Nazareth, the people in the synagogue exclaimed, 'Isn't this Joseph's son?' (Luke 4:22). They could not believe that a local boy like Jesus could be the Messiah, and they attacked him physically because of the claims he made for himself.

• *Jesus ate, drank and feasted* (see Luke 5:33–35). The Pharisees (like the disciples of John) lived a strict life that included fasting. Jesus, on the other hand, did not do this. The Pharisees did not see how Jesus could call himself a religious leader if he went to parties and drank.

• *Jesus had power.* Jesus healed people, cast out demons and worked miracles. The Pharisees were jealous of this. Some said that Jesus' power came from the Devil (see

Luke 11:14–28), but Jesus showed that this was not the case.

● *Jesus was from Galilee.* The English make jokes about the Irish. The French make jokes about the Belgians. The Germans make jokes about the Scots. The Jews in Jesus' day made jokes about people from Galilee. The Galileans were considered to be rough northerners who were a bit thick. They spoke in a funny accent. There would have been some prejudice against Jesus because of this.

Jesus, the outcast

Jesus suffered more than prejudice. In some ways he actually *became* an outcast. In doing so, he **identified with outcasts** everywhere, whatever their problems. In what ways was Jesus an outcast?

● Jesus was illegitimate. Joseph was not his father (Luke 1:26–38).
● There was no room for Jesus at the inn: he was born without a home (Luke 2:4–7).
● Jesus and his parents became refugees. They had to flee to Egypt until King Herod had died (Matthew 2:13–14).
● Jesus was rejected when he preached in his home town of Nazareth (Luke 4:13–30).
● During his ministry, Jesus had no home of his own, no money and no job (Luke 9:58).
● Jesus was rejected by the religious and political leaders of his day (Luke 14).
● Jesus died a criminal's death 'under God's curse' (see Deuteronomy 21:23). This was one of the most horrible of all Roman punishments (Luke 23:26–49).

Question time

1. List the things that some of the Pharisees and scribes said about Jesus.

2. Why were so many of the Jewish leaders prejudiced against Jesus?

3. In what ways was Jesus himself an outcast?

To do

Design a public poster entitled **Jesus the outcast**. The aim is to inform people about what Jesus does and who he mixes with, so that they will know about his claims and will not be influenced by him. Include warnings about disregard of the Sabbath law.

UNIT 10.3

Teaching about Outcasts in Luke's Gospel

Jesus welcomed outcasts. Jesus identified with outcasts. And Jesus taught about outcasts. Some of Jesus' teaching about outcasts is to be found only in Luke. In fact, two of the most famous stories in the whole Bible – *the good Samaritan* (Luke 10:30–37) and *the lost son* (Luke 15:11–32) appear only in Luke. They are part of the special Lucan material that scholars call 'L'.

In this unit, we will look at three of Jesus' stories about outcasts.

Jesus chose the lonely road between Jerusalem and Jericho, with its bandit country, as the scenario for his story of the good Samaritan. The point was that 'loving our neighbour' means helping anyone at all who happens to be in need. To underline the point he chose a Samaritan, belonging to a race the Jews despised, as the one who helped the injured Jew.

The good Samaritan

READ LUKE 10:30–37 

Here is a summary of the story:

- A man was on his way from Jerusalem to Jericho.
- Suddenly he was attacked by robbers. They took everything and left him for dead.
- A priest came along. But when he saw the man he crossed to the other side of the road and passed by.
- Then a Levite came along. He did exactly the same thing.
- Finally a Samaritan came along. He stopped and helped the man.

● He bandaged him up and helped him to his feet.
● He put him on his donkey.
● Then he paid for the man to stay at an inn until he was better.

What is special about this story?
● The Jews hated the Samaritans. They would not have liked the idea of a Samaritan helping them.
● The priest and Levite were religious figures, devoutly upholding the Law, and yet they failed to do what the Law strongly stressed – show love to their neighbour. By contrast, the Samaritan (who had the 'wrong' religion, according to Jewish teachers) stopped and put himself out for the wounded man. The Samaritan, with his donkey and money, was clearly a rich man, and therefore a target for robbers, yet he took the risk of stopping to be a true neighbour.

A modern version of the good Samaritan story might begin with a scene like this one . . .

The lost son

READ LUKE 15:11–32

The story goes like this:
● There was a man who had two sons.
● The younger son asked for his share of his father's will (in advance) and left home. He proceeded to live it up.
● Soon a famine hit that country. The young man had no money left.
● Finally he managed to find a job looking after some pigs. He was so hungry that he even wanted to eat the pigs' food.
● Eventually he decided to go home. He was not sure what his father would say.
● But, as he approached home, his father saw him from a distance.
● The old man ran and greeted him with great joy.
● He organized a party for his son and dressed him in the best clothes he could find.
● The older brother was jealous. He had worked solidly for his father for many years. But the father told the older brother to rejoice. It was as if the younger brother had come back from the dead!

What is special about this story?
1. The Jews had been commanded by God to have a lot of respect for their parents. The younger son had rebelled. In the Old Testament (see Deuteronomy 21:18–21) the Law stated that such a rebellious son should be stoned to death.

Instead, Jesus presents the father as loving and forgiving. This is a new and powerful picture of God's character which Jesus' Jewish listeners would have found surprising.

2. The Jews were allowed to eat certain animals and were not allowed to eat others. Pigs were 'unclean' animals according to Jewish Law. The fact that the younger brother went to look after pigs showed how far he had fallen. He really had become an outcast.

In the story of the lost son, the younger boy fell so low that he took a job feeding the pigs – and he was so hungry he would gladly have shared their food, even though he had been brought up, like all Jews, to regard pigs as unclean creatures, on the list of forbidden food.

The Pharisee and the tax collector

READ LUKE 18:9–14

Here are the essentials of the story:

- Two men went up to the Temple to pray.
- One was a Pharisee. The other was a tax collector.
- The Pharisee thanked God that he was better than other people – especially the tax collector.
- The tax collector was too ashamed to look up.
- He bowed his head and said, 'Have mercy on me, God, a sinner.'
- Which one did God look kindly on?

What is special about this story?

1. The Pharisee was rich, powerful and religious. He had everything going for him. The tax collector was just the opposite. Yet, because the tax collector was honest in his prayers and genuinely sorry for the bad things he had done, he was forgiven by God.

2. Jewish people looked up to the Pharisees. They looked down on tax collectors. The Pharisees did the right things – they kept the Law and gave offerings to God. The tax collectors did the wrong things – they worked for the Romans and kept a lot of the people's money for themselves. In this story, however, it is the tax collector, the outcast, who is forgiven by God.

Other stories of Jesus

There are some other stories about outcasts that Jesus told. In Luke 15, the story of the lost son is the third story in a trio. The other two are the lost sheep and the lost coin. The lost coin and the lost son are found only in Luke.

The lost sheep. Read Luke 15:1–7. A shepherd leaves his ninety-nine sheep and goes in search of just one that has wandered off into the wilderness.

The lost coin. Read Luke 15:8–10. A woman loses a coin and won't rest till she finds it. It is very unusual in the Bible to find God pictured as a woman, as in this story.

The rich man and Lazarus. Read Luke 16:19–31. Lazarus, a beggar, goes to heaven, while the rich man goes to the world of the dead. In this story, the outcast comes out on top.

These stories show God seeking and rewarding the lost and the outcast. This aspect of God's character was something new that Jesus revealed. It must have surprised many of his listeners and still challenges people today.

FOLLOW UP

Question time

1. Why is the story of the Good Samaritan important? Here is a list of possible answers. Choose two answers and say why you think they are important for the Christian church today.

The story of the good Samaritan is important for Christians because . . .

- It says that religious people do not always do the right thing, so it makes the church think about its own faults.
- It says that there should be no prejudice against different races, so it teaches Christians to accept everyone equally as God's people.
- It teaches that the most unlikely people do the work of God, so the church should not be quick to say who is a good person and who is not.
- It teaches that real 'neighbours' have to go out of their way in terms of time and money and effort, and that the church should do the same to help those in need.

2. The parable of the lost son (Luke 15:11–32):

- If you were the father what would you have done in the situation?
- How does this illustrate Jesus' teaching on outcasts?
- How relevant to modern life is the story?
- With whom do you sympathize most in the parable?

To do

Find out about Christians who are helping outcasts today – for example, Cicely Saunders, Sally Trench, Dr Barnardo's homes, Tear Fund . . .

The Status of Women in New Testament Times

Luke, more than any other Gospel writer, records stories about women. This is especially interesting because at the time of Jesus (as in most other periods of world history), women had low status in society.

Women and marriage

In marriage, a woman was regarded more as a possession than as a person with her own rights. She was handed over to her husband by her father. Her husband could have other wives. Men could exercise the power of divorce freely; women could not. A woman could get a divorce if her husband was impotent or he refused to have sex with her or he restricted her movements unbearably – but, even so, the divorce was the husband's act and not the wife's.

Traditionally, women could divorce only on the grounds of adultery. But, by the time of Jesus, the religious teachers, the rabbis, disagreed about the grounds for divorce. The religious school of Shammai kept to the traditional teaching, but the school of Hillel was different. According to Hillel, divorce could happen for many reasons, great or small. For instance, a man was justified in divorcing his wife if she burned his meal. He could also divorce his wife if he desired another woman.

Women and society

There were rules in society about the behaviour of women in public. A man was not allowed to be alone with a woman. He could not exchange a glance or even greet a woman in public. Women were classed with children in legal matters, and were not allowed to give testimony in court.

Women and education

By the time of Jesus, a girl's education was entirely her mother's concern. This happened in the home and was limited to learning domestic skills like sewing, cooking and looking after babies or children.

A boy received his education at a school attached to the synagogue. He started his education at about the age of six. He learned the Jewish scriptures and the history, geography and literature of the Jews. In particular, he learned the Jewish religious Law contained in the Torah (the first five books of the Bible).

In contrast, a girl was in no circumstances to be taught the Torah. As one teacher put it: 'May the words of the Torah be burned, they should not be handed over to a woman.'

Women and religion

For a synagogue to be formed, there had to be a minimum of ten men. Women did not count. They stayed in an area apart from

the men, and, during the time of Herod's Temple, women were not allowed to go beyond the Court of the Gentiles and Women. If a woman was menstruating, she could not go even this far. If she had just given birth, she could not enter the Temple for forty days after childbirth.

At the time of Jesus, Jewish women had no rights or status of their own. A woman's place was defined first in relation to her father, then to her husband.

Women in the Gospels

The Gospel writers portray Jesus as a radical in the way he related to women.

• In John's Gospel
Jesus shows no social embarrassment when he asks a Samaritan woman (a social outcast) to give him a drink. He is alone with her, she is a Gentile, and they have a long conversation. In a society where there were strict rules separating the sexes, Jesus disregards the conventions of the day.

• In the synoptic Gospels
Jesus is surrounded by a crowd of people and he speaks to a woman with a haemorrhage of blood. She touches him and he speaks kindly to her. Not only is Jesus at ease with physical contact, but he says nothing of his being 'unclean' because he has touched a woman who has an issue of blood. Normally this would be considered contaminating and the man would have to purify himself before he could take part in any religious ritual.

• In Matthew's Gospel
Jesus teaches something new and different about married men desiring other women. He goes further than the different religious 'schools' when he says that even to look at a woman and want to possess her is committing adultery in the heart.

• In Mark's Gospel
(Mark 10:11),
when Jesus says that a man can commit adultery against his wife, he is saying something entirely new. The rabbis only recognized adultery as being a sin *against the husband*.

• In all four Gospels
Jesus' attitude to women was revolutionary for the time in which he lived. Luke, more than any other Gospel writer, included special material relating to women. In the next unit we will look at passages about women which are found only in Luke.

FOLLOW UP

Question time

1. What was the status of women in Jesus' day? Answer the following questions:

- In marriage the woman was regarded as ____________.
- Men could divorce women for ____________.
- In public there were rules about women such as ____________.
- A woman's education consisted of ____________.
- Women did not enjoy the same rights as men in religion, for instance ____________.

2. In what ways did Jesus disregard the social and religious conventions of his day in respect of women? Give examples from Matthew, Mark and Luke.

To do

Prepare a talk for the class on one of the following subjects:

A woman's work is to look after the home.
A woman should first and foremost have children and bring them up.
One woman is worth ten men.
Women and men are equal.
Society is against women.

Luke and Women

Luke's special material

Throughout his Gospel, Luke includes material which is concerned with women. The following passages are unique to Luke:

- **Mary, the mother of Jesus** (Luke 1)
Mary's story about becoming pregnant, her feelings, and her personal experience are all recorded. They are not recorded by Matthew. Compare the two stories. Mary's song of praise, the Magnificat, is used in many Christian churches week by week. Where did Luke get this material from? No one else has recorded it.

- **Anna the prophetess** (Luke 2)
Anna was an old lady of eighty-four. She worshipped God daily. When she saw the baby Jesus, she recognized him as someone special who would set Jerusalem free. She had insight that few others had.

- **The widow of Zarephath** (Luke 4)
Luke includes this story about a widow. In the Old Testament, the widow of Zarephath received help from God because of the prophet Elijah (1 Kings 17:10–24).

- **The widow of Nain** (Luke 7)
Luke mentions another widow who had lost her only son. Jesus performed a miracle at the funeral because he had pity on her.

- **The women who accompanied Jesus** (Luke 8)
Luke includes information about women who went with Jesus on some of his travels with the disciples. These were: Mary Magdalene (who had been healed of evil spirits), Joanna (whose husband Chuza was an officer in Herod's court) and Susanna. Luke also says that there were other women who helped Jesus and his disciples by sharing their resources.

- **The 'sinful woman'** (Luke 7)
Luke tells the story of a 'sinful woman' (probably a prostitute) who showed her love for Jesus by washing his feet and using expensive ointment. This was a custom at the time – travellers often walked on foot along dusty roads, and normally their host would provide a service like this. But Jesus' host, a Pharisee, did not do this, and it was left to this woman to wash his feet. Jesus showed no embarrassment by this intimate contact with such a woman. He said that her loving actions showed she was forgiven. This offended the customs of the day.

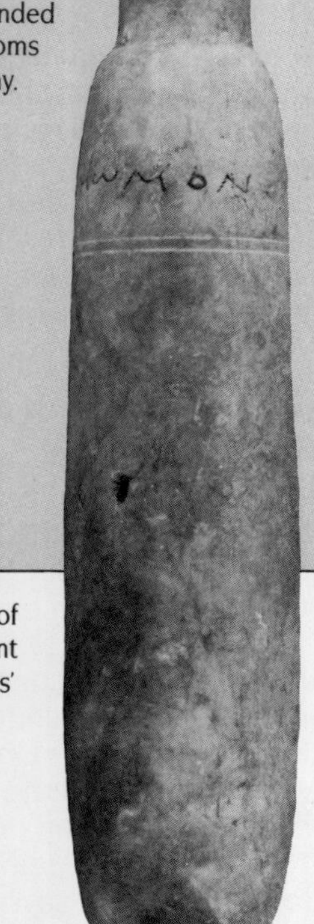

A scent-bottle, like the flask of expensive perfumed ointment the woman poured over Jesus' feet in the story recorded in Luke 7.

Luke's shared material

In some places Luke shares some stories with the other Gospel writers, but his accounts are different because he includes more detail. Here are two examples:

- **The parable of the unfaithful servant** (Luke 12:41–48 and Matthew 24:45–51)
Luke includes a mention of servants being both men and women, whereas Matthew only talks about men servants.

- **The parable of the lost coin** (Luke 15:8–10)
Both Matthew (chapter 18) and Luke include a parable about lost sheep. This relates very much to men who were shepherds. But Luke has included a parable about the woman who had lost a coin. It is a similar parable but, when reading his Gospel, women would easily relate to the story. Luke is thoughtful of women who hear or read his Gospel, as well as men.

Women at the crucifixion

All four Gospels record that there were women present when Jesus was put to death on the cross. But Luke includes something the other Gospel writers do not.

READ LUKE 23:27–31

Here, Jesus blesses a group of women who were probably outcasts. At the time of Jesus, people believed that if a woman was childless then she must have done something very wrong because children were a blessing or a gift from God. Barrenness (childlessness) must be a result of sin. Luke includes Jesus' blessing on women who were childless. He singled them out as he was on his way to be crucified.

Women as witnesses of the resurrection

All four Gospel writers include the account that women were the first to witness the resurrection of Jesus from the dead. In a society where women were not formally educated and not taken seriously, no one would have been convinced by women witnesses of anything that needed to be proved. Yet all four Gospel writers say that women witnessed the resurrection before the disciples or any other men.

In his account, Luke (chapter 24) differs from Mark. Mark says that the women failed to deliver Jesus' message to the disciples because they were afraid. But Luke says that they made a full report to the others of what they had seen and heard. Luke also mentions Joanna again – she is there at the resurrection with Mary Magdalene and Mary the mother of James.

Jesus and women

In the Gospels, and especially in Luke, Jesus communicated with all kinds of people – Pharisees and prostitutes, Romans and rebels, tax collectors and widows, housewives and fishermen. All this showed that God's Kingdom broke down all the barriers that separated people – because of race, poverty, politics or sex. Jesus' message brought liberty to everyone – including women as much as men.

Jesus related openly to women at a time when this was not acceptable. Jesus accepted help from women. Jesus had private conversations with women. Jesus enjoyed the company of women and, according to Luke, Jesus raised the status of women when he told Mary, the sister of Lazarus, that she had chosen well in listening to his teaching rather than doing all the household chores. Usually only the men seriously listened to a teacher – it was felt that wise words would be wasted on women.

In the next unit we will discuss attitudes to women in the Christian church today.

The stereotype woman. In Jesus' day women were regarded as useful possessions. Luke's Gospel records how different Jesus' attitude was. He treated women as people in their own right.

FOLLOW UP

Question time

1. What do we learn about Luke from the special material he includes on women?

2. What do we learn about Jesus from Luke's special material about women at the crucifixion (Luke 23:27–31)?

3. Women were the first witnesses of the resurrection. What was significant about this in the society of Jesus' day?

To do

Write a letter from one of the women who was a witness to the resurrection of Jesus from the dead. Use Luke chapter 24 for your information, so that your letter is accurate. The letter is from one of Jesus' followers to a friend, telling the story of the empty tomb.

Women in the Church Today

One of the most important disputes in the church today is about the ordination of women as priests and ministers.

The church is divided on the issue:

The Roman Catholic Church rejects the ordination of women entirely (although there is pressure from a minority of Catholics).

The Church of England (Anglican Church) Some parts of the Anglican Church have women priests – e.g. the United States, Canada, New Zealand and Hong Kong. But if women want to be ordained they have to go to these countries to train for ministry. Then they can practice as full ministers only where it is allowed. They cannot practice in other parts of the church.

Free Churches Some Free Churches, e.g. Methodists and Baptists, ordain women.

The Orthodox Church does not as yet see the issue as an important one.

Why is the ordination of women so controversial?

There are many reasons people have for objecting to women having the same status as men in the church. Some of these are *theological* reasons and some of them are *social* or *cultural*.

● *Theological objections* are to do with what people think about religious truth and God. Here are some theological reasons for rejecting women's ministry:
– The priesthood is chosen by God.
– God is always referred to as Father and is therefore male.
– His Son Jesus was male and he chose all male disciples.
– The Bible (especially St Paul) says that women should submit to their husbands and be silent in the churches (Ephesians 5:21–24).
– If the Anglican church allows women to be fully ordained, it will divide the worldwide church further because there will be an even greater split between Roman Catholics and Anglicans.

● *Social and cultural objections* are to do with how women are seen in society or in their cultural background. The place of women in society has changed. A hundred years ago it would have been impossible for a woman to be a doctor, let alone a Prime Minister. Although there have been big changes and women now have many more opportunities and greater status, there are still attitudes which are less progressive.

Here are some of the social and cultural reasons for rejecting women's ministry:
– Women are not cut out to be priests as they have babies. Looking after their children would take up valuable time – time they should be spending on looking after their congregations. Priests should be single-minded.
– Women are more emotional than men and so could not cope as well with the job.
– Women would not have the same respect as men if they were priests.
– Women should not be in charge of men; it's not right.
– It's easier for a man to advise a woman than for a woman to advise a man.

What are the arguments for the ordination of women?

● *Theological arguments*
– Because of what Jesus has done, there is

Barbara Harris, the first woman bishop, celebrates the Eucharist on the occasion of her ordination and consecration in Boston. The whole idea of women bishops is fiercely opposed by many in the church. But the issue is more than a sexist one.

no difference in God's eyes between men and women (Galatians 3: 26–28).
– The Bible recognizes only *two* kinds of priesthood: the priesthood of Jesus and the priesthood of all believers.
– Women had a high place in the early church before the priesthood became established.
– Women were amongst the followers of Jesus (Luke 8:2–3).

- *Sociological arguments*

– Women can now do jobs which were thought impossible in the past.
– Women are now leaders in a way that they never were before.
– Many women sincerely believe that they are called by God to be priests. Why should they be barred?

FOLLOW UP

Question time

1. Find out what reasons are given by the church against the ordination of women today.

2. What answer would you give to someone who said that women should not be ordained, because in the Bible Jesus was male and so were his disciples?

3. If you were a woman who thought that she had been called by God to be ordained a minister, what would you do in this situation? Consider the following:

- What would be your arguments for being ordained?
- What might you feel about the situation?
- What alternatives would there be to minister for God?

For example, would you consider being ordained elsewhere? Would this be the same thing? Why? Why not?

To do

Write a letter to a church newspaper complaining about the recent move to ordain women in the Church of England. Then write a reply to your letter from someone who disagrees with you.

Jesus and the Teachers of the Law

Who are the leaders in your community? Imagine for a moment that they all get together for a meal. They are just beginning to relax and enjoy themselves when one of their guests turns and begins to say:

'Outwardly you all look respectable, but inwardly your thoughts are evil . . .'

'You stuff yourselves full of food – you should be giving to the poor . . .'

'You love to be seen to be important but when people come near you they are corrupted by you . . .'

In Luke 11:37–54 a scene like this happens. Jesus is pictured sitting down with Simon the Pharisee for a meal. And over the meal, Jesus delivers a hard-hitting message against the Pharisees and the teachers of the Law. Remember that the Pharisees were the respected religious leaders of the day. They were concerned to keep God's Law (the Torah) that had been handed down to the Jewish people. Jesus said seven things about them . . .

Full of violence and evil

'You Pharisees clean the outside of your cup and plate, but inside you are full of violence and evil. Fools! Did not God, who made the outside, also make the inside? But give what is in your cups and plates to the poor, and everything will be ritually clean for you' (Luke 11:37–41).

For the Pharisees, religion meant obedience to the Law. Jesus said that 'external' obedience (keeping rules and instructions) was not enough. Laws can only control what a person *does*; they do not change what he or she *is*. It is no good appearing to be respectable on the outside, while inside you are full of bitterness or hatred.

Neglecting love and justice

'How terrible for you Pharisees! You give God a tenth of the seasoning herbs, such as mint and rue and all the other herbs, but you neglect justice and love for God. These you should practise without neglecting the others' (Luke 11:42).

The Pharisees were anxious to keep the commandments and pay their tithes. Usually the tithes (religious offerings) consisted of a proportion of agricultural produce. But the Pharisees were extremely scrupulous and also gave a proportion of their herb gardens, just in case they were not giving enough. Jesus told the Pharisees that they kept these laws down to the last detail, but neglected to do justice to others and to love God. In their concern to obey the *details* of the Law, they had neglected what the Law was really all about.

Unmarked graves

'How terrible for you Pharisees! You love the reserved seats in the synagogues and to be greeted with respect in the market-places. How terrible for you! You are like unmarked graves which people walk on without knowing it' (Luke 11:43–44).

Good teachers of the Law (rabbis) explained its true meaning to ordinary people, in Jesus' time as they do today. Those Jesus attacked were the ones who made it hard to understand, and who laid impossible burdens on people.

In Jewish Law contact with death made a person ritually unclean. Because of this, graves were painted white to prevent people from walking over them. Jesus called the Pharisees 'unmarked graves' – their outward reputation for holiness concealed the fact that they were like death. Their influence defiled other people.

This was an insult on the epic scale. It must have been a scandalous thing to say. One of the teachers of the Law objected: 'Teacher, when you say this, you insult us too!'

But Jesus didn't withdraw this insult. He went on to say how the Pharisees defiled other people . . .

Loading people down with rules

'How terrible also for you teachers of the Law! You put loads on people's backs which are hard to carry but you yourselves will not stretch out a finger to help them carry those loads' (Luke 11:46).

Jesus attacked the religious burdens which the teachers of the Law put on the backs of ordinary people. He may be referring to rules like those concerning the Sabbath, where the Law said that God required each person to have a day of rest from work. The Pharisees and teachers of the Law had added to the Old Testament Law by specifying hundreds of categories of 'work' that could not be done on the Sabbath.

Jesus did not accuse them of setting up a standard for others which they themselves could not keep. He accused them of loading others down with religious rules and not helping them to carry the extra weight. A religious system that makes the leaders ignore the suffering of ordinary people is wrong.

The descendants of murderers

'How terrible for you! You make fine tombs for the prophets – the very prophets your ancestors murdered. You yourselves admit, then, that you approve of what your ancestors did; they murdered the prophets, and you build their tombs' (Luke 11:48).

The Pharisees and teachers of the Law were prepared to build monuments to dead prophets, but because they insisted on their own particular interpretations of the Old Testament Law, they were not willing to receive a prophet who brings something new from God. This was exactly the way their ancestors saw the prophets. They too were guilty of the murder of the prophets from the first, Abel (in the Book of Genesis) to the last, the prophet Zechariah.

Locking the door

'How terrible for you teachers of the Law! You have kept the key that opens the door to the house of knowledge; you yourselves will not go in, and you stop those who are trying to go in!' (Luke 11:52).

The teachers were meant to unlock the Scriptures so that people could know about God. Instead, by concentrating on the small details of the Law, they ignored the really important issues. Instead of helping others to find God, they closed the door to them and threw away the key.

How did the Pharisees and teachers of the Law react to all these charges? What was their response?

They fiercely debated with him (Luke 11:53).

They laid traps for him (Luke 11:54, etc).

They plotted against him (Luke 19:47).

They had him put to death (Luke 23).

FACT·FILE

Other occasions when Jesus confronted the Pharisees . . .

- **A warning against hypocrisy**
'Be on guard against the yeast of the Pharisees – I mean their hypocrisy' (Luke 12:1–2).

- **Jesus warns against the teachers of the Law**
'Be on your guard against the teachers of the Law, who like to walk about in their long robes and love to be greeted with respect in the market-place; who choose the reserved seats in the synagogues and the best places at feasts; who take advantage of widows and rob them of their homes, and then make a show of saying long prayers! Their punishment will be all the worse!' (Luke 20:45–47).

Was Jesus for or against the Jewish Law?

Some people think that because Jesus was so critical of the Pharisees and the teachers of the Law, that he must have been against keeping the Law itself. However, Jesus did not say that he was critical of *the Law*, but rather of those who *interpret* it. This saying of Jesus shows his positive attitude towards the Law:
'It is easier for heaven and earth to disappear than for the smallest detail of the Law to be done away with' (Luke 16:17).

FACT·FILE

Some scholars think that it is unlikely that Jesus gave a single speech against the Pharisees, or that he did it whilst a guest in a Pharisee's house. Instead they think that the 'Woes' (verses 42–52) are a collection of Jesus' sayings which Luke put together to show Jesus' attitude towards the religious leaders of his day.

We do not know which of the Pharisees Jesus is speaking against. It is unlikely that Jesus was against the Pharisees as a group: he was criticizing those who were wrong.

To look up: occasions when religious leaders confronted Jesus

- Luke 20:19–26 **The question about paying taxes**
- Luke 20:27–40 **The question about rising from death**

Tradition holds that this is the tomb of the prophet Zechariah. Jesus told the Pharisees that they built fine tombs for the prophets whom their ancestors murdered.

FOLLOW UP

Question time

1. Where was Jesus when he delivered his message against the Pharisees?

2. Write a summary of Jesus' accusations against the Pharisees.

3. What did Jesus mean by saying '. . . You are like unmarked graves which people walk on without knowing it'?

4. Who were the Pharisees?

To do

Jesus attacked the misuse of the Law. We call this sort of attack a polemic. What might he have said to our twentieth-century world? Are there misuses of civil and religious law today? Write your own polemic against the misuse of the law, or the state of the church, and explain why you feel so strongly. What should happen instead?

UNIT 12.2

Jesus and the Sabbath

For the Jewish people the Sabbath was and still is a very important day. If you were in Israel on a Sabbath, you would find all Jewish shops closed. Jewish taxi drivers would not be available to take you anywhere. Tourists to Israel sometimes forget that the Sabbath (from sundown on Friday evening to sundown on Saturday) is a serious business and they get stuck without transport.

At the time of Jesus, the Sabbath was taken very seriously indeed. Its roots can be found in the first five books of the Bible, referred to by Jews as the Law of Moses (or the Torah).

THE SABBATH...

Started: 6 p.m. on Friday

Ended: 6 p.m. on Saturday

Sabbath

The Hebrew word for 'Sabbath' comes from *shabat*, meaning 'to cease' or 'to desist'. In the Bible the principle is laid down that one day in seven is to be observed as a day holy to God. Everyone is to 'cease' or 'desist' from work on that day. Here are some important passages:

Genesis 2:2 The work of Creation took six days, and on the seventh God rested. This set the pattern for a human day of rest.

Exodus 20:11 The Ten Commandments (given by God to the people of Israel) say that the Sabbath day is holy to the Lord and should be kept.

Deuteronomy 5:12–14 The people of Israel are told to keep the Sabbath in the way that the Lord has commanded them.

Numbers 15:32–36 This is the story of a man caught gathering sticks on the Sabbath and therefore he is seen as working when he should be ceasing from work. He is put to death.

As the Jewish religion developed, oral teaching about the Law was added to the written law. The Talmud is a collection of Jewish civil and ceremonial law. It includes two works: the Mishnah and the Gemara. In the Mishnah, the spoken teachings were written down, and we can discover what was taught about the commandment to honour the Sabbath day. God's Law said everyone was to take a day off in the week to rest and worship God. The Pharisees at the time of Jesus interpreted this as meaning no work at all on the Sabbath. This meant among other things that people could not walk more than about one kilometre from their own town. They were not allowed to carry a load, or light a fire in the home. They developed over 600 rules and regulations about the Sabbath.

This was what Jesus confronted. He did not ignore the importance of the Sabbath, but rather he saw that these added restrictions hid the true significance of the Sabbath day. Too many rules took away the true meaning of the Sabbath. It was meant for rest and relationship with God. Jesus not only broke the regulations but he seems to have *gone out of his way* to break them.

There are four occasions in Luke's Gospel where Jesus is in confrontation about the meaning of the Sabbath.

Healing two people

Jesus started his ministry by healing two people on the Sabbath: the man with an evil spirit and Simon Peter's mother-in-law.

READ LUKE 4:38–39

The first two cures that Jesus performed were on the Sabbath. This was against the Pharisees' interpretation of the Law, which allowed a doctor to work on the Sabbath only if life was actually in danger.

Picking ears of corn

READ LUKE 6:1–5

The Pharisees asked Jesus: 'Why are you doing what our Law says you cannot do on the Sabbath?' Jesus answered them in two ways:

He referred them to the story in 1 Samuel 21:1–26. The bread of the presence was twelve loaves which were placed in the Temple every Sabbath. Only the priests were allowed to eat this holy bread (Leviticus 24:9), but David and his men ate it when they were in great need of food. Jesus argued that extreme need comes before keeping religious rules. At their best the Pharisees would have agreed with this, but they would never have agreed with Jesus' next statement . . .

'The Son of Man is Lord of the Sabbath. Here Jesus went beyond anything that was acceptable to the religious leaders of his day. He claimed that he himself had the right to say what is the proper use of the Sabbath.

Healing the man with a paralyzed hand

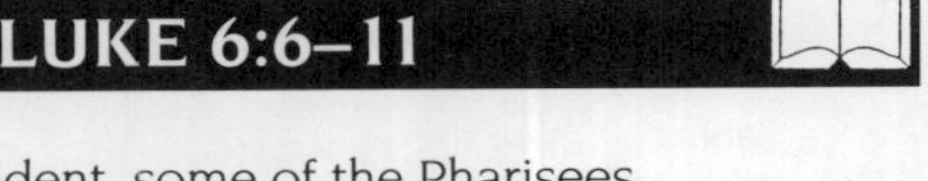

In this incident, some of the Pharisees waited to see if Jesus would heal on the Sabbath. Jesus took the initiative with a question that blew the wind out of their sails: 'I ask you: What does our Law allow us to do on the Sabbath? To help or to harm? To save a man's life or destroy it?' There was only one possible answer to this. Who could possibly say it was better to let someone suffer than rescue them?

Jesus heals a sick man

READ LUKE 14:1–6

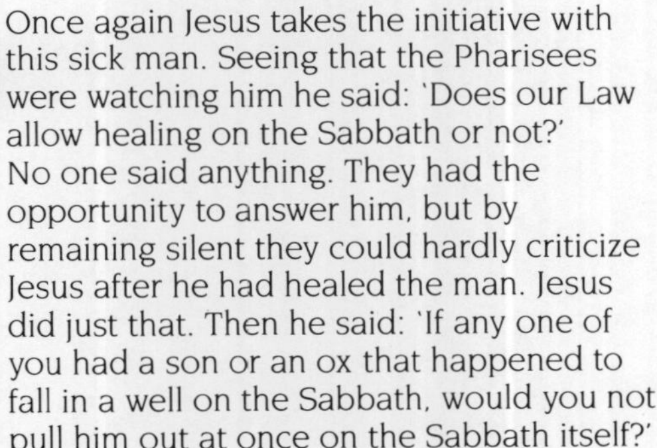

Once again Jesus takes the initiative with this sick man. Seeing that the Pharisees were watching him he said: 'Does our Law allow healing on the Sabbath or not?' No one said anything. They had the opportunity to answer him, but by remaining silent they could hardly criticize Jesus after he had healed the man. Jesus did just that. Then he said: 'If any one of you had a son or an ox that happened to fall in a well on the Sabbath, would you not pull him out at once on the Sabbath itself?'

The rabbis would discuss just how far a person could go without breaking the Sabbath law. Some of them would say that the law of mercy took first place on the Sabbath, so that if an animal was in pain and needed help it should be helped. Jesus meant that if it is possible to 'work' on the Sabbath by helping a distressed animal, how much more is it right to help a person who is in pain!

FOLLOW UP

Question time

1. What is the Jewish Sabbath?

2. What does the word 'Sabbath' mean?

3. Read the story of Jesus' disciples plucking ears of corn on the Sabbath (Luke 6:1–5). Then say whether the following statements are true or false. If they are false substitute the sentence with the correct answer.

- Jesus was walking through some cornfields on the Sabbath. True/False
- He and his disciples began to pick ears of corn and eat the grain. True/False
- The Sadducees accused them of breaking the Law. True/False
- Jesus reminded them of King David who had eaten bread offered to God when he was hungry. True/False
- Jesus concluded by saying that the Son of Man is Lord of the Sabbath. True/False

4. What is the meaning of Jesus' saying: 'The Son of Man is Lord of the Sabbath'?

5. What do we learn about Jesus' attitude to the Sabbath from the story of the healing of the sick man in Luke 14:1–6?

To do

Sabbath survey. Is the idea of a Sabbath day of rest a good thing? Take this survey round your school, community or church and find out how important the Sabbath is for today's world. (The Jewish Sabbath is Saturday. The Christian day of rest is Sunday. If you are Jewish, answer as for Saturday.) Tick which sentence you most agree with:

- A day of rest is out of date. We don't need this sort of thing nowadays.
- Sunday is the most important day of the week, because you can catch up on everything and you don't have to work.
- If Sunday was a work day we would get no rest and we would be exhausted.
- It is very important to have time to rest and worship God.
- Sundays are boring. I can't see the use of them.

Discuss your findings in class.

UNIT 12.3

Jesus and the Forgiveness of Sins

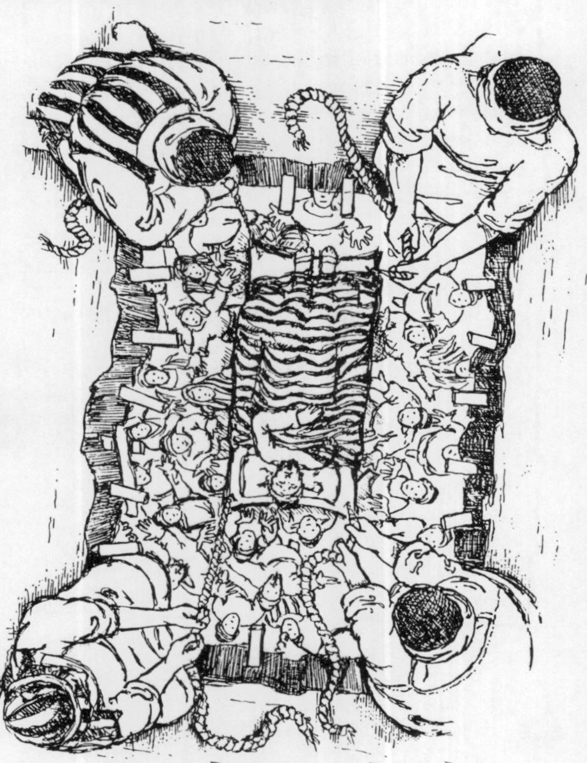

Jesus was radical. In his attitude to the Sabbath and in his discussions with the ultra-religious of his day he was non-conformist. Nowhere is this seen more than in Jesus' claim that he could forgive sins. There are two stories given in Luke's Gospel which tell us about Jesus forgiving sins.

Jesus heals a paralyzed man

READ LUKE 5:17–26

In this story, 'the power of the Lord' is with Jesus to heal. There is an enormous crowd gathered to see what will happen. Jesus was staying in a house. Luke does not specify where that is, but Mark's Gospel tells us that Jesus was in Capernaum (Mark 2:1–12). The story is memorable. Some men brought a paralyzed man to Jesus on a stretcher. They tried to get into the crowded house but there were just too many people. So, not to be put off, they climbed onto the flat roof, made an opening in the tiles and let the man down in front of Jesus.

Instead of saying anything about healing, Jesus first said: 'Your sins are forgiven, my friend.' The teachers of the Law and the Pharisees immediately responded by saying among themselves 'Who is this man who speaks such blasphemy! God is the only one who can forgive sins!'

Jesus knew their thoughts and replied: 'Why do you think such things? Is it easier to say, "Your sins are forgiven you", or to say, "Get up and walk?" I will prove to you then, that the Son of Man has authority on earth to forgive sins.' So he said to the paralyzed man, 'I tell you, get up, pick up your bed and go home!'

At once the man picked up his mattress and went home, praising God. Everyone was completely amazed.

There are several things worth noticing in the story:

> Jesus pronounced the man's sins were forgiven because of *the faith of his friends*. In biblical thought there is an emphasis on interdependence. This means that what one person does or is can influence others, or even the whole community. Luke does not say that the paralytic man had faith himself, but that his friends did. Their faith influences him.

Jesus diagnosed that the man's illness was *psychosomatic* (a physical illness caused by mental or emotional strain). In this case the man needed to know freedom from guilt and to feel forgiven. At the time of Jesus, people commonly thought that one cause of illness was that the sick person had sinned and that the illness was the consequence of this. Jesus believed that this was true of this man.

The Pharisees and teachers of the Law said that only God can forgive sins and that Jesus was blaspheming. Blasphemy is when someone insults or belittles God. How could Jesus say that he himself could forgive sins when only God can do that? Luke, Matthew and Mark all agree (Matthew 9:1–8; Mark 2:1–12) that Jesus claimed to have delegated authority from God to forgive sins. The proof of this was evident when the man was completely healed.

It is interesting that Luke's version of the story is slightly different from Mark's. In Mark the house was a Palestinian house with a mud-plastered roof, which the man's friends had to dig through. In Luke's Gospel, it is a Roman-style house with tiles and a central opening. Either roof would have enabled the friends to make an opening without too much difficulty and lower their friend into the house.

Jesus' feet are anointed by a sinful woman

READ LUKE 7:36–50

Simon the Pharisee respected Jesus. He called him *Rabbi*, which means 'teacher', and he invited him to dinner. However, Simon did not welcome Jesus fully. It was a custom to supply a footbath for the comfort of the guest. The roads were dusty and, in a hot land where travellers wore sandals, a footbath was essential to comfort.

At feasts and banquets it was quite normal for the doors to be left open to admit all sorts of people. Beggars would come in search of food, and others came to listen to the discussions of the rabbis. The guests would recline on low couches, their sandals removed and their feet behind them.

Into this scene came a woman who stood behind Jesus at his feet and crying. She used her tears to wash his feet, and then let her hair down to dry them. It was a show of great intimacy. No respectable woman would do such a thing – especially to let her hair down in public.

- Jesus accepted the woman's attention. This was *not* respectable.

- Simon the Pharisee was shocked. If Jesus really were a prophet he would know that this woman lived a sinful life (she was most likely a prostitute).

- Jesus told Simon a story – the parable of the two debtors. He asked him the question about who would love more – a man who was forgiven a debt of fifty silver coins or a man who was forgiven a debt of 500? Simon answered that the one who was forgiven more would love more.

Jesus used this parable to show his host how great love can be the product of great forgiveness. The woman's display of affection was a sign of her gratitude for the message of forgiveness. Perhaps she had heard Jesus before or perhaps she hoped to ask for his forgiveness. Jesus then said to the woman, 'Your sins are forgiven.' The others sitting at the table said to themselves, 'Who is this, who even forgives sins?'

Forgiveness of sins and the church today

Part of the gospel (the good news) which the church believes and proclaims is the message that Jesus forgives sins.

● **All Christians** know and say the Lord's Prayer. This includes the words, 'Forgive us our sins as we forgive those who sin against us.'

● **Some denominations** believe that forgiveness of sins is the most important part of the gospel message and that unless a person receives God's forgiveness for their sins, then they cannot be a proper Christian.

● **Roman Catholic Christians** go to confession. They openly confess their sins to a priest who listens and then administers God's forgiveness to them.

● **In the Church of England and the Roman Catholic Church** there are set prayers to confess sins to God and to ask for forgiveness and mercy. Here is a very famous prayer from the Church of England liturgy. It is called the prayer of General Confession:

> Almighty God, our heavenly Father, we have sinned against you and against our fellow men, in thought and word and deed, through negligence, through weakness, through our own deliberate fault. We are truly sorry and repent of all our sins. For the sake of your Son, Jesus Christ, who died for us, forgive us all that is past; and grant that we may serve you in newness of life; to the glory of your name. Amen

The object of our sin	● we have sinned against you ● and against our fellow men
The nature of sin	● in thought and word and deed
The cause of sin	● through negligence ● through weakness ● through our own deliberate fault
The response to sin	● we are truly sorry ● and repent of all our sins
The means of forgiveness	● for the sake of your Son, Jesus Christ, ● who died for us
The request to God	● forgive us all that is past; ● and grant that we may serve you in newness of life to the glory of your name. Amen

FOLLOW UP

Question time

1. Give an example of how Jesus forgave sins.

2. Give examples of how Christian teaching on the forgiveness of sins might be applied in practice in the church today.

3. Why is the forgiveness of sins important to the Christian church? Give reasons for your answer.

To do

Write and broadcast a 'News at Ten' item on the healing of the paralyzed man (Luke 5:17–26). You will need a reporter, one or two eye-witnesses from the crowd, and perhaps the man who was healed or one of the friends who took him to Jesus. Perform it for your class or use it for discussion.

Jesus Prepares for his Journey

If you read a story, it usually has three parts – a beginning, a middle and an end. That might seem obvious, but it shows that each story has a *plan*. Whoever has written the story has thought hard about its *shape*, and has put the events in a certain order.

Luke did this too. The events in his Gospel have a special order. Luke has chosen stories, happenings and sayings from Jesus' life, and arranged them to show clearly who Jesus is.

We have seen how Luke used different sources to write his Gospel. He combined these sources to have an effect on his readers. Luke was, after all, not just telling a *good story*, he was giving *good news*.

Perhaps a year had now passed since Jesus had called his first disciples. They had heard his words, seen his power and known him as a person. And yet they were still troubled about him. They knew he was a great prophet and a teacher. But was that all? Soon Jesus was about to make a change. But before he did so he performed one last great miracle in Galilee.

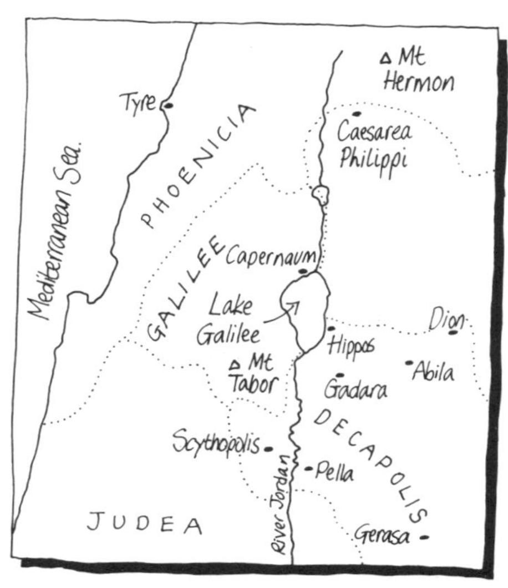

The feeding of 5,000 men

READ LUKE 9:10–17

This is a remarkable miracle. It is another example of Jesus' power over nature. Miraculous food did have a place in the Old Testament. After Moses had led God's

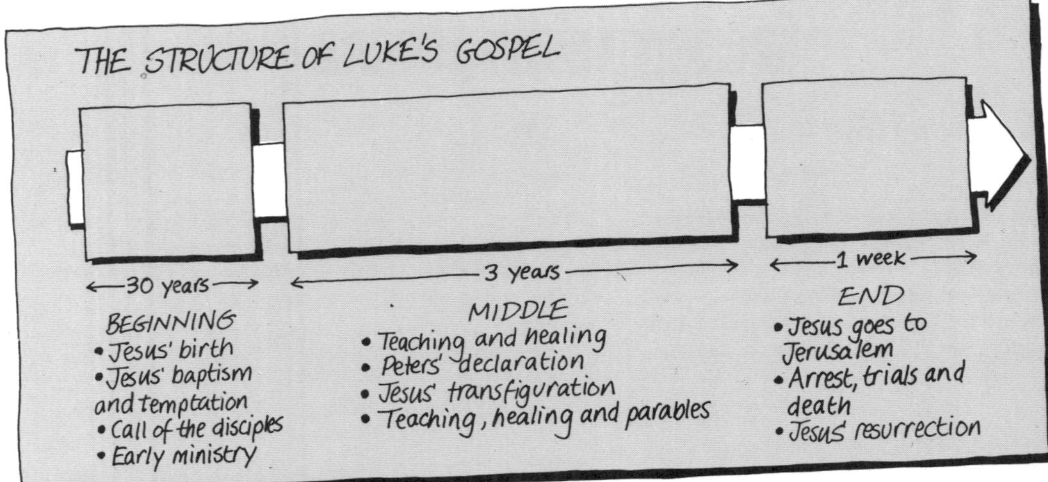

Luke records how Jesus made a meal of five small loaves and two fish enough to feed a crowd of 5,000 men.

people out of slavery in Egypt, God had given the people a special kind of food called manna to eat in the desert (Exodus 16; Numbers 11).

Traditionally, however, the Christian church has seen this miracle as a graphic symbol of:

- The feast of the Kingdom of God – a preview of the heavenly celebration happening here on earth.
- A preview of the Lord's Supper – when Jesus broke bread and gave wine to his disciples the night before he was crucified.

How can we understand this miracle?

There are a number of different interpretations of this event:

- Some believe this was a real miracle. Jesus created the food to feed the crowd of hungry people.
- Some scholars believe that this story was added to the Gospel as a *preview* of the Lord's Supper. This means that some people think it was 'invented' to point towards the Passover meal that Jesus shared with his disciples (Luke 22).
- Some scholars believe that the real miracle was that Jesus encouraged the crowd to share the food they had already brought – that nothing supernatural happened.

Mark and Matthew have *two* separate feeding accounts. These may refer to two separate events.

- The feeding of 4,000 **people:** Matthew 15:32–39; Mark 8:1–10.
- The feeding of the 5,000 **men:** Matthew 14:13–21; Mark 6:30–44.

The second account is the one Luke uses. John also has an account of the feeding of the 5,000 men (John 6:1–14). John's story seems separate from the others, however, and he may have used an independent source.

The feeding of the 5,000 men was the last miracle that Jesus performed before the great turning-point in Luke's Gospel. At last Jesus was ready to reveal who he really was. At last he was ready to begin his final journey.

So far, Jesus had given hints of who he was. He had healed and taught. He had cast out demons and calmed the storm. He had even forgiven sins. But his followers and the crowds were beginning to ask questions about who he was. They knew that he was a teacher, a prophet and a miracle-worker. But things were about to change.

Peter's declaration about Jesus

READ LUKE 9:18–20

This is a very important moment in the Gospel story. Peter finally realizes who Jesus is – he is the Messiah.

It was only after Peter's realization that Jesus began to teach his disciples some new things, and began his long journey to Jerusalem. Look at the story closely:

Jesus was *praying alone*. Luke always shows Jesus praying before an important event or decision.

Jesus asked his disciples who the crowd thought he was.

The crowd thought Jesus was a great prophet – like Elijah, John the Baptist, or one of the other great Old Testament prophets come back to life.

Peter said, 'You are God's Messiah.'

At the time, the Jews were expecting the Messiah to be an *earthly king* or a *heavenly saviour*. Jesus was not like either of those figures. After spending so much time with Jesus, however, Peter had decided that Jesus was the Messiah. His *way of seeing* Jesus had changed.

Read Matthew 16:13–20 and Mark 8:27–30.
What are the differences between these accounts of Peter's declaration about Jesus?

Both Mark and Matthew give the location of Peter's declaration about Jesus as Caesarea Philippi. Luke does not mention this.

Matthew (16:17–18) includes the words, 'Good for you, Simon son of John! . . . You are a rock, and on this rock foundation I will build my church.' Luke omits these verses, but they are important in the history of the Christian church.

- Roman Catholics believe that Peter *really was* the foundation on which Jesus was going to build his church. Peter was, in effect, the first Pope. Because of this, the Roman Catholic Church believes it has an authority and a tradition that the other Christian churches do not have.

Here are some other ways of interpreting the text:

The feeding of the 5,000, like so many other events of Jesus' ministry, took place among the hills around Lake Galilee.

Jesus was only making a joke. The Greek word for 'rock' is *petros* – which is Peter's name in Greek. So Jesus' saying here is actually a pun. Perhaps Luke is only showing Jesus' delight and humour at Peter's realization.

The story is not historical. Some people believe that this story was added later by the early church. They think that it was only the early Christians who began to believe that Jesus had been the Messiah. No one – not even Peter – could have guessed this about Jesus when he had been alive.

It is Peter's faith that is the important point here. It was faith like Peter's – exercised by *all* Jesus' followers – that would be the rock on which the Christian church would be built.

FOLLOW UP

Question time

1. What do you think about Peter's declaration about Jesus (Luke 9:18–20)?
Answer the following:

- What was Jesus doing when the disciples came to him?
- What did Jesus ask his disciples on this occasion?
- What did the disciples reply (fill in the sentence)?

'Some say that ______________ they answered, others say that you ______________, while others say that one of the ______________.'

- What was Peter's declaration about Jesus?

2. Look at the Synoptic accounts of Peter's declaration – Matthew 16:13–20; Mark 8:27–30; Luke 9:18–20. What are the differences between these accounts?

3. Give three ways in which Christians have interpreted the text about Peter's declaration.

To do

Imagine that you are a spectator at the feeding of the 5,000 (Luke 9:10–17). You write a letter to a friend telling them what you experienced and saw. Use the Gospel account to help you construct your letter. Use the first person ('I') in your account. Include the following:

- the location
- the atmosphere
- what happened
- what people said afterwards

Did everyone perceive it as a miracle or were there differing views?

Suffering and Glory – Jesus Sets his Face towards Jerusalem

After Peter's important declaration that Jesus is the Messiah – Jesus went on to speak about his suffering, death and resurrection. These were things he had not talked about to his disciples before. It may have been that Jesus thought his disciples now had enough faith in him to believe his words.

Jesus speaks about his suffering and death

READ LUKE 9:21–27

The first thing that Jesus did after Peter had confessed him to be the Messiah was to order his disciples *not* to tell anyone else about it. But why did he do this?

If the crowd had thought that Jesus was the Messiah, there might have been a riot. They might have thought that he had come to save them from the Romans. Jesus did not want the crowd to know that he was the Messiah because they would have the *wrong idea* of what Jesus had come to do.

If the Jewish leaders had thought Jesus was calling himself the Messiah they might have arrested him on a criminal charge. It would have been dangerous (in a political *and* a religious sense) for Jesus to call himself the Messiah.

Jesus then went on to talk about his suffering, death and ressurrection. In doing this, Jesus drew on some ideas.in the Old Testament. He said that he was:

The Messiah, the Davidic king that the Jews were expecting

The Son of Man – the heavenly figure written about in the Book of Daniel

The Suffering Servant mentioned in the Book of Isaiah. The Jews believed that Israel was the Suffering Servant, but here Jesus applies the title to himself.

In this passage Jesus said that:

- the Messiah must suffer
- the Messiah's disciples must be prepared to share his suffering
- the Messiah and his disciples will be glorified. They will receive a blessing and a reward from God.

The Suffering Servant is a prophetic figure who appears in the Book of Isaiah. The Jews believed that Israel was the Suffering Servant. The Christian church, however, has traditionally seen the writings about the Suffering Servant as prophecies about Jesus (see Isaiah 52:13–53:12).

The transfiguration

READ LUKE 9:28–36

After Jesus spoke about his suffering, death and resurrection, something extraordinary happened: Peter, James and John (the three disciples closest to Jesus) were given a glimpse of Jesus' heavenly character. The story unfolds like this:

The mountain of Jesus' transfiguration was most probably Mt Hermon, in the far north of Palestine.

- Jesus goes with Peter, James and John up a hill to pray. As always in Luke when prayer is mentioned, something important is about to happen.
- Jesus' appearance changes. His face alters and his clothes become bright and white.
- Moses and Elijah (two of Israel's great leaders from the Old Testament) appear beside Jesus and talk with him.
- Peter, James and John have fallen asleep – but they wake up and see what is happening.
- Peter starts talking about making three tents – one for Jesus, one for Moses, and one for Elijah.
- Then a voice begins to speak from a cloud. The voice tells the disciples to keep quiet and listen to Jesus.
- When the voice stops speaking, Jesus is alone. The disciples tell no one what they have seen.

Once again, this story has a special meaning and a special place for Luke in his Gospel.

- Jesus goes up to pray on a hill. This is like Moses in the Old Testament going up Mt Sinai to meet God.
- Jesus is suddenly no longer like an earthly man, but a *heavenly figure*.
- Moses and Elijah appear beside him. Moses represents the Law; Elijah represents the prophets. The phrase 'the Law and the Prophets' was a Jewish way of summing up the whole of the Old Testament. In the Old Testament Moses left this life by dying on top of a mountain. Elijah was taken up to heaven in a fiery chariot – he did not die. These powerful parallels with these key moments in the Old Testament show that something very important is about to happen.

● The voice from heaven links the transfiguration with Jesus' baptism in Luke 3, where a voice from heaven spoke. The transfiguration is another important step in Jesus' life.

● The three tents may refer to the tent Moses made for God in the wilderness (Leviticus 23:42, 43). This was where God was worshipped while the Israelites were travelling through the desert.

● Jesus talks to Moses and Elijah about dying in Jerusalem. The word for 'death' used here is *exodos*. *Exodos* means 'being delivered'. In the Old Testament, Moses led the Israelites from their slavery in Egypt into the Promised Land. In the New Testament, Jesus is about to lead his people from bondage to Satan and his kingdom into the promised Kingdom of God.

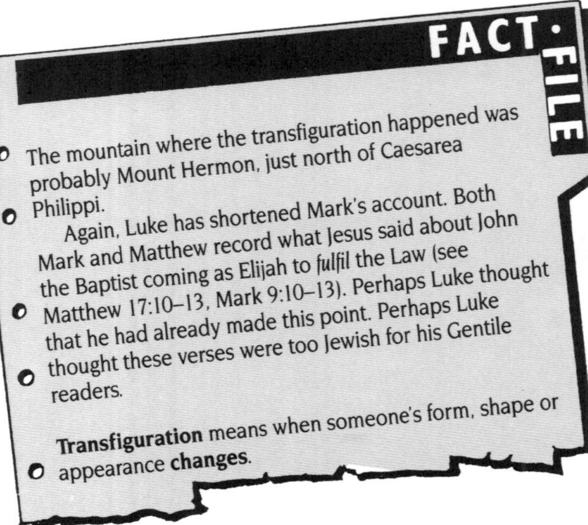

FACT · FILE

The mountain where the transfiguration happened was probably Mount Hermon, just north of Caesarea Philippi.

Again, Luke has shortened Mark's account. Both Mark and Matthew record what Jesus said about John the Baptist coming as Elijah to *fulfil* the Law (see Matthew 17:10–13, Mark 9:10–13). Perhaps Luke thought that he had already made this point. Perhaps Luke thought these verses were too Jewish for his Gentile readers.

Transfiguration means when someone's form, shape or appearance **changes**.

Jesus heals a boy with an evil spirit

READ LUKE 9:37–43

Jesus returned from the silence of the mountain to the noise of the crowd. He was asked to cure a boy with an evil spirit whom his disciples could not help. Jesus was angry – even now, after all that he had told them and shown them, his disciples still did not have enough faith to heal this boy.

FOLLOW UP

Question time

1. What reasons are given for Jesus telling his disciples to keep his identity as the Messiah a secret?

2. Write an account of the transfiguration.

3. Explain what is meant by 'transfiguration'. Why is this story important? What Old Testament symbols lie behind the event?

4. What do you think about Peter's declaration of faith in Jesus? Was Peter the rock on which Christ would build his church? Is Jesus making a joke? Is this a belief of the early church which has been added later, or is there some other explanation? Discuss the issue and argue for one viewpoint.

To do

Write a character reference for Peter. From what you have read of him so far in Luke's Gospel, construct a reference for Peter. Details should include:

- occupation
- approximate age
- home town
- leadership qualities, e.g. shy/outspoken, etc.
- does he get on well with other people?

Include any other information you know from the other Gospels, and after each sentence quote the verse of the Bible which gives you the information about his character.

The Journey to Jerusalem

The story of Jesus in Luke's Gospel changes after Peter's declaration that Jesus is the Messiah.

First of all, Jesus tells his disciples that he must suffer, die and be raised to life again. This will happen in *Jerusalem*. Jesus is pictured talking to Moses and Elijah about this (Luke 9:30–31).

Then, in Luke 9:51, Luke writes: 'As the time drew near when Jesus would be taken up to heaven, he made up his mind and set out on his way to Jerusalem.'

This pattern is common to Matthew, Mark and Luke. But, in Luke's Gospel, the journey to Jerusalem has to be looked at carefully.

Luke's approach

Until now, Luke has been following the shape of Mark's Gospel fairly closely. Suddenly he stops doing this. From Luke 9:51–19:28, Luke uses

- the writings common to Matthew and Luke (Q)
- and material that only Luke himself uses (L)

Luke is doing something particular here. He is putting some of the material he has (parables, miracles, stories and teaching) into a *narrative* – the story of Jesus and his journey to Jerusalem. This material is ten chapters long, one third of Luke's Gospel.

Jesus now sets his sights on Jerusalem. And Luke's readers know that Jesus is going to Jerusalem to *die*.

How does the journey to Jerusalem work?

On a geographical level, the story leaves a lot of questions unanswered. Luke keeps reminding his readers that Jesus is going to Jerusalem (Luke 9:51, 13:22, 17:11, 19:28). But there are two problems.

Jesus starts out from Galilee on the short route through Samaria, but arrives in Jerusalem by the longer route through Jericho (see map).

In between Jesus is first in Bethany (a few miles from Jerusalem) and later he is found on the borders of Samaria and Galilee. This would imply he was travelling *away from* Jerusalem.

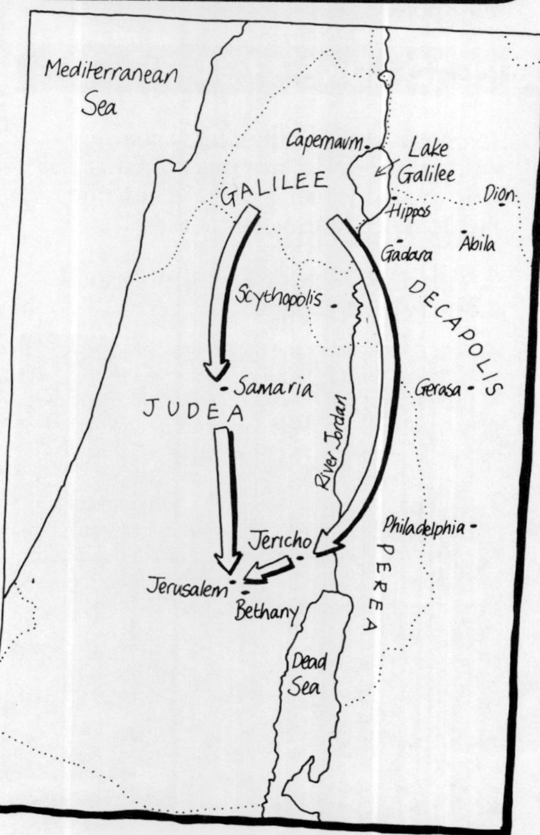

It could be that Luke knew something of John's tradition. In John, Jesus makes several visits to Jerusalem during the final year of his ministry in order to take part at the great feasts.

Or perhaps Luke keeps reminding his readers that Jesus is going to Jerusalem in the same way that John continually talks about 'the hour which had not yet come' – a reference to Jesus' death.

Why did Jesus want to go to Jerusalem?

Jerusalem was (and is) the most important city for the Jews. Politically, Jerusalem was the capital, and religiously, it was the place where the Temple stood. Jerusalem was the centre of the Jewish faith and Jewish power. Jerusalem was where Jesus would be acclaimed and accused.

Pilgrims went to Jerusalem for the great Jewish feasts – especially the Passover. It would have taken Jesus about three days to walk there.

READ LUKE 13:31–35

Here Jesus speaks about Jerusalem:
- He calls Herod a *fox* – this is a bad insult.
- He mentions that it will take him three days to reach Jerusalem.
- He predicts his death.
- He shows his love for Jerusalem and is sad that the Jewish religious centre of faith has rejected him.
- He talks about the destruction of the Temple.

The events of the crucial last week of Jesus' life took place in the city of Jerusalem.

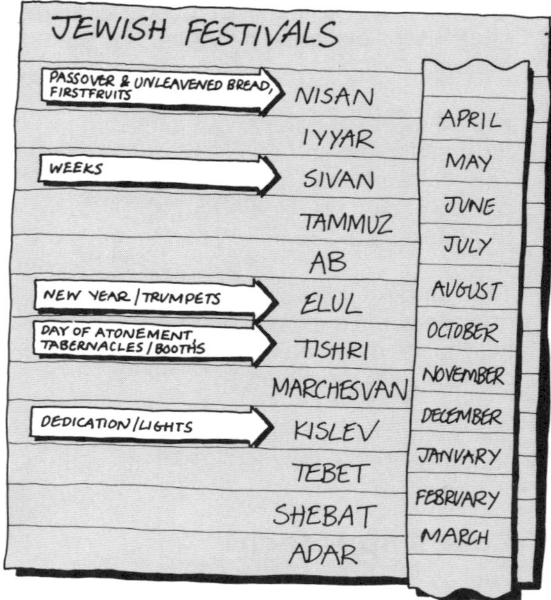

FOLLOW UP

Question time

1. Why is the journey to Jerusalem important in Luke's Gospel?

2. How is Luke arranging his material in the journey narrative?

3. What is 'Q' material?

4. What is 'L' material?

To do

- Copy the illustration from unit 13.1 to show the overall structure of Luke's Gospel.
- Using a map of Israel in New Testament times trace Jesus' journey according to Luke.

UNIT 14.1

Jesus Arrives at Jerusalem

What happens *in your town* when someone important arrives? Do they . . .
- hang out flags?
- have a brass band playing?
- roll out the red carpet?

What happens *at your school* when someone important arrives?
- Does your head teacher make a speech?
- Are you told to behave properly?
- Is the school cleaned up?

What happens at *home* when someone important arrives? Does . . .
- your father put on a suit?
- your mother put on her best clothes?
- the best china come out?

When someone important arrives, it is a special occasion. People are excited – they want to see what is going to happen.

When Jesus arrived in Jerusalem, he arrived as someone important. He did not just arrive as a pilgrim, he arrived as a king. This is a high point in Luke's story of Jesus.

After Peter's declaration that Jesus is the Messiah (Luke 9:20), Jesus ordered his disciples not to tell anyone who he was (Luke 9:21). Now Jesus prepared to enter Jerusalem openly as the Messiah.

Jerusalem was the goal of Jesus' travels.

Jerusalem, the symbol of the Jewish faith and home of the Jewish Temple, now becomes the symbol of Jesus' rejection and persecution. Though Jesus prepared to enter the city as a king, Luke's readers also know that Jesus had come to suffer and die.

Jesus enters Jerusalem

READ LUKE 19:28–40

How are we to understand the event? There are a number of different views.
- The story of finding the colt or donkey shows Jesus' prophetic knowledge.
- Jesus is showing prophetic power, like Samuel, the great prophet in the Old Testament (1 Samuel 10:2–9).
- This story was written later and is included to show how special Jesus was.

Jesus was arriving in Jerusalem for the Passover feast. This was the most important feast of the Jewish year. Many pilgrims came to Jerusalem for it.

It was also the time of year when the Jews believed that the Messiah would appear. So there were a lot of Jews in Jerusalem at this time. They were *nationalistic* and *anti-Roman*. It must have been a very tense time, with the potential for violence.

There is a prophecy in the Book of Zechariah in the Old Testament (Zechariah 9:9–10) saying that one day a king would

As Jesus rode into Jerusalem on the first Palm Sunday, crowds waved great branches of palm in excited greeting.

come to Jerusalem riding on a donkey. This king would rule the world by peace, not by force.

When Jesus rode on a donkey into Jerusalem:

- He was fulfilling the prophecy of Zechariah
- He was showing his kingship
- He was showing that he came to bring *peace* and not *war*.

Once again, Luke showed that Jesus was no threat to Roman rule.

The crowd acclaimed Jesus. The procession was like a coronation with Jesus as king. Even though the Pharisees opposed him (Luke 19:39) Jesus said that even the creation must sing his praises (Luke 19:40).

FACT FILE

- The colt was a young horse. For readers of the Septuagint (the Greek version of the Old Testament), the word would have been *donkey*. The animal was young and unbroken. It was therefore fit for a *sacred purpose* (see Numbers 19:2, Deuteronomy 21:3; I Samuel 6:7).
- Luke takes the quoted words of Psalm 118:26 and changes them. He changes *peace on earth* to the idea of *peace in heaven*. These words were the priest's blessing to pilgrims coming to Jerusalem. Luke adds the word 'king' to the quotation to show his readers exactly how Jesus was arriving.
- Luke gives a shorter account of Jesus' entry into Jerusalem than the other Gospel writers. Matthew (Matthew 21:4) and John (John 12:15) both quote a prophecy from Zechariah (Zechariah 9:9–10). Mark and Luke do not.

Roman soldiers were garrisoned in Fort Antonia, close to the Temple, ready for swift action if the excited crowds that flocked into the city at festival times got out of hand.

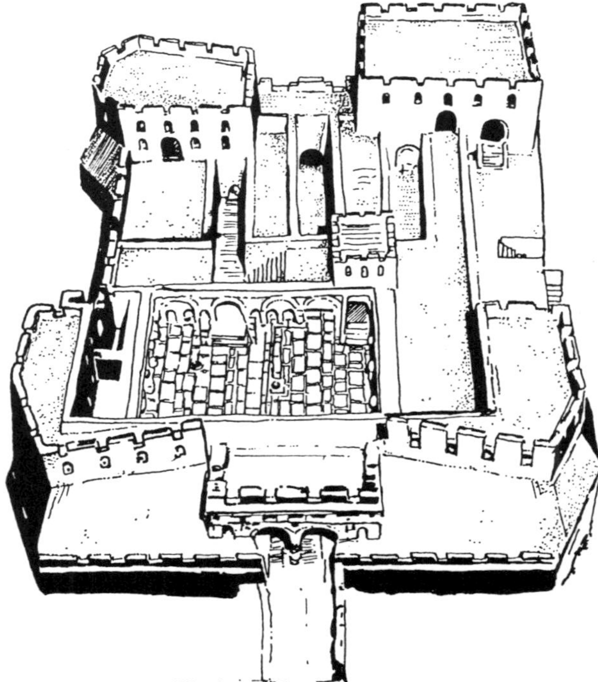

Did Jesus know he was fulfilling Zechariah's prophecy?

Many scholars argue that Jesus knew himself to be the Messiah, but others believe that the idea that Jesus was the *Messiah* came from the early church. They think that no one – not even Jesus himself – would have claimed that he was the Messiah while he was still alive.

According to this viewpoint, the story of Jesus riding on a donkey into Jerusalem is, therefore, a kind of *drama*. Luke uses the story to show Jesus coming as a king to Jerusalem – the city that would reject and kill him.

- It is possible that Jesus did know of Zechariah's prophecy and rode the donkey into Jerusalem to show the people who he was.

- It is also possible that Jesus entered Jerusalem on a donkey and it was only afterwards that the early church put the prophecy and Jesus' action together. This is what John says in his Gospel (John 12:16).

Why didn't the Romans get alarmed?
Perhaps the Romans knew that Jesus wasn't a threat. He was a Jewish problem and they were not interested in him.

Perhaps they did not even notice Jesus' procession. Many pilgrims would have been arriving for the Passover. Jesus was just one more.

In the Christian year, Jesus' entry into Jerusalem marks the beginning of *Holy Week*. This is the week leading up to Easter. *Palm Sunday* celebrates Jesus' entry into Jerusalem. Often Christians make crosses out of palms on this day or have palm branches in their churches. Luke does not mention that the crowd spread palm branches down in front of Jesus – a bit like a red carpet today. But see Matthew 21:8; Mark 11:8.

FOLLOW UP

Question time

1. Read Luke 19:28–40 and then answer the questions:

- Jesus came near to ____________ at the Mount of Olives.
- He sent ____________ ahead with instructions.
- They were to find a ____________.
- If someone asked them what they were doing they had to say ____________.
- As Jesus went down the Mount of Olives a large crowd of disciples began to praise him in loud voices saying ____________.
- Then some of the Pharisees said to Jesus ____________.
- Jesus answered them, 'I tell you ____________.

2. What prophecy from the Old Testament was being fulfilled when Jesus rode into Jerusalem?

3. What day in the Christian year (today) marks Jesus' entry into Jerusalem?

4. In what way do Christians remember this special day?

5. What is the importance of Jesus riding into Jerusalem on a donkey? What does this action show?

To do

Find out about Palm Sunday and Holy Week. Interview your local vicar/priest/minister and find out what happens in church.

Jesus at Jerusalem

Jesus had arrived at Jerusalem as a king. But what would the king do? The moment that Jesus entered Jerusalem, Luke shows him doing *two* things:

Jesus weeps over Jerusalem

READ LUKE 19:41–44

Jerusalem is the symbol of the Jewish faith. It is the city that will reject Jesus. Luke shows that in rejecting Jesus, Jerusalem is also rejecting *God's salvation*. Instead of saving the city, God will judge it. Jerusalem will be destroyed.

Jesus was heartbroken about this. He wept over the city's coming fate. He did not want Jerusalem to be destroyed; he wanted the city to be saved.

There are two opinions about this passage:

This is an authentic prophecy – Jesus really spoke these words. It may not have been difficult, given the tense political situation, for Jesus to prophesy the destruction of the Temple.

Some believe that this reference to the destruction of the Temple shows that Luke's Gospel was written after the destruction in AD70. Luke put the words into Jesus' mouth.

JERUSALEM

The picture shows a reconstruction of the city as it was in the first century, based on archaeological excavations.

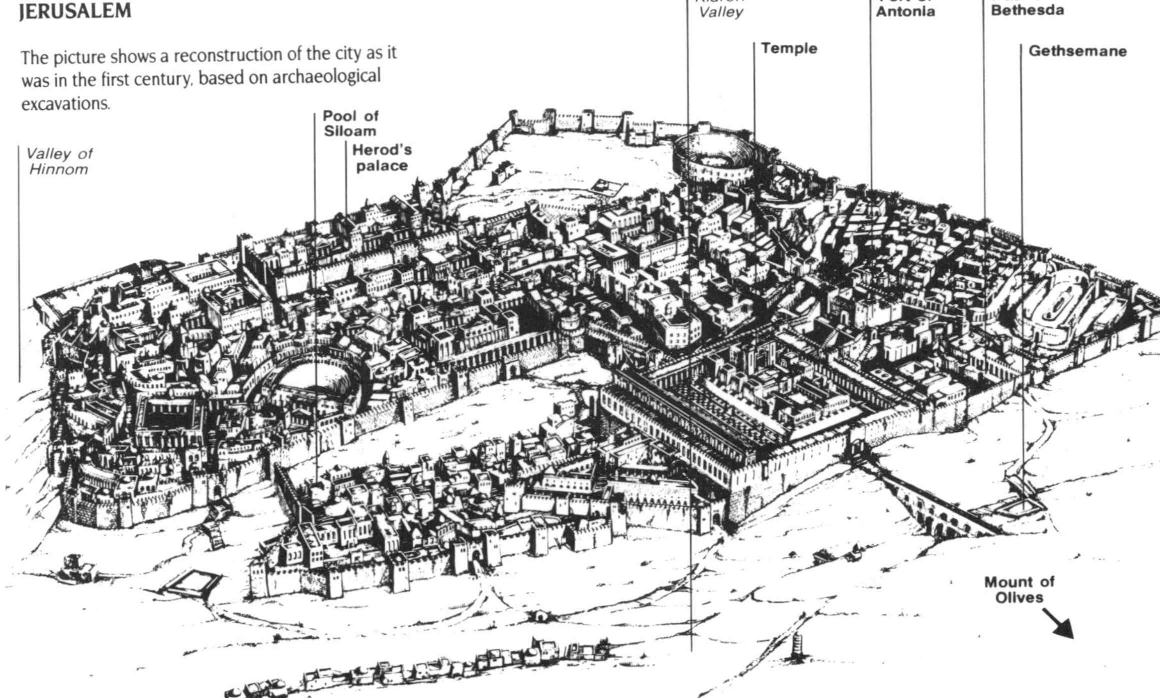

The mosque known as the Dome of the Rock stands on the ancient Temple site in present-day Jerusalem.

We have a description of the destruction of the Jerusalem Temple written by the Jewish historian Josephus. Jesus' prophecy does not go into *detail*, certainly not the kind of details that Josephus gives us. In fact, Jesus' prophecy is very general, and similar to other prophecies found in the Old Testament (Isaiah 29:3; Ezekiel 4:2; Psalm 137:9).

Did Jesus predict the fall of Jerusalem?

Jesus clears the Temple

READ LUKE 19:45–48

The Temple has an important place in Luke's story of Jesus.

- Zechariah is in the Temple when an angel appears to him and announces the birth of John the Baptist.
- Jesus is presented in the Temple, where Mary and Joseph meet Anna and Simeon.
- The boy Jesus remains in the Temple when he is twelve years old, while his parents return to Nazareth after the Passover feast.
- Jesus' long journey to Jerusalem reaches a high point with his arrival in Jerusalem and his entry into the Temple.

The Temple authorities had allowed a market to grow up there. This market was held in the Court of the Gentiles. Having it there meant that the Temple was not 'a light to the Gentiles', as it should have been. Pilgrims exchanged their everyday money for *temple coins*, in which a half-shekel tax had to be paid. Half a shekel was a small coin, but the money-changers charged a lot to change the people's money for this special coin.

Pilgrims could also buy animals for sacrifice which were 'without blemish' (Leviticus 1:3).

Jesus was angry that the Temple was being given over to money-making and not to prayer.

Luke has shortened Mark's account of this incident. In Mark the clearing of the Temple happens *the day after* Jesus' entry into Jerusalem. In Mark, it is a separate act.

The clearing of the Temple is given more importance in the other Gospels. It certainly seems to have helped the Jewish authorities finally decide to get rid of Jesus.

Non-Jews (Gentiles) were forbidden to enter the inner courts of the Temple, on pain of death. This is one of the warning notices, in Greek, from the time of Jesus.

Jesus at the Temple

Luke shows that Jesus taught every day at the Temple. Large crowds came to hear him and hung on his every word.

The Jewish leaders could not *ignore* him, or *remove* him. Jesus was a popular teacher. If the Jewish leaders had tried to interfere with him, there might have been an incident. But they did try to trap him by argument . . .

READ LUKE 20:1–8

This story shows Jesus' cleverness in arguing. The Pharisees wanted to trap Jesus into giving an answer that would:

make him unpopular with the crowd

give the Jewish leaders an excuse to arrest him.

Instead, Jesus turned their question around, so that it trapped the Pharisees and other Jewish leaders.

They could not answer that John's authority came *from God*, because Jesus would then ask why they did not believe him.

They could not answer that his authority came only *from man*, because the crowd would have turned against them. Many people strongly believed that John was a prophet.

So Jesus continued to teach in the Temple. Meanwhile, his enemies grew more bitter against him.

FOLLOW UP

Question time

1. When Jesus weeps over Jerusalem, what do you think Luke is trying to show in his Gospel?

2. Jesus said that Jerusalem would be destroyed. Was he prophesying the future?

3. How important is the Temple in Luke's Gospel? Give examples of how he mentions it in the life of Jesus.

4. Jesus is angry when he sees what is happening in the Temple. Why is this? Do you think this story could be relevant to the church today? How?

To do

- *Improve your self-awareness* and get to know yourself better. Jesus was angry at the injustice he saw in the Temple. What makes you angry? Do you express it? How? If you don't, what happens to the anger? Does it affect you? Could you handle things differently? Fill in the chart and discover more about yourself:

At school I get angry when (tick the appropriate line):
– I am blamed for doing something I didn't do.
– I am bullied by others.
– I can't understand the work and I'm accused of being lazy.
– I am bored most of the time.
– I ____________ (your own answer).

I usually respond to this by ____________.
In future I could try an alternative and ____________.

With my friends I get angry when:
– They talk about me behind my back.
– They let me down.
– They pretend to like me but really don't.
– They borrow things and don't give them back.

I usually respond to this by ____________.
In future I could try an alternative and ____________.

In society I get angry when:
– I see animals being treated badly.
– The poor are given nothing and the rich have everything.
– Criminals get away with murder.

I usually respond to this by ____________.
In future I could try ____________.

- Imagine you were a pilgrim at the Temple when Jesus clears it out. Write a letter to a friend describing what you saw, heard and felt.

UNIT 14.3

Jesus Debates in the Temple

After Jesus' entry into Jerusalem and the clearing of the Temple, Luke goes on to record some of the discussions that Jesus had in the Temple and the teaching that he gave.

After Jesus' authority had been questioned by the chief priests, elders and teachers of the Law, Jesus went on to tell a parable.

The parable of the tenants in the vineyard

READ LUKE 20:9–18

As usual, Jesus drew his parable from life. In Palestine, occupied as it was by the Romans, many foreigners must have owned large estates. No doubt the Jews resented this.

It was the law that if the owner of the property died and there was no *heir* – no person to take over the property – the tenants had the first chance of buying it. Jesus' listeners would have known this.

Though Jesus drew his parable from life, he may have also had in mind Isaiah's *parable of the vineyard* (Isaiah 5:1–7) in the Old Testament. In that parable, the vineyard represents Israel.

The Jewish authorities knew that Jesus had told this parable against them (see verse 19). That made them even more angry and more determined to arrest Jesus.

The early church has often used an *allegorical* interpretation of this parable. An *allegory* is a story in which the events and characters are all *symbols*. Usually this is not true in a parable. But one tradition of interpreting this parable is:

The landlord is God.

The servants are the prophets in the Old Testament.

The son is Jesus.

The tenants are the Jewish leaders.

The other, new, tenants are the Gentile church – the new Christians.

Traditionally, the church has believed Luke thought that the son in the story represented Jesus.

In Mark's version of this story (Mark 12:1–12) the son is killed inside the vineyard and his body is thrown over the wall.

Luke, like Matthew, alters this ending (Matthew 21:33–46). The death of the son happens **outside the vineyard**. This makes the death of the son more like the death of Jesus who **died outside the city** (Hebrews 13:12). The cry of the bystanders, 'Surely not!', is added by Luke. Perhaps it helps to point up this parable as an *allegorical* forecast of the fall of Jerusalem in AD70.

Luke 20:17 once more shows how, in rejecting Jesus, the Jewish leaders are rejecting their salvation.

The question of taxes

READ LUKE 20:20–26

Again, the Jewish leaders were eager to trap Jesus. They bribed men to ask Jesus

HEROD'S TEMPLE

This was the Temple of Jesus' day, begun by Herod the Great. It took many years to build and was a magnificent sight. The artist's drawing gives an idea of what it looked like.

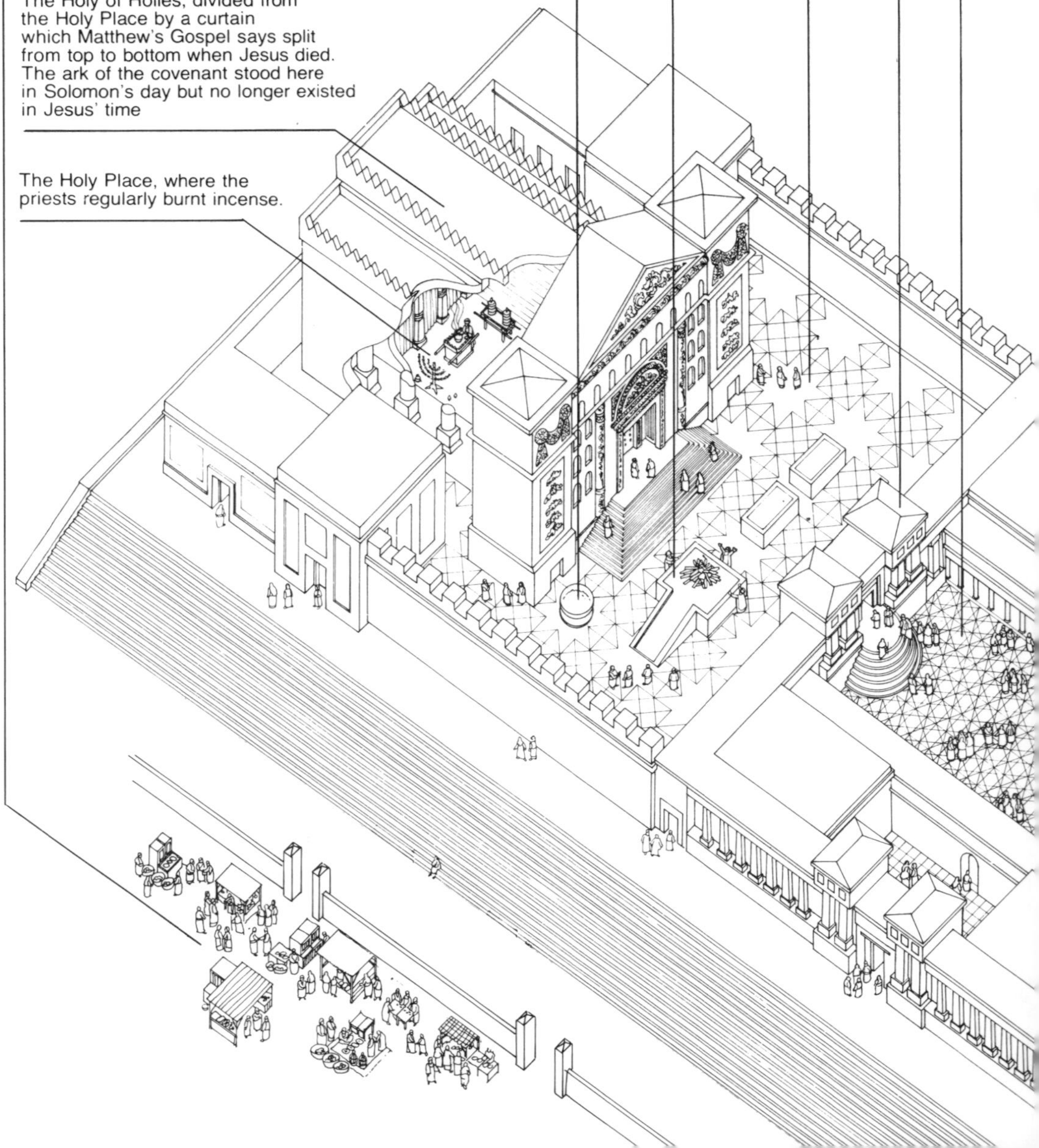

The court of the Gentiles. This was the only part in which non-Jews were allowed. The traders and money-changers worked here, and were turned out by Jesus

The altar where animals were sacrificed. Jesus was described by John the Baptist as being 'the lamb of God that takes away the sin of the world'

A bowl for ritual washings

The court of the women. Women were not allowed any further into the temple.

The court of Israel, reserved for male Jews

The court of the priests

The Holy of Holies, divided from the Holy Place by a curtain which Matthew's Gospel says split from top to bottom when Jesus died. The ark of the covenant stood here in Solomon's day but no longer existed in Jesus' time

The Holy Place, where the priests regularly burnt incense.

a difficult question. But why was this question so difficult?

● The Jews were anti-Roman. The Zealots (a group of extreme revolutionaries), believed that loyalty to Caesar meant disloyalty to God. God or Caesar was the choice – there was no other.

● The Jews hated the taxes that they had to pay the Romans. It hurt their national pride.

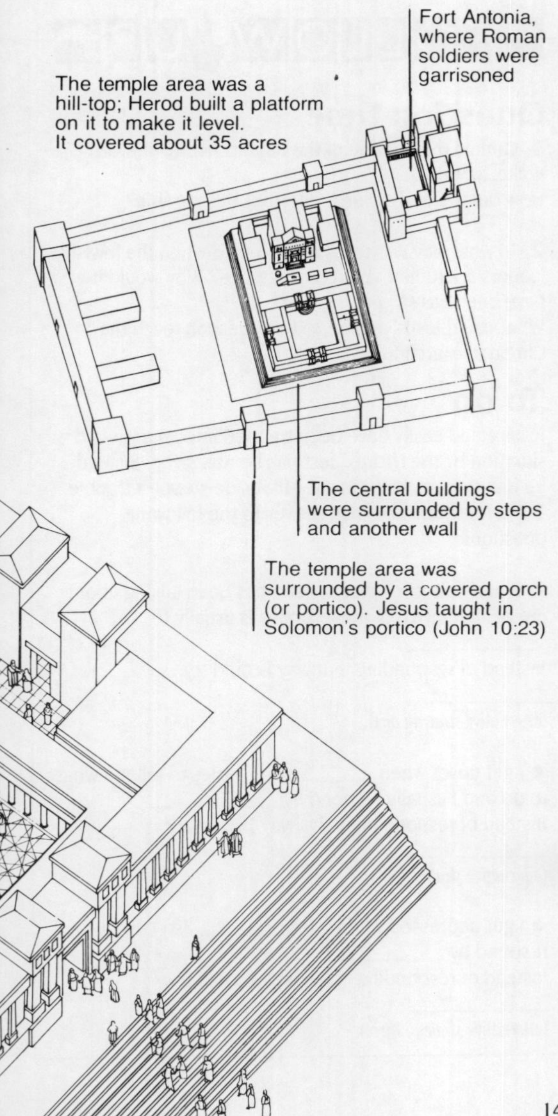

Jesus answered a tricky question about paying tax to Rome by asking his questioners to look at a coin, stamped with the emperor's image.

● One of the strict Jewish commandments was not to make an image of anything or anyone (Exodus 20:4). The silver coin (which Jesus asked for) had the head of the emperor on it. Copper coins in Palestine were issued *without* the head of the emperor. This was in deference to the Jewish Law.

● If Jesus said, 'Yes, pay taxes to Caesar,' he would become unpopular with the crowd. If Jesus said, 'No, it is against the Law to pay taxes to Caesar,' he could be arrested as a criminal. It seemed a case of 'heads I win, tails you lose'. Either way, Jesus lost the argument.

Jesus' answer was not only clever, it said something that is important, even today. Jesus did not see that Roman rule and God's rule cancelled each other out. A person can be faithful in both civil duties and religious duties. Just by possessing a silver coin, Jesus' questioner showed that he had in some way accepted Caesar and Roman rule. Once again, Luke is showing that Jesus was no threat to Roman rule.

The question about the Messiah

READ LUKE 20:41–44

The Jews were expecting the Messiah to be a king like King David in the Old Testament. Here Jesus showed the Jewish leaders that their ideas about the Messiah were too limited.

Jesus said that the Messiah would be more than just a son of David. Even in the Old Testament it was clear that the Messiah would be *greater* than David. He would do more than share the throne of David, he would share the throne of God.

Traditionally, the Jews believed that Moses had written the Torah, the first five books of the Bible, and that David had written all the psalms. Nowadays most Christian scholars disagree with this view.

Jesus, however, obviously speaks as if David did write Psalm 110. And many people see this as revealing Jesus' *humanity*.

Jesus, in many ways, was like the other people of his time. He knew, felt and thought what they did. As a Jew he was part of Jewish culture and belief. He is speaking here as a first-century Jew, not a twentieth-century theologian.

Jesus warns against the teachers of the Law

Again, Jesus attacks the Jewish leaders for their hypocrisy. Again, in the context of Jesus' teaching in the Temple, this must have made Jesus' enemies even angrier.

The widow's offering

Note the features of this story. The incident describes:

- a woman
- a widow
- a poor person

She is alone. She is the kind of person to whom Jesus is preaching the Kingdom of God. She is in sharp contrast to the rich people around her. They give out of *what they have*. The widow gives out of *what she doesn't have*. Her offering is a real sacrifice because she will not have much else to live on.

Some people think this incident was a story *Jesus told* (see Luke 20:47) which became a story *about Jesus*.

Now the time of teaching is past; the time of trial is about to begin.

FOLLOW UP

Question time

1. Outline the parable of the tenants in the vineyard (Luke 20:9–18).
How did the early church interpret this parable?

2. In what way was Jesus being tested when the Jewish leaders asked him about paying taxes? Why would it have been easy to get trapped?
What could Jesus' answer to this question teach the Christian church today?

To do

Jesus could easily have been trapped into an awkward situation by the tricky questions he was given. Instead he found an *alternative* answer that side-stepped trouble. Try to find your own alternatives to the following questions:

- When I discover that a friend has been talking about me behind my back my response is usually to
______________.
Instead of responding that way I could try
______________.
(alternative strategy one)

- I get upset when ______________ tries to tell me what to do and I usually respond by ______________.
Instead of responding in this way I could try
______________.
(alternative strategy two)

- I get depressed when ______________, so I usually respond by ______________.
Instead of responding in this way I could try
______________.
(alternative strategy three)

The Upper Room: Preparing for Passover

READ LUKE 22:1–13

The Passover Festival was central to the Jewish faith. It recalled the story from the Jews' history recorded in the book of Exodus. The Jewish people were slaves to the Egyptians in about the twelfth century BC. The Passover recalls the events that led to freedom and escape for the Israelites.

The Passover Festival happened every year and lasted for a week. It began on the 14th Nisan (the first month of the Hebrew year), around the month of April. The Feast of Unleavened Bread (Leviticus 23:6) began on the 15th and lasted until the 21st.

Jewish people still celebrate the Passover today in much the same way as they did at the time of Jesus. Each year there were certain preparations to be made and every Jew in Jerusalem would have been getting ready for the feast . . .

Two days before Passover all the leaven (the yeast that makes bread rise) was taken out of the house.

Lambs were killed (this part of the Festival changed when the Jerusalem Temple was destroyed). The blood of the lamb recalls the blood which the Israelites put on their doorposts, so that the angel of death passed over their houses on the night when the first born of each Egyptian household died.

Every Jew attended the Passover in Jerusalem each year if possible. Some Jews could not do this because they lived in other countries. But everyone wanted to make the pilgrimage at least once in a lifetime.

The climax of the celebration was the passover meal. The Jewish people still celebrate their escape from Egypt every year in the Feast of the Passover (or H*agadah*, as it is called in Hebrew). On the eve of Passover there is a service in every Jewish home which is called the *Seder*. The family gather together for a special meal. On the table are symbols of food:

- **An egg**
- **Matzot** Three pieces of bread without yeast known as ('unleavened' bread). This reminds them that God's deliverance came so quickly that there was no time for the bread dough to rise.
- **Roasted lamb bone** A reminder of the lambs which were slain on that night long ago.
- **Bitter herbs** This recalls the bitterness of slavery.
- **Salt Water** A symbol of blood on the doorposts and of the tears of slavery of Israel in Egypt.
- **Parsley** reminds them of the hyssop which was the plant dipped in the blood to mark the doorposts.
- **Haroset** is a muddy-looking mixture of apples, spices and honey. It represents the mud out of which the bricks were made when Israel had to be slaves and build for the Egyptians.
- **Four cups of wine** are drunk at the Seder, each one representing a different promise given to Israel by God through his servant Moses in Exodus 6:6–8:

'So tell the Israelites that I say to them, "I am the Lord: I *will rescue you* and *set you free* from your slavery to the Egyptians. I will raise my mighty arm to bring terrible punishment upon them, and I *will save you*. I *will make you my own people* and I will be your God." '

This is a modern celebration of the Passover festival, by a family of Askenazi Jews in Israel.

Josephus, a first-century historian, records one Passover when 256,000 lambs were slain. The Jewish Law stated that there had to be at least ten pilgrims for each lamb. This suggests that there were over two and a half million people in Jerusalem at that time.

Luke's people

Notice the people who are in this passage in Luke 22:1–13.

The chief priest and the *teachers of the Law* Luke tells us that they were afraid of the people. This means that they wanted to arrest Jesus, but they could not do it because they were afraid the people would riot.

Judas Iscariot Mark and Matthew in their Gospels imply that Judas betrayed Jesus for money, but John and Luke say that 'Satan entered' Judas. The early church believed that from the time of Jesus' temptations, Satan had been trying to destroy him. They saw Jesus' death on the cross as the final battle between God and Satan. Judas was one of the twelve disciples. He was a close friend of Jesus. Why did he betray him? Was it for the money? Was Judas disappointed that Jesus had not started a violent revolution?

Peter and John were sent to get the Passover meal ready.

The man carrying a jar of water would have been an unusual sight. Normally only women carried water. Jesus arranged this secret sign so that he could be sure of having a final meal with his disciples, uninterrupted. The scene is set for the last meal in Jesus' life. This meal has been remembered throughout the ages by Christians by breaking bread and drinking wine. In relating it, Luke tells us what Jesus' life was about, and what he achieved through his death.

FOLLOW UP

Question time

What do you know about the Passover Festival? Answer the following:

1. How long did the Passover Festival last?

2. What did the Festival of Unleavened Bread celebrate?

3. Who attended Passover?

4. What symbolism lies behind the unleavened bread at Passover?

5. What did the blood of lambs recall in the history of Israel?

To do

Illustrate the Passover meal by drawing the different food/drink and then giving each part a label, saying what is being symbolized.

UNIT 15.2

The Last Supper: A New Covenant

How would you like to be remembered?
- For your beauty or your good looks?
- For your outstanding sporting achievements?
- For your intelligence?
- For your kind deeds to others?
- For your loyalty and friendship?

Some rich people like to be remembered for what they have given to charity. They leave money to libraries or hospitals and often a part of the building is named after them – The Alfred Purbeck Ward, or The Gladys Pring Room.

Others prefer to be remembered for what they have loved. On Wimbledon Common there are benches inscribed with names of people who loved the beauty of the Common. Either they have left money in their will, or close friends and relatives have donated the bench in their memory.

Memories are powerful. They can make us laugh or cry. In some way they bring to life, even for a moment, the person or the event in mind.

The Last Supper

READ LUKE 22:14–20

During the last meal he ever ate, Jesus said he wanted to be remembered in a special way by his friends. He wanted his followers to remember him by eating a special meal together. As they ate bread together they would remember his body. And as they drank wine, they would remember his blood.

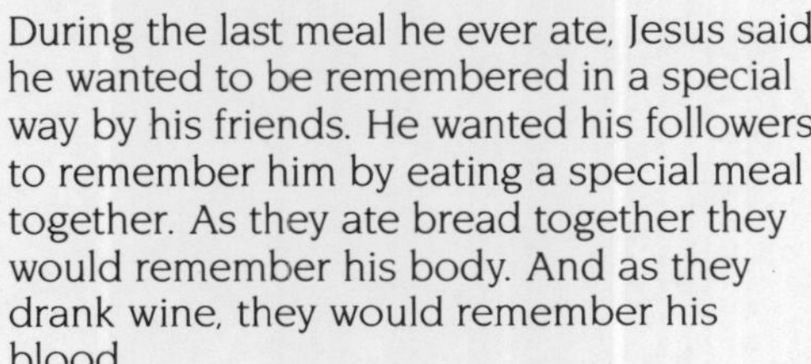
'This is my body, which is given for you. Do this in memory of me.'

'This cup is God's new covenant sealed with my blood, which is poured out for you.'

Jesus and the disciples would have reclined at table, Roman style, as they ate their last supper together.

Jesus was talking about the meaning of his death. Jesus' death was to be no ordinary death, but through his death God was going to make a new covenant (or agreement) with the world. God was going to do something new for people through the death of Jesus. What did Luke think this was?

A clue can be seen if we compare Luke's account with the other Gospels, particularly John. Verses 7–13 describe how the Passover meal was prepared. The lambs were killed a day earlier (14th Nisan) in preparation – but in Luke's account everything seems to be happening on the same day.

Why is this? Is there a confusion of dates?

- It may be that Jews used different calendars for celebrating their feasts and that therefore nowadays we do not really understand the order of events at the time of Christ.

- Or perhaps Luke is giving us a clue about his thinking in the way he has written the account. He has Jesus' last meal coinciding with the Passover meal, which remembers *people being set free from slavery.*

Leonardo da Vinci, painting the Last Supper, set the scene in his own time.

Luke sees God's new covenant through Jesus' body and blood as setting people free, so perhaps the symbolism is more important than a precise time-sequence. If you read John's Gospel you will see that the crucifixion is placed a day earlier than in the synoptic Gospels. He portrays Jesus dying at the same time as the Passover lambs were being killed in the Temple.

Luke and the Last Supper

Most scholars think that Luke used Mark's Gospel as one of his sources. If you compare the two accounts of the Last Supper given in Mark and Luke you will see some differences. These differences can give us information about Luke's special emphasis in the story.

- **Only Luke** uses the welcome from Jesus at the beginning of the meal: 'I have so much wanted to eat this Passover meal with you before I suffer!'
- **Only Luke** names Peter and John as the ones who prepare the feast.
- **Only Luke** has the words of Jesus about his betrayal at the end of the meal. Matthew and Mark have it at the beginning. And Luke leaves out Mark's harsh words about the betrayer: 'It would have been better for that man if he had never been born.'
- **Only Luke** expands the story of the Last Supper by adding the teaching of Jesus on being a servant, along with the prediction of Peter's denial and the conversation with the disciples (verses 24–38).
- **Only Luke** points to a future supper which will be given in the Kingdom over which Jesus is to rule.

FOLLOW UP

Question time

1. What do you know about the Last Supper? (Luke 22:14–20)

- Jesus took a cup, gave thanks to God, and said, '______________.'
- Jesus told his disciples that he would not drink this wine until ______________.
- Jesus took a piece of bread, gave thanks to God, broke it, and gave it to them, saying '______________

2. What did Jesus mean when he said, 'This cup is God's new covenant sealed with my blood, which is poured out for you'?

3. What are the differences between Luke's account and Mark's account of the Last Supper? Can you think of any reasons why Luke should shape his material in this way?

To do

What might the disciples have been thinking and feeling during their last meal with Jesus? Did they suspect it was their last time together? Choose two disciples and write a possible conversation between them.

Bread and Wine in the Church Today

The first Christians were accused of cannibalism. Their enemies misunderstood the language they used. When Christians spoke of eating the 'body' and 'blood' of Christ – some who heard them took it literally!

The Eucharist is central to the Christian church. The word means 'thanksgiving'. The Eucharist is the service which celebrates the death of Christ through the bread and the wine. Sometimes the Eucharist is called different names: Holy Communion, Mass, The Lord's Supper, The Lord's Table, or The Breaking of Bread. These different names reflect different beliefs about the Eucharist.

The history of the Eucharist

At first the Eucharist was simply part of a meal shared by the early believers. During the meal the bread and wine were shared as a reminder of the death and resurrection of Jesus. When Christians did this they believed that in Jesus' death they had 'died' to sin, and in his resurrection they were 'raised' to a new life. In other words they 'participated' or 'shared' in Jesus' death and resurrection.

- In later centuries the church in the West put more importance on celebrating the 'Eucharist' or 'Mass'. They came to believe that power came from this 're-living' of Jesus' sacrifice. The Eucharist was now no longer part of a simple meal together. It had become a formal church service.

- Then in 1215 the Fourth Lateran Council said that: 'The Body and Blood are truly contained in the Sacrament . . . under the appearance of bread and wine, after the bread has been changed into the Body, and the wine into the Blood, through the power of God.'

  In other words, they believed that somehow when the bread and wine were offered to God they *became* the Body and Blood of Christ. Eventually, ordinary Christians were seen to be unfit to drink the wine, because it was the blood of Christ. Popes could threaten rebellious rulers with exclusion from the Eucharist, which meant exclusion from heaven.

- In the sixteenth century, there was a great movement for reform in the church – called 'the Reformation'. Martin Luther was one of the leading reformers. He insisted that Christian believers should be given both bread and wine.

Jesus told his disciples, as they ate bread together, to remember his body, given for them; and as they drank the wine, to remember his blood, poured out for them.

Protestants and Catholics

The different understandings of the Eucharist is one of the main differences between the Roman Catholic Church and the Protestant churches. Even today this difference exists. Some Protestant churches follow the approach of Zwingli. He was another reformer who went further than Luther in his rejection of Roman Catholic ideas. He said that the bread and the wine were only signs. According to Zwingli, the words said by Jesus, 'This is my body', meant: 'This stands for my body'.

Eucharist in the church today

In the Roman Catholic Church the service is called Mass.

It is the most important service. Roman Catholics believe that the bread and wine actually in some way become the real body and blood of the risen Christ, although they look the same.

The bread is a small wafer and the priest breaks it in public view of the people. A small piece of the wafer is dropped into a special cup of wine. The people go to the front of the church and the priest gives them a piece of wafer to eat.

In some churches only the bread is given to the people and only the priest drinks the wine.

During Mass, incense is burnt. It scents the church. Incense is a symbol of prayers rising to God.

MORE OVERLEAF

In the Church of England (Anglican Church) the service is usually called Holy Communion.

It is normally held on Sunday morning. The people usually go to the front of the church to receive communion kneeling at the 'communion rail'.

Each person is first given a small piece of bread to eat. They are then given the cup or chalice which is full of wine, and each person takes a sip.

In other Christian denominations the service is called 'The Lord's Supper' or 'The Lord's Table'.

The services are usually held less often than once a week (although some churches, such as the Brethren, hold the service every Sunday).

Many of the other denominations do not use alcoholic wine; they use a non-alcoholic fruit juice.

The bread is usually ordinary bread, cut into small pieces, rather than wafers.

The wine is usually given out in small individual glasses.

In some churches the people sit in their seats and the bread and the wine are brought to them.

It is not unusual for the people to take individual glasses and wait so that all drink together at the same time, to show that in the sight of God they are all equal and to emphasize fellowship with one another.

FOLLOW UP

Question time

1. How important is the celebration of the Eucharist to Christians today?

2. What would be your response to someone who said that the bread and the wine become the body and blood of Christ during the Eucharist service? Would you agree? Why? Would you disagree? Why?

To do

- *Write a poem*. What could believers be experiencing and thinking as they wait for the Eucharist? Here are two poems written by fourth-year pupils. Write your own.

It is so quiet
I can even feel my heart beating.
All I can hear are the ancient words, 'The Body of our Lord Jesus Christ'
'The Blood of our Lord Jesus Christ'
Is it? Is it his Body?
Some say so. I don't know.
All I know is that when I eat this bread, it's like nothing else on earth.

I don't know why I'm here, I really don't.
I could be doing all sorts of things.
I could be out with friends, I could be fishing,
And yet I'm here.
Why? What is it that draws me to this table?
Why should someone's death two thousand years ago affect all my Sundays?
And yet it does.
Because somehow this is different.
Somehow this is special.
It's as if Jesus still breaks it
And gives it to me himself.

- *Design a church poster* advertising the Eucharist service on the church noticeboard. Include:
  - the name of the church
  - what time the service begins
  - the title of the service

Draw a picture to symbolize the bread and wine.

Remember to be accurate. If you choose a Baptist Church it's no good calling the Eucharist 'Mass' – you could offend a lot of Baptists!

UNIT 16.1

Jesus in the Garden

Jesus had eaten his last meal with his disciples. He knew that he had only a short time left with them. He knew that soon he was going to die. The Kingdom of God that he had talked about was to be entrusted into the hands of his new followers.

It was night. Jesus went out with his disciples to pray. He felt evil and darkness closing in.

Jesus prays

READ LUKE 22:39–46

This passage shows Jesus' darkest hour. Often these verses are referred to as the 'agony in the garden'. Here Jesus is shown struggling with doubt, begging that God's will be done.

The usual position for prayer was *standing*, but Luke records that Jesus knelt down. This picture of Jesus kneeling perhaps shows us something of the depths of feeling that Jesus was experiencing at this point.

Jesus tells his disciples (in verse 40): 'Pray that you will not fall into temptation'. These words echo two scenes from earlier in Jesus' ministry:

The temptations in the desert (Luke 4). Jesus' third temptation suggests that God will protect his Son. The Devil has not been far from Jesus all through his ministry. Now Jesus knows that the Devil is very close and the powers of darkness are coming nearer. Here Jesus is warning his disciples against the Devil's power.

This section in Luke also ends with the same reminder (verse 46).

The Lord's Prayer (Luke 11:4) 'Lead us not into temptation.' This is the prayer that Jesus taught his disciples to say. Jesus was possibly reminding his disciples of his teaching, warning them not to forget him during this dark hour.

How does Luke present Jesus in his agony?

Luke, as we have seen again and again, is interested in presenting people in their situations. At this point in the Gospel, Luke is careful to show Jesus at his most human.

Luke shows Jesus in doubt

Jesus is prepared to die, but he is not sure if his death is God's will. Although Jesus has foretold his own death, now, in the garden, he is not sure.

Jesus prays earnestly that God's will be done. Perhaps, at this point, Jesus cannot see how the Kingdom of God will come about through his own death.

Luke shows Jesus in agony

Luke is the only Gospel writer who records that Jesus' sweat fell like great drops of blood to the ground (verse 44).

As the New Testament describes Luke as a doctor, perhaps here Luke's professional eye is describing the physical appearance of an inward experience. In any case, it is clear that Luke shows that Jesus was undergoing very great suffering.

Jesus went out *as usual* to the Mount of Olives to pray. Presumably Jesus and his disciples did this every night. Only tonight was different. Jesus separated himself from his disciples and went to pray on his own. Luke emphasizes Jesus' *aloneness* – in Mark's Gospel, Peter, James and John are also mentioned.

Mark says that Jesus prayed three times in Gethsemane, an olive orchard on the side of the Mount of Olives across the Kidron valley from Jerusalem.

Luke mentions only the Mount of Olives and recounts only one prayer.

Why was Jesus in agony?

Apart from the obvious reasons why a person might not be able to face death calmly, it may be that:

- *Jesus feared being cut off from God.* Jesus saw death as a consequence of *sin*. The result of this would be that Jesus would be separated from God. As Jesus had never been separated from God, the prospect of this was too awful to bear.

  The appearance of the angel, however (in verse 43), shows that God was with Jesus even in his suffering.

- *Jesus felt increasingly alone.* As Jesus prays, his disciples fall asleep. Luke provides an explanation for this – he says that it was nervous exhaustion.

  The Jews were not supposed to fall asleep during the Passover celebrations as it broke their fellowship: perhaps there is an echo of this belief here in this section.

  Little by little, as the darkness closes in, Jesus is becoming truly alone.

Jesus is arrested

READ LUKE 22:47–53

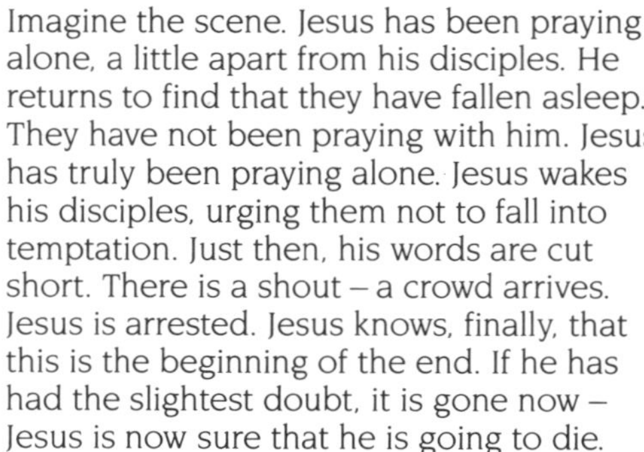

Imagine the scene. Jesus has been praying alone, a little apart from his disciples. He returns to find that they have fallen asleep. They have not been praying with him. Jesus has truly been praying alone. Jesus wakes his disciples, urging them not to fall into temptation. Just then, his words are cut short. There is a shout – a crowd arrives. Jesus is arrested. Jesus knows, finally, that this is the beginning of the end. If he has had the slightest doubt, it is gone now – Jesus is now sure that he is going to die.

Most people experience the pain of rejection at some time or other:

“My mum walked out on me.”

“My dad left for another woman.”

“My boyfriend turned round and told me to drop dead.”

“My best friend let me down.”

“She promised not to tell and then told everybody.”

Probably all of us have had the bad experience of being let down by someone we love and trust – not just in a little way, but in a very important way. Often such experiences damage our trust when it comes to others. We feel safer when we keep ourselves to ourselves. We realize that it is dangerous to be open – able to be hurt.

Jesus had opened himself to his disciples throughout the three years of his ministry. Now one of them, Judas, had come with a crowd to betray him. How do you think Jesus felt about this? How would you have felt?

What did Jesus do?

The other Gospels record that Judas kissed Jesus. This was the usual kind of greeting a disciple would give to his rabbi (teacher). Yet Luke records that Jesus fended off Judas' greeting with a question. Jesus did not allow Judas to kiss him. This may have been because a kiss was the greeting used by the Christians in the early church and Luke did not want it damaged by this recollection.

Jesus stopped the violence

It might have been possible to fight and escape. But Jesus knew that they would come for him another day. The disciples were prepared to fight for Jesus (though not to pray for him) – yet Jesus stopped them.

Again, Jesus showed that he was a leader unlike other leaders. His way was not the way of armies and fighting.

Jesus healed the servant's ear

Luke is the only Gospel writer who records the healing of the servant's ear. Even when he was threatened, Jesus still tried to bring peace and healing to a violent situation.

Jesus recognized what was happening

Mark records that a mob arrived to arrest Jesus. Luke is aware that some of the Jewish officials must have been included in this crowd. Luke writes that the chief priests, the officers of the Temple guard and the elders were present. These people were, of course, symbols of law and order. Yet instead of performing their task by day, they had chosen to come for Jesus under cover of darkness.

Look at Jesus' question. Jesus pointed out that he had been in the Temple teaching every day, but none of the Jewish officials had had the courage to arrest him there. Instead, they had come at a time when no one could see what they were doing.

Amongst the ancient olive-trees in the Garden of Gethsemane, Jesus agonized in prayer as he faced imminent death.

FOLLOW UP

Question time

1. What do you know about the arrest of Jesus? Answer the following questions:
- What had Jesus been doing just before he was arrested?
- What had the disciples been doing?
- What did Judas do?
- When the disciples saw that Jesus was about to be arrested, what did one of them do?

2. What did Jesus say during his time of agony in the Garden of Gethsemane?
Fill in the following quotations:
- When he arrived at the place, Jesus said to them (his disciples), 'Pray that ____________.'
- 'Father,' he said, 'if you will ____________.'
- He went back to the disciples and found them asleep. He said to them, 'Why are you ____________? Get up and ____________.'

3. How did Peter deny Jesus? Give an account of what happened.

4. Using both Mark's and Luke's Gospels write an account of the arrest and trial of Jesus using these points in your work:
- Jesus prays on his own.
- Jesus prays in the Garden of Gethsemane.
- Jesus prays three times.
- Jesus kneels down.
- The disciples sleep because they are exhausted.
- Jesus is mocked before the Jewish trial.
- Jesus is hit and spat upon.

5. What do we learn about Luke's attitude to Rome from his account of Pontius Pilate?

6. How valuable is Old Testament prophecy for Luke's understanding of Jesus' suffering?

To do

Write a diary. Imagine you are one of the disciples and you are recording the events surrounding the agony and the arrest/sentence of Jesus to death. Record the events from the perspective of close friends. What happened? When? What did you feel? What were your hopes and fears? (If you want to, you can choose to be Judas – but you will need to angle things differently!)

UNIT 16.2

Jesus Before the Council

After Jesus had been arrested, Luke records that it is Peter, out of all the disciples, who followed on behind to see what was going to happen to Jesus. We have to remember that Peter was perhaps closer to Jesus than any of his other disciples. Peter was the one who recognized Jesus as the Messiah (Luke 9:18–20) and Mark and Matthew state that Jesus told Peter he was the rock on which he was going to build his church.

We must also remember that Jesus had predicted that Peter would deny ever knowing Jesus. Jesus said this to Peter during the Last Supper. Peter was upset by Jesus saying this and promised that he was ready to die for Jesus.

With this in mind, Luke goes on to tell the sad story of how Peter denied Jesus.

Peter's denial

READ LUKE 22:54–62

From now on, Luke changes Mark's order – perhaps making more sense of the events that occurred immediately after Jesus' arrest. In Mark, Peter's denial comes *after* Jesus' trial, whereas Luke places it before. Luke does not write about Peter's oaths and curses. Instead he gives a quieter, perhaps more moving version of the story. As in Mark, Peter does deny Jesus, and the servant girl recognizes his accent – accusing him of being from Galilee and a follower of Jesus.

What Luke adds gives weight and compassion to the story – that after Peter had denied Jesus, Jesus turned and looked straight into Peter's eyes just before the cock crowed. Peter had done what he said he would never do.

Some manuscripts, though not all, record that Peter went out and wept *bitterly*. Luke again is clear in showing the feelings of the people involved in this scene.

Jesus is mocked and beaten

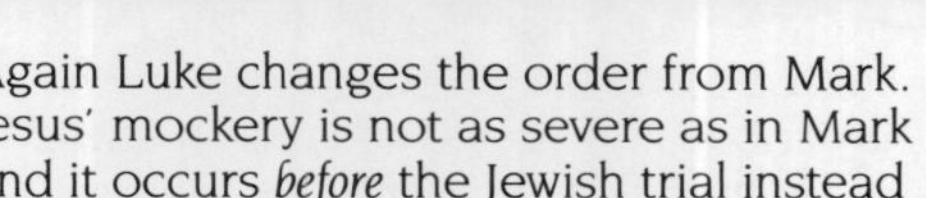

Again Luke changes the order from Mark. Jesus' mockery is not as severe as in Mark and it occurs *before* the Jewish trial instead of after.

Luke's account of Jesus being beaten is, however, clearer than the accounts in Mark and Matthew. In Mark the blindfold is mentioned, but not the soldiers' questions. In Matthew the questions are mentioned, but not the blindfold (look at Matthew 26:67–68 and Mark 14:65).

We have already looked at the title *Suffering Servant* which the early church attached to Jesus. The Songs of the Suffering Servant, recorded in the Old Testament book of the prophet Isaiah include these verses:

'We despised him and rejected him;
he endured suffering and pain.
No one would even look at him –
we ignored him as if he were nothing.
But he endured the suffering that
should have been ours,
the pain that we should have borne.'
Isaiah 53:3,4

'He was arrested and sentenced and led off to die,
and no one cared about his fate.'
Isaiah 53:8

The early Christians found passages from the Old Testament which they were convinced applied to Jesus as *prophecies*. From the very first days of the church, these verses were given a special meaning in relation to Jesus' treatment at the hands of the soldiers.

Jesus before the Council

The Council that Jesus was brought before was called the Sanhedrin. The Sanhedrin was the highest Jewish court.

The people who were on the Sanhedrin were the most important Jews. They included the chief priests and the scribes (the scribes interpreted the Jewish Law). The Sanhedrin had seventy members in all.

The Council would have sat in a semi-circle in front of Jesus. They would have met in the 'Hall of Hewn Stones' in the inner court of the Temple.

Strictly speaking, Jesus' trial did not take place according to correct legal procedure. The Jewish leaders had already made up their minds. They wanted to be rid of Jesus. The problem was finding a reason to accuse him.

The Jewish leaders wanted to force Jesus to admit that he thought he was the Messiah. Then they could accuse him both of blasphemy and of inciting rebellion against the Romans.

The term 'Messiah' was a *political* title in the minds of the Jews and the Romans. Especially at Passover time, when so many Jews were in Jerusalem, there was danger of a rebellion if anyone appeared claiming to be the Messiah.

Yet Jesus did not confirm or deny the Sanhedrin's suspicions. Jesus listened to their accusations, but refused to commit himself. Instead, he said: 'But from now on the Son of Man will be seated on the right of Almighty God' (Luke 22:69).

Jesus was saying that he had passed beyond the Sanhedrin's authority. Jesus believed the Sanhedrin had no more power to hurt him. He now knew that he would be with God, and would soon be in a position to judge the very people who had judged him so unjustly.

It is clear that these religious leaders had no time for Jesus. They did not want to listen to him. They had already decided what was to become of him. Their problem was that the Romans had taken away from them the legal power to condemn someone to death. Because of this, they now had to bring Jesus before Pontius Pilate, the Roman governor. And they had to convince Pilate that Jesus had claimed to be the Messiah.

FOLLOW UP

Question time

1. What did the Jews believe about 'The Suffering Servant'?

2. What is a prophecy?

3. What sort of authority did the Sanhedrin have?

4. How did Jesus respond to the Sanhedrin?

5. Complete the following sentences about the Sanhedrin:
The Sanhedrin were ____________.
The only thing the Sanhedrin could not do was ____________.
The Sanhedrin had ____________.
The people in the Sanhedrin were ____________.

To do

Look at the account of Peter's denial (Luke 22:54–62). Choose one of the following activities:

- Draw the story in picture form with speech bubbles for the main characters.
- Narrate the story with a different speaker for each main part.

Jesus is Condemned to Death

Jesus is brought before Pilate

READ LUKE 23:1–5

Pontius Pilate was Governor of Judea from AD26–36. He was appointed by the Emperor Tiberius and was also 'Procurator' (Governor) – that is, he was responsible for raising the right amount of taxes to send back to Rome. He was known to be violent and cruel.

Mark shows Pilate as a weak man.

Matthew shows Pilate as (literally) washing his hands of having to decide about Jesus.

As we have already seen, Luke is always eager to show that Christianity is no threat to Rome. Perhaps because of this Luke records that Pilate found Jesus innocent *three times*. Pilate said: 'I find no reason to condemn this man' (Luke 23:4).

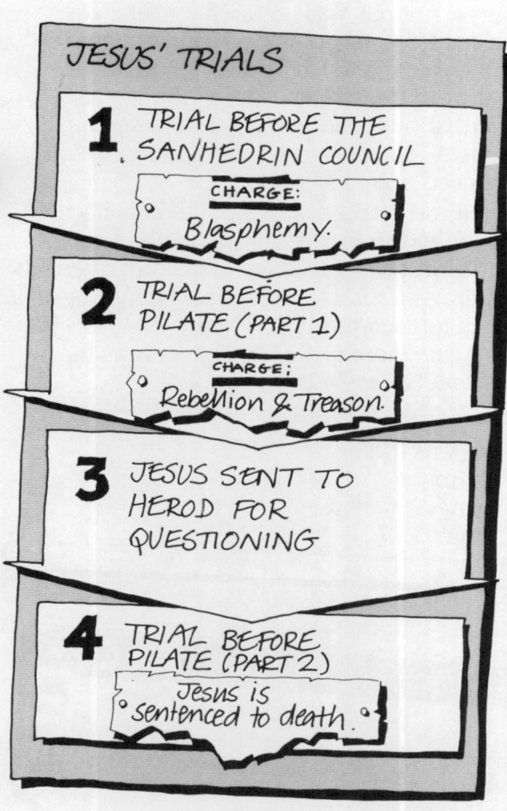

The charges that the Sanhedrin presented against Jesus before Pilate were *political*. A *religious* charge of blasphemy would not have interested Pilate at all. The charges were:

trying to cause a revolt

telling the people not to pay their taxes to Rome

claiming to be a king – the Messiah.

Luke showed very clearly, of course, that Jesus did not want to be a political figure. Jesus did not try to cause a rebellion. He did not tell people not to pay their taxes (quite the opposite). And he did not want to be a powerful king. The Jewish leaders had taken the opposite of what Jesus had said, and presented this as the truth to Pilate.

Pilate had a problem. He did not want to condemn Jesus. He believed that Jesus was innocent. But at the same time he knew that the religious leaders could stage a riot if he didn't agree to their demands. So when Pilate heard that Jesus was from Galilee (a region ruled by Herod Antipas) he decided to send Jesus to Herod for judgment. In fact, to save face, Pilate decided not to decide.

Jesus is brought before Herod

READ LUKE 23:6–12

Herod Antipas was 'tetrarch' or ruler over Galilee from 4BC to AD39. The Jews hated him almost as much as they hated Pilate.

Herod treated Jesus as a joke. He had heard about Jesus and wanted to see a miracle. Jesus, however, did nothing. He did not even open his mouth.

Herod Antipas was the one who had had John the Baptist put to death. And, earlier in Luke's account, Jesus had referred to him as 'that fox'. This is probably why Jesus refused to talk to Herod.

Again, here is the idea of Jesus as the *Suffering Servant* in Isaiah:

> 'He was treated harshly, but endured it humbly;
> he never said a word.'
> Isaiah 53:7

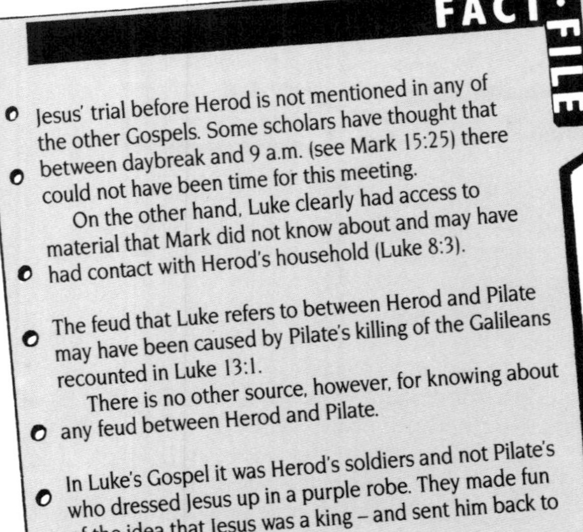

FACT·FILE

- Jesus' trial before Herod is not mentioned in any of the other Gospels. Some scholars have thought that between daybreak and 9 a.m. (see Mark 15:25) there could not have been time for this meeting.
  On the other hand, Luke clearly had access to material that Mark did not know about and may have had contact with Herod's household (Luke 8:3).
- The feud that Luke refers to between Herod and Pilate may have been caused by Pilate's killing of the Galileans recounted in Luke 13:1.
  There is no other source, however, for knowing about any feud between Herod and Pilate.
- In Luke's Gospel it was Herod's soldiers and not Pilate's who dressed Jesus up in a purple robe. They made fun of the idea that Jesus was a king – and sent him back to Pilate.

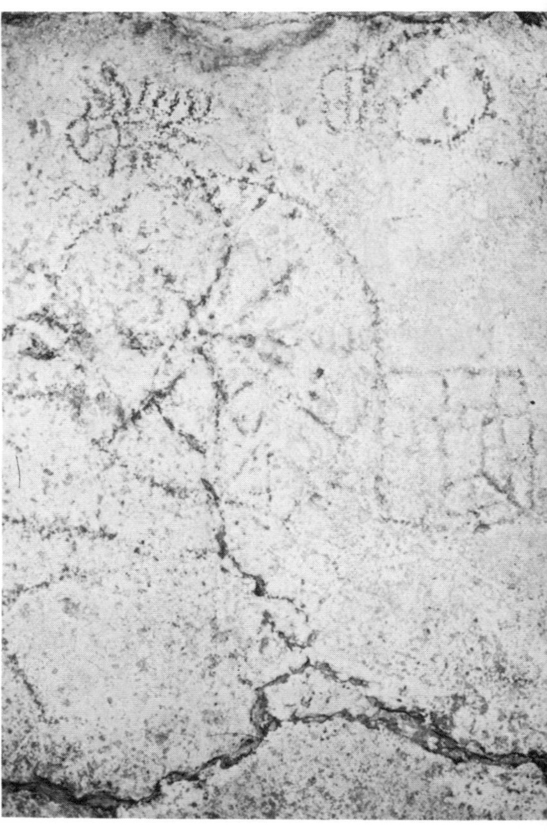

This is the Roman pavement of Fort Antonia, scratched with the soldiers' games. It was here that Jesus was rough-handled when he was brought before the Roman governor, Pilate.

Jesus is sentenced to death

READ LUKE 23:13–25

Pilate stated three times that he found Jesus innocent. He was happy to have Jesus whipped and to let him go. Luke may be trying to show Pilate in a favourable light, with an eye to Roman readers. But Pilate did not have his way.

Luke shows how normal justice has been turned upside down. The crowd shouted for the release of Barabbas – a known terrorist wanted on several counts.

This inscription, found at Caesarea, was the first reference to Pontius Pilate known outside the Gospels.

The crowd shouted for the guilty man to be released; they shouted for the innocent man to be condemned.

At last, Pilate gave in to the demands of the religious leaders. Perhaps he wanted to save face; perhaps he was afraid of a riot. We know what kind of violent man Pilate was from other sources.

Finally, Jesus was condemned to death.

FOLLOW UP

Question time

1. What do you know about Pontius Pilate?

2. How does Luke present Pontius Pilate in his Gospel?

3. What do you know about Herod Antipas?

4. What part do the crowd play in condemning Jesus to death?
- a very important part? If so – why?
- a very small part? If so – why?
- other – why?

To do

Design a poster showing the charges against Jesus. For example, 'This man has been found GUILTY of ______________.

From Luke's Gospel design a Personal Profile of Pontius Pilate. Include an imagined picture of him and job details, character, popularity with others, political views, etc.

The Way to the Cross

Have you ever been blamed for something you didn't do? Often the louder you say that you didn't do it, the more other people believe you did. Then you feel hurt, trapped and angry. Why won't people believe you when you tell the truth? It's not fair.

Have you ever seen anything really terrible happen to another person – an accident perhaps, an illness, or an attack? It's terrible to see someone in great pain – especially when we can do nothing to help. And why should something so awful happen to them – to anyone? It's not fair.

In his Gospel, Luke shows how Jesus' death was not fair. Jesus was innocent and he did not deserve to die.

Luke writes that the Jewish leaders had plotted against Jesus:

- because he was a threat
- because he was popular
- because he wanted to change things.

Jesus had been tried and now he had been condemned.

Jesus' journey to the cross was terrible and bitter. Luke tells the story and, as usual, he concentrates on the *people* who were there. Luke shows how they reacted to Jesus, and how Jesus responded to them.

Simon of Cyrene

READ LUKE 23:26

Death by crucifixion was a terrible punishment. The Romans reserved it for the worst of their criminals.

- First the condemned man had to carry a cross bar of rough wood over his shoulders to the place of execution.
- Then large nails were driven through his wrists into the wood.
- After that his feet were nailed to the upright post and the cross was raised from the ground.

It was an agonizing punishment – and usually a death by slow suffocation. Hanging by your arms cuts off the air supply to your lungs. So to breathe you have to push down on the nails through your feet – which of course is agony. Often criminals took hours or even days to die.

And people came to watch and look.

The Romans had the right to ask civilians to help them. Jesus was obviously too exhausted to carry his cross any further, because of the flogging he had received. So the Romans pulled Simon of Cyrene out of the crowd and ordered him to carry it.

Cyrene was a town in North Africa where many Jewish people lived. Simon may well have been in Jerusalem for the Passover.

Often Christians have looked on Simon of Cyrene as a picture of what Jesus' disciples have to do. Jesus had told his disciples that they would have to share his suffering. In this verse, Simon of Cyrene carries Jesus' cross. The church has drawn inspiration from this passage and seen it as showing how Christians today should be following in Jesus' footsteps closely – even to the place of death.

A Good Friday procession carries a cross through the narrow streets of the Old City of Jerusalem, remembering the death of Jesus nearly 2,000 years ago.

The women

READ LUKE 23:27–31

Luke's 'camera' picks out the women following Jesus on the way to his death. All through his Gospel Luke has written about women, and he does not forget them here. The women were more than upset – they were weeping and crying – just as they would at a funeral. They were acting as though Jesus were already dead.

But Jesus turned to them. He told them not to cry for him, but for themselves. He told them that a time was coming that would be so bad that it would be better if they had no children.

Jesus' message was clear and terrible. If Jesus, an innocent person, could be condemned and suffer so much – how much more terrible would be the sufferings of guilty Jerusalem when God decided to punish the city?

The likeness to a skull in this rocky outcrop convinced General Gordon that it was the place of Christ's crucifixion.

The two thieves

READ LUKE 23:32–43

Finally Jesus was crucified between two thieves in the place called 'The Skull'.

The thieves were at the end of their lives. They had been condemned and were being executed. They had nothing more to lose, but – perhaps – everything to gain.

The thieves showed two completely different attitudes to Jesus.

- One of them hurled insults at Jesus, telling him to save himself. He did not

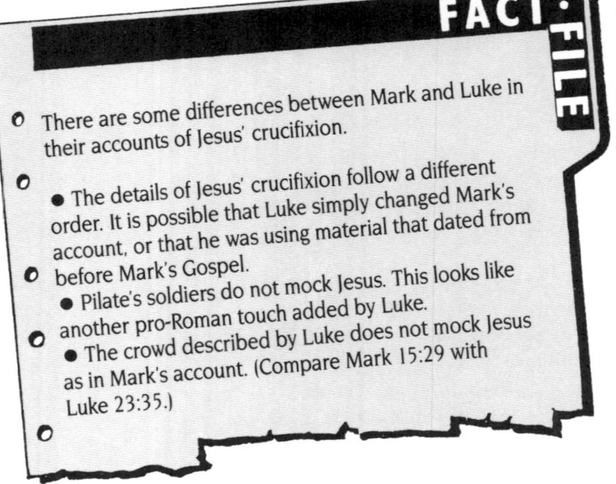

The scene at the cross

The crowd at the cross	Jesus and the crowd
● The crowd watch silently	● Jesus asks God to forgive them
● The women wail	● Jesus tells them to cry for themselves
● The Jewish leaders jeer while Herod's soldiers divide Jesus' clothes and jeer	
● One thief mocks Jesus; the other accepts him	● Jesus promises salvation to a thief

believe that Jesus was the Messiah. He did not care.

● The other knew that Jesus was innocent – he knew that Jesus was the Messiah, a king. And he asked Jesus to remember him. Jesus said that he would do more than that. He promised the dying man that he would be with Jesus in Paradise.

One thief dies bitter; the other dies with the promise of new life.

This story is found only in Luke (although the criminals are mentioned in Mark 15:27).

All the while that Jesus was on the cross suffering, there was an inscription above his head:

This was in fact who Luke believed Jesus to be. But Pilate had had the inscription placed there to get his own back on the religious leaders.

FOLLOW UP

Question time

1. Describe the importance of the following people in the story of the crucifixion. Who were they? What did they do and say?

- Simon of Cyrene
- The women who mourned for Jesus
- The Roman soldiers

2. Who said what? Fill in the correct answer:

'Save yourself if you are the King of the Jews!'
____________.

'Aren't you the Messiah? Save yourself and us!'
____________.

'Remember me, Jesus, when you come as King!'
____________.

'I promise you that today you will be in Paradise with me' ____________.

'Forgive them Father! They don't know what they are doing' ____________.

3. Where was Jesus crucified?

4. What are the differences between Mark's and Luke's accounts of the crucifixion? How do you account for these?

5. What did Luke think about Jesus' death?

UNIT 17.2

Death on the Cross

The end of hope

Jesus' disciples had followed him for three years. They had eaten with him, they had listened to him teach, and they had watched him perform miracles. Now Jesus was hanging on a cross, dying.

What about the Kingdom he had preached – where was that now?

What about the salvation he had offered – what was that worth now?

And God's love – where was God's love in the painful death of an innocent man on a cross?

The disciples were beaten. Their hopes were gone. Their spirits were broken. They had nothing left.

Jesus dies

READ LUKE 23:44–49

In many countries, when someone important dies the flags are lowered to half-mast.

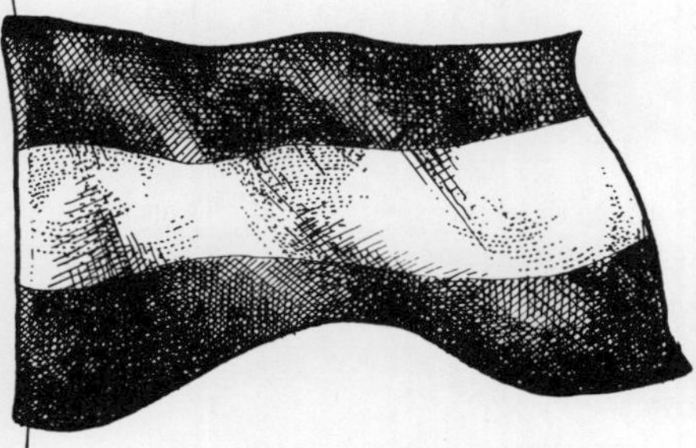

When we remember the people who died in two world wars we observe a silence.

When Jesus died, the sun stopped shining.

The people in the ancient world believed that the deaths of important people were accompanied by supernatural events. This part of Luke's story would not have seemed strange to them. Some people think that this happened, just as Luke describes it, others that the description is symbolic, used by Luke in order to highlight what had happened.

When Jesus died, the Temple curtain was torn in two.

The Temple curtain separated the everyday worship of the Temple from the holiest place – the place where the High Priest was allowed to go only once a year on the Day of Atonement.

This dramatic event could be symbolic of two things:

- the coming destruction of the Jerusalem Temple
- that Jesus' death had somehow opened up the way to God for *everybody*. Now everyone could go in to the holiest place (Hebrews 10:19).

When Jesus died, he did not scream or cry. Instead, in contrast to the crowd and the supernatural signs that Luke describes, Jesus died peacefully. In fact he uttered the kind of prayer that a Jew would say before going to sleep.

The Roman centurion, standing close by, said, 'Certainly he was a good man.

FACT·FILE

Luke and Mark

In this account of Jesus' death, Luke follows Mark, but he rearranges the material. Some people say that Luke simply edits Mark; others that Luke was using his own special sources.

- Jesus' cry of desolation and the reference to the coming of Elijah are omitted in Luke
- The tearing of the Temple curtain is brought forward in Luke to link up with the darkening of the sun
- Jesus' final words (see Psalm 31) are found only in Luke
- Luke has different words for the centurion
- The description of the crowd leaving is new
- Luke does, however, follow Mark's account of Jesus' burial very closely.

Finally the crowds left – sadly. Luke mentions the women – the same women who had an important part to play in the next stage of the story. Luke pictures the disciples standing, watching from a distance. They *witnessed* the event of Jesus' death, but they did not get involved in it.

The diagram shows a rock-cut first-century tomb like that in which Jesus was buried. A heavy stone was rolled across the entrance to seal and secure it.

The burial of Jesus

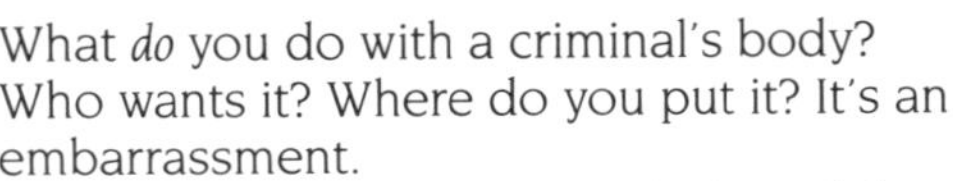

What *do* you do with a criminal's body? Who wants it? Where do you put it? It's an embarrassment.

Worse than that, the Jews believed that the body of a criminal had to be buried before nightfall. Jesus had died like a criminal *under God's curse.* If the body was not buried quickly, the belief was that the curse passed on to the land (Deuteronomy 21:22–23).

● **Joseph of Arimathea** is described as a wealthy man and a devout Jew. In many ways he is much the same kind of good person as Zechariah and Elizabeth, Anna and Simeon – the people who appear at the beginning of Luke's Gospel.

Joseph of Arimathea believed that the Sanhedrin, the Jewish Council, had acted wrongly in condemning Jesus. Joseph was a member of the Council, but he wanted to separate himself from their decision. He came forward for the body when no one else showed any interest at all in Jesus.

He was allowed to claim Jesus' body and to put it in an unused tomb.

● **The women** prepared the traditional spices and perfumes to dress the body. But

the following day was the Sabbath. On that day they could do nothing. So they stayed at home and rested, according to Jewish Law.

The unused tomb, like the unridden colt, meant that it was fit for a sacred purpose.

Where were the disciples?

The disciples were shattered by Jesus' crucifixion. Their hopes were gone. By rights the Messiah should be a powerful king – not a defeated criminal.

So what had gone wrong? Was Jesus really who he said he was? And what would happen to them now? When the authorities moved in, the disciples moved out. The disciples had watched the crucifixion *from a distance* (Luke 23:49). They did not seem to want to be involved. And none of the disciples came forward to ask for Jesus' body for burial. It was left to Joseph of Arimathea – someone not mentioned in Luke's Gospel up to this point.

Jesus had died. The story seemed done. But it was not over.

Question time

1. What is meant by crucifixion?

2. According to Luke, what supernatural events happened when Jesus died?

3. What was the Temple curtain? What was the significance of its being torn in two?

4. Who were the spectators at the crucifixion? Why did Luke include them?

5. Write a sentence about Joseph of Arimathea.

To do

- Imagine you were an eyewitness to the crucifixion. You can choose to be anyone at the scene. Write a letter to a friend describing the events and your own feelings about what happened.

- Design a front-page news headline for the *Jerusalem Sun*. Include pictures of the event, headlines and sub-headlines, and one or two interviews with people who were there. In particular, cover topical issues – for example, why was Jesus dying? Where were his friends/disciples? What did different people think about Jesus?

The Meaning of the Cross

There are some beliefs that people will live or die for. At the very heart of the Christian faith is the belief that Jesus died on a cross. This is an historical event that no serious scholar doubts. It happened. People saw it. They remembered it.

But so what? Many people die (many good people die) for what they believe in. That is something that has happened throughout history and happens even today. So why is Jesus' death any different? How can a man's death 2,000 years ago have any effect on the world today?

In the history of the Christian church, the cross has been seen not just as an *event*, but as an *experience*. The cross is not just a matter of *fact*, it is also a matter of *faith*.

What is important for Christians is not just that Christ died, but that his death has a meaning. Christians believe that Jesus' death changed the world.

Oh, yeah?

If you describe an event, normally you do not just say *what* happened, you also *interpret* the facts. Sometimes if you hear someone describing an event you have seen you might interrupt and say, 'No, it wasn't quite like that,' or 'No, that's not quite what he meant.'

The facts alone are usually not enough. We need more than the facts, we need a *meaning*.

The story of Jesus' death was told over and over again from the very earliest days of Christianity. It was written down and used as part of worship when Christians met. It became part of the Gospels – probably the most important part. From the earliest days of the Christian faith, Christians insisted on two things:

Jesus' death was historical. Jesus was not a legendary figure or a divine, mythical being. He really lived, and he was actually crucified.

Jesus' death has a meaning. For the early Christians, Jesus' death was vitally important for several reasons:

Jesus fulfilled the Old Testament prophecies. He died as the Suffering Servant written about by the Prophet Isaiah. This belief has, to some extent, coloured the writing of the Gospel accounts of Jesus' death.

All the Gospels link Jesus' death with Psalm 22 and Psalm 69. The parting of Jesus' clothes and the insults hurled at him come from Psalm 22:18 and Isaiah 53:3. Jesus' death had been foretold centuries before. What had been planned long ago was finally happening. That is one meaning that the Christian church has traditionally found in the death of Jesus.

What did Luke think about Jesus' death?

It is fair to say that the Gospel writers are more concerned to tell the *story* rather than the *meaning* of Jesus' death.

But Luke did alter Mark's account of Jesus' death in some significant ways. Luke is not concerned to show Jesus dying as a *ransom* for the world (Mark 10:45). Instead, Luke is interested in Jesus as the Messiah, offering salvation to the world. It is more important to Luke *who Jesus is* rather than *how he dies* – though Luke's story clearly pictures Jesus as the Messiah – a fact that the crowd are blind to. Only the disciples, the women, the thief and the centurion realize who Jesus really is.

How do Christians understand Jesus' death?

Many people have been inspired by Jesus' death to live lives of sacrifice and self-giving. Different traditions of the Christian church have developed different *doctrines* about Jesus' death. A doctrine is a belief or teaching about the character of God or Jesus, or about an event to do with God or Jesus.

The beliefs that surround the death of Jesus are not just *theories*. They have come about as people have read and understood the New Testament, and as they have experienced the power of the story. Here are some of the ways Christians understand Jesus' death:

• Jesus died as an example

Just as Jesus showed people how to live, he also showed people how to die. Jesus lived and died an *example* – a model of how a human being should behave.

• Jesus defeated Satan

Though Jesus' death on the cross appeared to be a defeat, in fact he *triumphed* over Satan. On the cross, Jesus destroyed the power that Satan and his angels had held over the world.

• Jesus died as a sacrifice

Jesus had come to Jerusalem to celebrate the Passover feast. At the Passover, lambs were sacrificed to God on behalf of the people who offered them. Because of their sins, people deserved to die, but the lamb died in their place.

Jesus was the lamb of God. His blood was poured out and he surrendered his life for many. In sacrificing himself, the people who should have been punished by God were spared and set free to enjoy the *new covenant*, the new relationship with God, that Jesus had come to offer.

• Jesus died in the place of each of us – as a substitute

Humankind had become separated from God because of *sin*. In dying on the cross Jesus was taking on himself the punishment for the sin of the whole world. He took the sins of everyone onto himself and endured the punishment for them – allowing everyone who believed in him a free pardon and new life.

• Jesus died as a ransom

This idea is stronger in Mark than it is in Luke. The Greek word for 'ransom' (*lutron*) means the price paid to buy back a slave into freedom. Jesus died to buy back

Many different pictures are used to bring out the meaning of Jesus' death. Here the lamb is the symbol of Christ, speaking of sacrifice; the flag is the emblem of his triumphant resurrection.

humankind from bondage to Satan and set people free to live new lives with God.

• Jesus died as an atonement

The word *atonement* means to make two things *at one*. Jesus' death brought humankind and God back together. They had been separate because of human sinfulness, but now they were free to communicate again. And more than that. In the new covenant that Jesus offered, a new kind of life with God was possible that had not been before. In dying Jesus completed his mission. He lived obediently. He did not sin. His death was not a defeat – it was a triumph.

USSR President Brezhnev shakes hands with US President Nixon. It is a gesture of reconciliation between former enemies. The New Testament sees Jesus' death on the cross as an act reconciling God and people, making them friends.

Down the centuries countless Christians have died for their faith. An outstanding example from our own time is Archbishop Janani Luwum of Uganda, who was killed under Idi Amin's regime.

FOLLOW UP

Question time

1. How did the early Christians interpret Jesus' death? Fill in the following sentences with the correct answers:

- Jesus fulfilled the ____________.
- He died as a ____________ prophesied by Isaiah.
- When his clothing was divided up it was a fulfilment of Psalm ______.
- All the Gospels link Jesus' death with Psalm ______ and Psalm ______ and believe that it was foretold centuries before.

2. What have Christians thought about Jesus' death down the centuries? Write an account of the ways in which his death has been understood.

3. How important is Jesus' death and crucifixion for Christians today?

4. What do you think about the crucifixion? Is it significant? Give your reasons.

To do

Draw a *portrait gallery* of 'Witnesses to the Crucifixion'. Divide your page into 'picture frames' and put in pictures of all the principal characters in Luke. Label them and use the chart for revision.

UNIT 18.1

He is Not Here

It is early morning – so early that the sun is still cold and no one is up. Quietly, sadly, some women are on their way to a tomb. They have got ready some spices and perfumes to prepare the body of their friend for burial, as is the Jewish custom. They have come to care for Jesus' body.

Jesus is dead. For a whole day the disciples and the women have lived with the knowledge that Jesus has died. The story is finished. The play is done. The Sabbath, the day of the week when no work can be done, is over. And now the women are doing all they can do – all there is left to do. They are going to prepare Jesus' body as a last act of respect and love.

Jesus rises from the dead

READ LUKE 24:1–11

Luke's account of the resurrection happens in this way:

- Early on Sunday morning the women make their way to the tomb.
- To their surprise, the stone has been rolled away.
- Puzzled, they enter the tomb and find that Jesus' body is no longer there.
- Suddenly, two angels appear and ask the women what they are doing.
- The women are afraid, but the angels remind them that Jesus had promised in Galilee that he would be raised again to life.
- The women rush back to tell the disciples what has happened.
- The women tell the disciples the news, but the disciples do not believe them.
- But Peter is not so sure.
- Peter runs to the tomb alone.
- There he finds the linen wrappings that had covered the body of Jesus – and nothing else. He is amazed.

The case of the missing body

Some stories have a twist. They end in a way you do not expect. Then you have to look at the story in a whole new light.

Jesus' story had a twist. He had come back to life. He had been dead, and now he had disappeared. No wonder the disciples found it difficult to believe the women.

The stone was rolled away and the body had gone! Impossible, you might think. But was it really more possible for the women to believe what had happened then, than it is for us now?

One of the interesting parts of this story is that it was the *women* who first learned that Jesus had risen. According to Jewish Law, a woman could not give evidence in

The picture shows the inside of the rock-cut Garden Tomb in Jerusalem. The broken slab is where the body would have been placed.

court. In other words, women were not to be believed.

But the story of Jesus' resurrection was first entrusted to women.

Look at the story closely

- The women go to the tomb – the account begins just like any other story.
- They find the stone rolled away and are *puzzled* – a normal human reaction.
- They go inside the tomb and two angels appear to them.
- The women return to tell the disciples what has happened. But none of them believe the women. Again, given the situation, this is an understandable reaction. The disciples had no hope left. They had seen Jesus die and now the women were saying that he had come back to life – impossible!
- Of all the disciples, it is only Peter who listens to the women and then runs to the tomb. He finds the empty linen wrappings and these convince him that Jesus has risen. He is amazed.

Remember, it was Peter who first realized that Jesus was the Messiah. Now he is the first disciple to realize that Jesus has risen from the dead.

Many people believe that angels appeared to the women just as Luke says.

Some think that the women had a hallucination.

Others say that Luke puts in the angels to highlight the importance of this part of the story.

The story of Jesus' resurrection is short and very human. Luke writes it simply. The story is presented as history, and again Luke concentrates on the people involved:

- the women
- the disciples
- Peter.

It is a story that is easy to understand – but perhaps difficult to believe. *Note* that the emptiness of the tomb is stressed very strongly in Luke (Luke 24:3).

FACT FILE

Luke's account of Jesus' resurrection is based on Mark – but Luke introduces new material:

- There are two young men at the tomb instead of one (see Mark 16:5).
- In Mark 16:7 the women are told that the risen Jesus is going ahead of them and the disciples to Galilee. Luke omits this. Luke simply writes that the angels *reminded* the women of the teaching that Jesus had given in Galilee about his suffering and resurrection.
- In Mark the women are given a message to deliver, but are too afraid to do so (see Mark 16:7). Luke writes, however, that the women made a full report to the disciples of what they had seen and heard.
- Finally, the list of names is different. Luke mentions *Joanna* as being among the women (Luke 24:10), whereas Mark has Salome (Mark 16:1).

FOLLOW UP

Question time

1. What do you know about Luke's account of the resurrection? Fill in the missing spaces:
Very early on Sunday morning the women went to the tomb, carrying ____________. They found that ____________. They went in but they could not find ____________. Suddenly, two men in bright shining clothes stood by them and said, '____________.' The women returned from the tomb and told all these things to ____________ but the apostles thought that what the women said was ____________. The women were Mary Magdalene, and ____________ and ____________. Peter got up and ____________.

2. Why were the women visiting the tomb?
What is the response of the disciples to the news?
What does Peter do?

To do

Find out about angels. Where do they appear in Luke's Gospel? Why? Do people still believe in angels?

UNIT 18.2

He is Risen

You don't believe everything you read, do you?

You don't believe everything you see on television, do you?

Has anybody ever said that to you? How *can* you know, then, if something is true? How can you know if someone is telling you the truth?

There are two ways:

● *Check your facts* Maybe you can read a book, look up a newspaper, or ask someone else in order to *check* a story that someone has told you.

● *Check your feelings* Do I trust the person who's telling me this story?' This is an important question. If we *trust* someone, we are much more likely to believe them when they turn round and tell us something unusual. This trust is based on what we know of their characer.

Jesus' resurrection was unusual – highly unusual. In fact, the Christian church has always claimed that Jesus' resurrection was *unique*. That means that nothing like it had ever happened before; and nothing like it has ever happened since. It was a one-off.

So how is it possible to talk about the resurrection, if there's nothing to compare it with? How is it possible to know if Luke was really telling the truth?

To begin with, we need to reconstruct the scene in Jerusalem . . .

The evidence

● Jesus had died

That was quite clear. In fact it was more than quite clear, it was quite historical. No one really doubts that. Some people might say that the story of Joseph of Arimathea was just a story, but we have no reason *from looking at the text* to doubt Luke at this point.

So far, so good. Now, the Sabbath day means that everyone has to rest. Everyone stays at home and the women don't go to the tomb.

But there is a problem. Where is the body?

● The disciples had the body

This is unlikely. Luke describes the disciples as being afraid. They had lost hope – and they did not believe the women.

What is more, the disciples *changed* when they finally believed that Jesus had risen and appeared to them. Many of the disciples went on to preach, teach and travel – spreading the gospel about Jesus. Many of them even went on to die for what they believed in.

It is highly unlikely that the disciples would have *changed* or *died* for a lie.

● The Romans had the body

This is a strange idea. Pilate wanted no trouble during the Passover feast – and no trouble meant having Jesus put out of the way. Why cause unnecessary trouble by stealing the body of someone who was more convenient dead?

● The Jewish leaders had the body

This is another strange idea. It was the Jewish leaders who had plotted to kill Jesus. All they had to do to silence the disciples when they started to preach that Jesus had risen was to produce the body – which they didn't do.

● Jesus wasn't really dead

It is hard to believe that Jesus was taken off the cross alive. It was the soldiers' job to see that the criminals were properly dead. It is even harder to believe that Jesus got up, took off his linen wrappings, rolled the stone to one side, and wandered away.

So what did happen? We have what Matthew, Mark, Luke and John have written down. For them, what the eyewitnesses at the time claimed from the very beginning is true.

Jesus died and rose again

The apostle Paul wrote in his first letter to the Corinthian church:

> 'And if Christ has not been raised, then your faith is a delusion and you are still lost in your sins' (1 Corinthians 15:17).

Traditionally the Christian church has always believed that Jesus rose *bodily* from death. Why?

- They believed it was a *historical fact*
- They believed it showed Jesus *had beaten death and the power of Satan*
- They believed it showed that *Jesus was who he said he was – the Messiah*
- They believed that it showed *the new resurrection life was now available to everyone who believed in Jesus* – for now and the life to come.

In Matthew's Gospel, the Jewish leaders are worried that Jesus' disciples will come and steal Jesus' body. They ask for a guard to be put on the tomb – and Pilate agrees (see Matthew 27:62–66).

Christianity is based on facts – but it is also about faith. Christianity takes history seriously – seriously enough to say that Jesus died and rose again *at a particular time and place in history*. But Christians do not simply remember historical facts about Jesus. They also have *faith* that Jesus' death and resurrection have a special meaning for them – even today.

Police File

Jerusalem police department

The 'Jesus' Case

1. The women – not worth bothering to question them as they can't give evidence.
2. The disciples – hard tracking them down. They ran off and hid after their leader's death.
3. The Jewish leaders – blaming us for the whole thing. They claim that the disciples have stolen the body.
4. Peter – denies everything.
5. Caution! We are still looking for two 'shining men' seen near the scene of the crime. They can't be ordinary grave-robbers as the linen wrappings (the most valuable bit) are still in the tomb.

FOLLOW UP

Question time

1. What explanations have been given for the disappearance of Jesus' body?

2. St Paul said that if Christ has not been raised then Christian faith is a delusion and Christians are still lost in sins.

Why do you think the resurrection of Jesus from the dead is so important to Christians? Do you agree with them? Give reasons for your answer.

3. Did Jesus rise bodily from the dead? Yes or No? What reasons are there for and against this view? What is your opinion?

To do

Draw and symbolize the resurrection story.
Artists throughout the years have tried to depict the resurrection. How would you do it? Here are some ideas – but you may have better ones of your own:

- The empty tomb.
- The two men in bright shining clothes saying, 'Why are you looking among the dead for one who is alive?'
- The linen wrappings lying on their own.

The Meaning of Easter

Every year there are Christmas holidays and Easter holidays. Christmas celebrates the *birth of Jesus*. Easter celebrates *Jesus' death and resurrection*. Christmas and Easter are the two most important festivals in the Christian year.

The background to Easter

Easter is a strange word. It does not come from the Bible. *Eostre* was a northern dawn-goddess. She was a symbol of *new life*.

Easter takes place in spring (in the northern hemisphere), the season of new life. The new life coming out of the ground is, in some way, linked with Jesus coming out of the tomb. Just as Christmas echoes an old pagan mid-winter feast, so Easter echoes old *rites* of *fertility*.

That is why we have Easter eggs. The egg is a symbol of life. It breaks and something comes out. In a similar way the tomb broke – and Jesus came out. Just as a seed falls into the ground, lies and grows – so Jesus died, was buried and came back to life again.

The egg is often used as an Easter symbol. Out of it comes new life – as Jesus was raised from death to life.

Easter also takes place at the time of the Jewish Passover. You may have wondered why Easter changes its date each year. That is because it takes place near the Jewish Passover, on the Sunday after the full moon that falls on or after 21 March. This date 21 March – is the *spring equinox* – the beginning of spring – in the northern hemisphere.

Easter events

All over the world, Christians celebrate Easter. Easter comes at the end of *Holy Week*. These are the events remembered in this special week.

Palm Sunday celebrates Jesus' victorious entry into Jerusalem, riding on the back of a donkey.

Maundy Thursday remembers the night of the Last Supper, when Jesus broke bread and drank wine with his disciples.

Good Friday remembers Jesus' terrible death on a cross.

Easter Sunday recalls Jesus' resurrection – the day he came back to life.

The Jewish Sabbath takes place on a Saturday – but the Christian Sabbath changed to Sunday – the day Jesus rose from the dead.

What Jesus said about his own death and resurrection

We have looked at the *evidence* for Jesus' resurrection. But what does it all *mean* for Christians? Here is what Luke records Jesus said about his death and resurrection:

Luke 9:22 'The Son of Man must suffer much and be rejected by the elders, the chief priests, and the teachers of the Law. He will be put to death, but three days later he will be raised to life.'

Luke 11:29 'How evil are the people of this day! They ask for a miracle, but none will be given them except the miracle of Jonah.'

Jonah was a prophet in the Old Testament. The story tells how he was swallowed by a large fish. Eventually the fish was sick and Jonah escaped. Jonah (who was in the belly of the fish for three days) is a picture of Jesus in the belly of the tomb.

Luke 12:50 'I have a baptism to receive, and how distressed I am until it is over.'

As we saw in Unit 3.2, baptism was a picture of dying and rising to new life. Jesus' baptism was not just a baptism of water – he actually had to die to bring in a new kind of life – resurrection life.

Luke 18:31–33 Jesus took the twelve disciples aside and said, 'Listen! We are going to Jerusalem where everything the prophets wrote about the Son of Man will come true. He will be handed over to the Gentiles, who will mock him, insult him and spit on him. They will whip him and kill him, but three days later he will rise to life.'

Soon after Jesus' death, his disciples came out of hiding and said that he had risen to new life. This is the very basis of the Christian faith: *Jesus died and rose again*. Whatever had happened, the disciples had certainly changed.

From being frightened and hidden away, they had emerged, bold and fearless. Jesus, the Messiah, who had died as a criminal, was now the *exalted Messiah* offering salvation to the whole world.

The disciples believed that Jesus had died. The disciples believed that Jesus had risen. What is more, the disciples believed that Jesus had appeared to them and talked with them. The Kingdom of God that Jesus had preached was not at an end after all. It was only just beginning.

Why is the resurrection important?

The resurrection is one of the central beliefs of the Christian faith. Why does it matter so much to Christians that Jesus rose from death?

- *The resurrection shows that Jesus really was the Messiah*. It is not a proof in a scientific sense, but the resurrection is a *sign* that Jesus was trustworthy, powerful and true.

- *The resurrection shows that there is life after death*. Jesus experienced death – and then returned. This new resurrection life is the same life Jesus offers to everyone who decides to follow him.

- *The resurrection shows that the powers of evil have been defeated*. All the way through his Gospel, Luke has shown how the Kingdom of God in Jesus has been defeating the Kingdom of Satan. Jesus' death on the cross looked like Satan's victory – but in fact it was Satan's defeat. The world that was bound to Satan is now free for God.

- *The resurrection shows that there is salvation*. Luke shows Jesus as *bringing salvation*. The resurrection shows that Jesus' salvation is not just for now, but for ever and for everyone.

Memory check

- **The resurrection is an event**

We have looked at some of the historical details surrounding the resurrection. The Christian church has always claimed that the resurrection was a historical event. The church has believed, traditionally, that Jesus really did rise from the dead.

• The resurrection is a belief

The resurrection is not just a matter of history; it is a matter of faith.

– Some people believe the resurrection happened just as Luke described.

– Some people *do not believe* that Jesus rose from the dead. Instead they claim that the resurrection story was only a legend that grew up about Jesus later on.

– Some people say that the resurrection story is only a *picture*. The disciples lost their faith in Jesus at the crucifixion and then – they found it again. Their way of picturing their new-found faith was to form the story of Jesus' resurrection – the story that Jesus had risen bodily from the tomb. What is important to these people is not Easter **fact** but Easter **faith**.

• The resurrection is an experience

Everyone has to agree that *something* happened to the disciples. They claimed that they had met and spoken with Jesus.

No Jew would ever have used the word *resurrection* to describe a new life after death. It was a *new* idea – and the Christian church used the word from its very beginnings.

It is important to remember that for Christians the event of the resurrection is not just **past history** but **present experience**.

– The resurrection is an **inspiration**.

– The resurrection is a **promise**.

– The resurrection is **power**.

Christians claim that the resurrection affects their lives even today – whether they believe in a bodily risen Jesus or not.

Note: The disciples did not preach the empty tomb; they preached the risen Lord.

Question time

1. Explain what happens in Holy Week. What do Christians remember during this time and why is it important to them?

2. What symbolism lies behind: a) the word 'Easter', b) Easter eggs?

3. What did Jesus say about his own death and resurrection? Display his sayings in quotations on a clean sheet of paper.

To do

Read the following Easter hymns. Can you identify the Christian beliefs contained in them?

Love's redeeming work is done;
Fought the fight, the battle won:
Vain the stone, the watch, the seal;
Christ hath burst the gates of hell.

Lives again our glorious King;
Where, O death, is now thy sting?
Once He died our souls to save:
Where's thy victory, boasting grave?

Soar we now where Christ hath led,
Following our exalted Head:
Made like Him, like Him we rise;
Ours the cross, the grave, the skies.

Charles Wesley 1707–88

Jesus lives! thy terrors now
Can, O death, no more appal us;
Jesus lives! by this we know
Thou, O grave, canst not enthral us.
Hallelujah!

Jesus lives! to Him the throne
High o'er heaven and earth is given;
We may go where He is gone
Live and reign with Him in heaven.
Hallelujah!

Jesus lives! our hearts know well
Nought from us His love shall sever;
Life, nor death, nor powers of hell,
Part us now from Christ for ever.
Hallelujah!

Jesus lives! henceforth is death
Entrance-gate of life immortal;
This shall calm our trembling breath
When we pass its gloomy portal.
Hallelujah!

The Walk to Emmaus

Luke believed that when Jesus rose from the dead, he did not simply vanish – he appeared to his disciples and spoke to them. Jesus' disciples claimed that they had met him. This experience lies at the very foundation of the Christian faith.

After Peter found the empty linen wrappings in the tomb, Luke switches the scene. We are outside Jerusalem, on a lonely road. It is later that same resurrection day. Jerusalem is buzzing with the rumour that Jesus has risen. Two disciples of Jesus are walking along, discussing what has happened. They are not prepared for what happens next.

The walk to Emmaus – Part 1

READ LUKE 24:13–24

Sometimes events that happen in our lives seem to have a special meaning. We tell them over and over again. They become stories. We have strong feelings about them. They become important incidents in our lives.

Two men are walking to Emmaus – a village outside Jerusalem. Notice how, once again, Luke focuses on *individuals*. He takes a story and makes something special out of it.

- Cleopas and the other disciple are busy talking about Jesus' death and the first rumours of his resurrection. It is clear that these events have been the talk of all Jerusalem.

- A stranger approaches them. It is Jesus, but neither disciple recognizes him. Jesus does not appear as a ghost, a spirit or an angel, *but as a man*. It is important that even after his death and resurrection Jesus does not stop being a man.

Either Jesus has disguised himself in some way, or perhaps Luke is making the comment that the disciples' *lack of faith* prevented them from recognizing Jesus. They are not fully sure about Jesus' resurrection. They do not quite believe that miracles like this can happen.

- Cleopas and his friend are sad. They believe that Jesus was a prophet. They also seem to think that Jesus was the earthly Messiah. They had hoped that Jesus would set Israel free – *politically*. They know that Jesus was a very great man but, even though they have followed him, they never really realized who Jesus actually was. Perhaps their blindness to Jesus' *true identity* is the cause of their blindness now.

- The two disciples tell Jesus the story of the empty tomb. They add that some of the disciples have gone to the tomb and found it empty, just as the women had said. But none of them has yet seen Jesus risen.

The walk to Emmaus – Part 2

READ LUKE 24:25–35

During his ministry, Jesus had often scolded his disciples for their lack of faith. Here Jesus does exactly the same thing to the two disciples he meets on the road.

- Jesus explains the Bible to them – starting at Genesis and working his way through. He explains how the whole of the Old Testament points towards the Messiah's suffering, death and resurrection.

Luke describes a meeting between Jesus and two of his followers as they took the road from Jerusalem to Emmaus on the first Easter Sunday.

● Cleopas and the other disciple invite Jesus to stay the night with them. They are hospitable. They offer Jesus a meal.

● When Jesus breaks the bread, Cleopas and the other disciple suddenly realize that the stranger they have invited to their table is Jesus.

● The breaking of the bread is like the breaking of bread at the Last Supper. Cleopas and his friend recognize Jesus' action even though they themselves were not present at the Last Supper.

● The symbolic act of breaking bread is something that Christians have performed from the very earliest days of the church. Perhaps in this scene Luke is making a reference to an early form of the eucharist.

● Jesus was with his disciples all the time – and they did not recognize him. Only when they talked about the incident afterwards did they realize that there had been something special about the stranger they had met on the road.

● Then Jesus vanishes. Though he still has a body, it no longer has normal human limits.

Some people say that the disciples had *new faith* in Jesus through the breaking of bread. After reading the Old Testament, they came to a realization of who Jesus really was and their faith was made new. They did not meet the risen Jesus *bodily*, but in their *experience*.

● Cleopas and his friend return to Jerusalem to find the disciples very excited. Jesus has now appeared to Simon Peter.

● Eagerly, Cleopas and his friend tell their own story.

Doubt has turned to faith: Jesus has risen and appeared. The disciples are amazed – and changed.

FOLLOW UP

Question time

Read Luke 24:13–35 and then answer the questions:

1. Who was making the journey to Emmaus?

2. Where was Emmaus?

3. What were the travellers talking about?

4. What did Jesus explain to them?

5. How did they recognize Jesus?

To do

In groups of three or four, write a drama script of the return of Cleopas and his friend to Jerusalem. What was the conversation about? Did the disciples believe them? Act it out.

Jesus Appears to His Disciples

It was not merely the empty tomb that convinced the disciples that Jesus had come back from the dead – it was the risen Lord.

That same resurrection evening, Cleopas and his friend were telling the disciples of their amazing experience on the road to Emmaus. The disciples had changed since the morning. Now they were ready to believe. They were ready to believe because Jesus had also appeared to Simon Peter.

Then, while Cleopas and his friend were still speaking, Luke says that Jesus appeared to all of them.

Jesus appears to his disciples

READ LUKE 24:36–49

Luke changes the scene once again. The disciples are gathered in a room somewhere in Jerusalem. They are discussing the astounding events of the day. Two other followers of Jesus rush in to say that they have seen the risen Lord, when Jesus appears to them all.

How did Jesus appear?

This is a question worth asking. After all, many people might say:

The disciples saw a ghost.

The disciples had an hallucination.

The disciples were fooled by a trick of the light.

Against these interpretations, Luke goes out of his way to stress that Jesus appeared *in bodily form* to his disciples. How does Luke show this?

Was Jesus a ghost?

Luke makes it plain that whatever Jesus was, he was *not* a ghost. For example . . .

- Jesus had *wounds*. That is what Jesus meant when he said to his disciples, 'Look at my hands and my feet . . .' (Luke 24:39).

- Jesus had *flesh and bones*. This is something that Jesus pointed out *specifically* to his disciples. Ghosts are not solid. They do not have flesh and bones.

- Jesus *ate with his disciples*. Jesus ate a piece of cooked fish. Ghosts do not eat. It was in order to show that Jesus was *not* a ghost that Luke writes that Jesus ate with his disciples.

Was Jesus an hallucination?

It is certainly possible that one or two people might have had an hallucination. The problem is that Jesus appeared to *many* people, and hallucinations do not normally happen in this way. Furthermore, it is not likely that all the disciples would have had the *same kind* of hallucination, or that they would have held the same beliefs about such an experience.

Was Jesus a trick of the light?

Luke does not write that Jesus simply appeared. Instead, Jesus spoke, taught and ate with his disciples. Or so Luke claimed.

It is not really possible to reduce the resurrection appearances to a simple trick of the light. After all, they were the very experiences that changed the disciples utterly and led to the birth of the Christian church. Something very powerful must have happened. But what?

No ghost – but a friend?

Jesus did not appear to his disciples as a strange ghost: he appeared as a familiar friend.

- Jesus' first words to his disciples were, 'Peace be with you.'
- Jesus asked why his disciples were alarmed.
- Jesus showed his disciples his wounds and ate with them. He wanted to convince them that it was *really him*.
- The disciples were not afraid – they were full of *joy* and *wonder*.

It is important to remember that while Luke presents his Gospel as being full of *history*, it is also full of *theology*. The episodes that Luke writes about often have a theological meaning.

Some critics do not accept that the resurrection appearances are historical in a *factual* sense. Instead, they view these stories as pictures of something important that happened in the *experience* of the disciples.

The disciples had no hope – then they had new faith. Jesus' resurrection, therefore, was *a resurrection of faith in them*.

Equally, Jesus' appearance to the disciples was *a sign that he was with them in their faith*. Jesus did not really appear, but the disciples' *way of seeing the world* changed and they felt that the Spirit of Jesus was with them, helping them and changing them.

Scholars who hold this view would believe that the risen Jesus acts in *human experience*, but that he does not act in *human history*.

Jesus teaches his disciples

Jesus taught his disciples in the same way that he had taught Cleopas and his friend on the road to Emmaus. Jesus said that:

- the writings of the Old Testament pointed to him
- he fulfilled the promises of the Old Testament
- the prophecies that the Messiah must suffer, die and come back to life on the third day had come true in him.

Jesus also gave his disciples a commandment. He told them to preach repentance and forgiveness to all nations. This was to begin at Jerusalem.

Luke's Gospel began with the preaching of John the Baptist to Israel. It ends with Jesus' disciples preparing to preach the gospel to the whole world – to the Gentiles.

To do all this, Jesus gave his disciples a promise of power. He promised that the Holy Spirit would be given to them. This Holy Spirit would be the power and presence of Jesus working through the disciples after Jesus had left them in bodily form.

Luke pictures this happening at the beginning of his second book, the Book of Acts, in chapter two.

FOLLOW UP

Question time

1. What answer would you give to someone who said that in the Gospels Jesus is presented as a 'ghostly figure' after his resurrection? Answer from your knowledge of Luke.

2. What did a) the Jews and b) the Greeks believe about the afterlife? How did belief in the resurrection of Jesus differ from these views?

3. What commandment did Jesus give his disciples when he appeared to them? What implications would this have for the church today?

4. Scholars have different ways of understanding the resurrection and Jesus' appearances afterwards. What do you understand to be the different views held? Fill in the spaces:

- *Scholars who accept the stories as being historically true* believe that Jesus really did ____________ and that the New Testament accounts are ____________. They believe that God acts powerfully in the history of the world.
- *Scholars who do not accept the stories as being historically true* say that they are true because they happened, not in a factual event, but in the ____________ of the disciples. Jesus' resurrection was therefore a resurrection of ____________ in them. Scholars who hold this view believe that God does not act in human history but rather in ____________.

To do

Draw up a witness list to testify to the resurrection of Jesus. You should include columns on:

– who the witness is
– what it was they saw
– what it was they heard
– where they were when this happened
– what the effect on them was
– whether they did anything afterwards

If you have time, look up the resurrection appearances in Matthew, Mark and John. These will add to your list.

- *Debate the issue in class*: 'This house believes that the resurrection of Jesus Christ from the dead was a spiritual resurrection and not a bodily one.'

Jesus is Taken Up to Heaven

Luke's Gospel ends with the resurrection appearances. And the story ends where it began – in the courts of the Temple in Jerusalem. But the end of the Gospel is not really an end – it is a beginning. For Luke wrote not one book, but two. And Luke's second book, The Acts of the Apostles, shows the Gospel message reaching out through the world. It records the birth and the early days of the Christian church.

Different resurrection accounts

All four Gospels record the resurrection of Jesus, but the accounts of the resurrection appearances are not the same in each of the Gospels.

- **Matthew's Gospel**

– Jesus appears to the women (Matthew 28:9–10).
– Jesus appears to his disciples *in Galilee* (Matthew 28:16–20).

- **Mark's Gospel**

There are three possible endings:

1. The women meet one angel at the empty tomb (Luke has two). The angel tells the women that they must give the message to the disciples that Jesus has gone to Galilee. The women, however, are afraid. They run away and tell no one (Mark 16:8). This is the earliest known ending to Mark's Gospel.
2. Jesus appears to Mary Magdalene, to two disciples, and to his own disciples when they are eating.
He is then taken up to heaven (Mark 16:9–20). This is one ancient ending to Mark.
3. The women tell Peter what they have seen. Jesus sends his message out to the world through his disciples. This is another possible ending to the Gospel.

PEOPLE WHO SAW JESUS

According to the Gospels, a great many people actually saw Jesus, alive again, after his death and burial.

- MARY MAGDALENE MET JESUS. She went to his tomb and the stone was rolled away. (John 20:1-2, 11-18)
- PETER AND JOHN followed and found the tomb empty. (John 20:3-10)
- TWO PEOPLE on the road to Emmaus met Jesus. (Luke 24:13-35)
- HIS DISCIPLES saw him in Jerusalem. (John 20:19-29)

- HE APPEARED TO HIS DISCIPLES AGAIN by Lake Galilee, and on several more occasions. (John 21:1-14)
- ON ONE OCCASION 500 PEOPLE saw him at once (I Corinthians 15:5-7)

- **John's Gospel**

In some ways the last episode of Luke's Gospel is very like John 20:19–29. Both accounts stress that Jesus appeared in *bodily* form. – Jesus appears to Mary Magdalene (John 20;11–18).
– Jesus appears to his disciples, who are hiding in a locked room (John 20:19–23).
– Jesus appears to seven disciples at Lake Tiberias (John 21:1–14).
– Jesus speaks to Simon Peter (John 21:15–19).

Jesus is taken up to heaven

READ LUKE 24:50–53

This last episode in Luke's Gospel is known, traditionally, as the *Ascension*. The Ascension is when Jesus is taken up to heaven. This event marks the *end* of Jesus' resurrection appearances. But it is not the end of the story.

- The birth of the church is yet to come.
- The gift of the Holy Spirit is yet to come.

The disciples have had quite a day, according to Luke! They have learned that Jesus is risen. They have actually seen him, eaten with him, and been taught by him. And now Jesus takes his disciples out of Jerusalem to Bethany.

- He *blesses* them.
- Jesus then leaves his disciples and is taken up into heaven.
- The disciples *worship* Jesus and return to Jerusalem.
- The disciples are filled with great joy. Joy is a constant theme throughout the Gospel of Luke.
- The disciples spend their time in the Temple at Jerusalem, giving thanks to God.

Note that *the disciples worshipped Jesus*. Now they were finally convinced that Jesus was not only a man – he was also God.

But how did Jesus go?

Did he jump? Did he fly? Did he just float away?

Now:
– If you have a girlfriend and you say, 'Her neck is like a swan's and her eyes are like stars,' do you really mean that she looks like this?
– If you have a boyfriend and you say, 'He's got legs of iron and hair like straw,' do you really mean he looks like this?

Probably not. What you are doing is:
– giving an impression
– communicating an experience
– using *pictures* in language to show what someone is like.

Luke is trying to write about an experience – an experience that is hard to put into words. That is one reason why these verses might seem so odd to us. Luke wants to show that:

- the resurrection appearances stopped
- Jesus went back to heaven.

Even if Jesus literally took his disciples out to Bethany and was taken up to heaven then and there in front of them, Luke may have interpreted the story.

FOLLOW UP

Question time

1. How do you account for the fact that Luke is the only Gospel to record all the resurrection appearances of Jesus in Jerusalem and not in Galilee. Why is Jerusalem so important to Luke?

2. Write an account of Jesus' ascension. How can this story be understood?

3. Why were witnesses so important to the early church?

To do

Design a poster entitled 'Witnesses of the Resurrection'. Include pictures of:
– the women at the tomb
– the friends on the road to Emmaus
– Jesus' disciples, etc.
Label them.

The Resurrection from the Dead

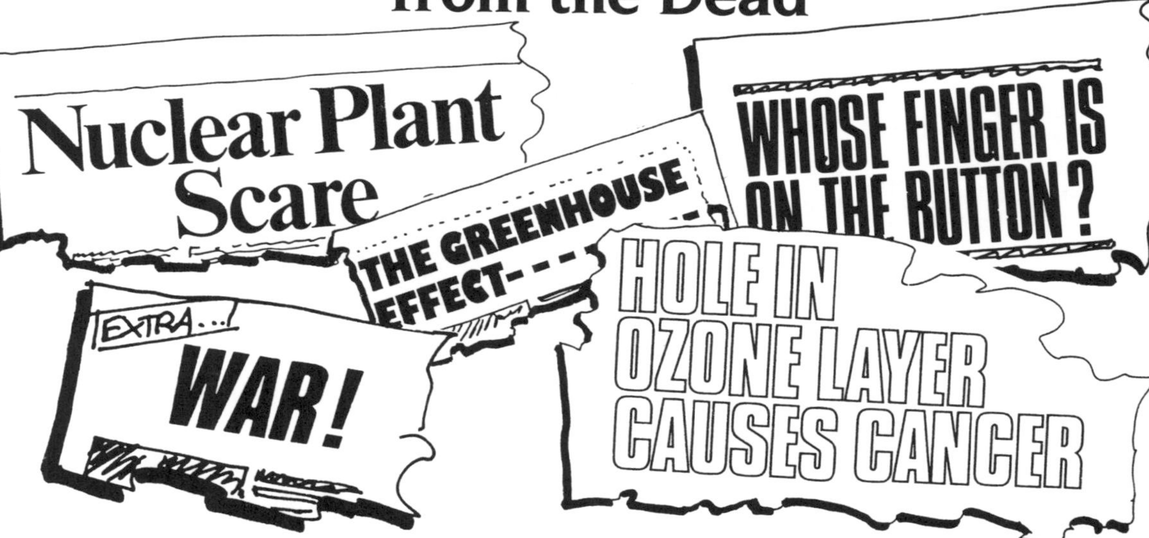

Sometimes the end of the world seems just round the corner. When we turn on the TV or open a newspaper there are items about nuclear bombs, wars, disease, pollution and other things that threaten our very survival.

Sometimes it seems that we haven't got long left.

There's a lot of gloom around – when, of course, people want hope. Yet no matter how bad things are, people want to believe in the future.

Stop the world, I want to get off

When the Jews were in exile in Babylon, some of them lost hope in an *earthly Messiah* (a great warrior or king) coming to save Israel from their enemies. Instead they looked to a *heavenly Messiah* to rescue them. This Messiah would

- be a heavenly King
- save the righteous and punish the wicked
- save Israel and punish Israel's enemies
- end human history and begin the rule of God.

The word for these kinds of ideas is *apocalyptic*. The Jews began to develop these ideas when they were in exile in Babylon.

Jesus the apocalyptic Messiah

Jesus' followers, the early Christians, came to believe that Jesus was the *heavenly* Messiah as well as the *earthly* Messiah. Although he was not a warrior or a king, they believed that Jesus came to preach God's kingdom on earth. They thought he was the 'son of David' (Israel's greatest king). But also

- Jesus cast out demons
- Jesus healed the sick
- Jesus showed great power over nature
- Jesus raised dead people to life
- Jesus rose to life from the tomb
- Jesus appeared to his disciples
- Jesus ascended to heaven

According to Luke, Jesus came to offer salvation to the whole world and to preach the Kingdom of God.

Luke believed that Jesus did not just offer a new life *now*. He offered a new life *after death* to all those who believed in him.

Similarly, Luke believed that Jesus not only preached that the Kingdom of God had arrived with him, Jesus preached that one day he would *return* and the Kingdom of God would be established in power for ever.

The early Christians believed firmly that *Jesus was coming back* – something many Christians still believe today. They believed that Jesus would not come back weak, but strong – not as a servant, but as a king.

Apocalyptic comes from the Greek word *apokalupsis*, meaning to 'uncover' or 'reveal' what was hidden. The Book of Revelation in the New Testament is also known as 'The Apocalypse'. It describes what happens when God shows his power at the end of the world.

Eschatology describes some of the things that will happen at the end of the world:

- Jesus will come back
- Jesus will judge the world
- Jesus will establish the Kingdom of God for ever.

What did Jesus himself say about these things?

'I assure you that there are some here who will not die until they have seen the Kingdom of God' (Luke 9:27).

This is an important verse. Luke writes that Jesus spoke these words just after Peter's declaration that he was the Messiah.

There are some scholars who believe that **Jesus was talking about his return** here. They think he was talking about the final coming of the Kingdom of God. That is possible. But if it is true, then it did not happen.

Others believe that **Jesus was referring to his resurrection** and the establishment of God's Kingdom through the birth of the church.

Matthew and Mark's accounts of these words are slightly different:

'I assure you that there are some here who will not die until they have seen the Son of Man come as King' (Matthew 16:28).

Many people wonder what, if anything, happens after we die. For anyone who has ever asked questions about life after death, Jesus' teaching makes fascinating reading.

'I tell you, there are some here who will not die until they have seen the Kingdom of God come with power' (Mark 9:1).

Luke has been accused of making his version of these words of Jesus sound *less apocalyptic*. Nevertheless, both views of the *meaning* of this verse are still possible.

The resurrection of the dead

In Jesus' day there was a lot of argument about resurrection from the dead. The two main groups of religious leaders were the Pharisees and the Sadducees. The Sadducees believed that only the first five books of the Old Testament (the Torah) were important. The Jewish Law was to be found in these five books, and it was widely believed that Moses had written them. The

Pharisees also believed the teaching of the prophets.

The Sadducees did *not* believe in life after death – the Pharisees did. In fact, it is true to say that there is not much *specifically* about life after death in the Old Testament. It was one of the beliefs that developed when the Jews were in exile in Babylon. In the Old Testament, the Jews believed in *sheol*, a shadowy place under the earth, where the spirits of people went after they died.

Jesus believed in an afterlife.

The question about rising from death

READ LUKE 20:27–40

Once again, Jesus showed how cleverly he could argue. The Sadducees asked a smart question. They wanted to show how stupid it was to believe in life after death. They were trying to make fun of the whole idea.

● Jesus answered the Sadducees seriously. He said that where there is no *death* there is no *need* for marriage or children. In the age to come, there would be no growing old and no dying. And there would be no property, no marriage and no children. So the legal question the Sadducees had asked was stupid, not the idea of resurrection.

● Jesus went on to claim that the first five books of the Old Testament *do* talk about an afterlife. God told Moses, 'I am the God of Abraham, the God of Isaac, and the God of Jacob' (Exodus 3:6). Although these men had long been dead, Jesus argued, God talks about them as though they were still alive.

Jesus seems to be arguing very finely about a point or a word, but this is exactly how the Sadducees argued. Jesus was beating the Sadducees at their own game.

Jesus believed in a resurrection from the dead. Christians say that Jesus did more than just believe it. He demonstrated this belief by rising from the dead himself.

FOLLOW UP

Question time

1. What is meant by the word 'apocalyptic'?

2. What is meant by 'eschatology'?

3. What is meant by 'the second coming' or 'the parousia'?

4. What did Jesus mean when he said, 'There are some here who will not die until they have seen the Kingdom of God'?

5. How do you know that Jesus believed in an afterlife? Answer from Luke's Gospel (Luke 20:27–40).

To do

Conduct a survey on *Beliefs about the afterlife*.

Find out what people believe in your class/school/community. First design your survey form, so that it is easy to fill in when you are talking to people. What details do you want to know? Are you going to give people a choice in their answers, or can they say what they like? Do you want just a Yes/No format, or do you want to know why they hold the beliefs they do?

When you have finished, compare and discuss your findings with others. Were you surprised at the results? Are there some beliefs which are more common than others?

Jesus Predicts the End-times

Some people claim to know the future. But do they? Can people really predict what is going to happen?

In Luke's Gospel, Luke shows Jesus as predicting the future. Jesus is presented as saying that life will get much worse. Terrible times are coming for everyone, but especially for his followers and for the people of Jerusalem.

Then, to end it all, Jesus will *return*. Jesus will return as a saviour and a judge. Human history will end and the Kingdom of God will begin – but this time for ever.

The belief that Jesus will return is called *the second coming* or the *parousia*.

Luke and the early church

As yet, Jesus has not returned. This is not a problem for us today, but it may have been a problem for the early church. One view is that Christians then believed that Jesus was coming back *soon*. They believed that his resurrection would be followed by his speedy return in power.

But Jesus did not return in power. And because Jesus did not return, some scholars believe that there was a *crisis* in the early church. The Christians reached a point where they were not exactly sure what to believe. Some argue that Luke helped solve this crisis by writing about the resurrection and the second coming as though they were two events that would be *far apart in time*.

Remember, Luke wrote not one book but two: the *Gospel of Luke* and the *Acts of the Apostles*. The Gospel of Luke is about Jesus' birth, life, ministry, death, resurrection and ascension. The Acts of the Apostles is about another birth – the birth of the Christian church. It is a *history* of the early church. It could be that Luke wanted to write about the age of the church taking place between the resurrection and the second coming as a *way of explaining* why Jesus had not returned straight away. But this is only one view.

If you believe that Luke was trying to deal with the problem of why Jesus had not come back, then you may try to show that Luke has made his Gospel *less apocalyptic* than Mark. There is apocalyptic material in Luke, but it is 'softer' than in Mark.

The apocalyptic prophecies of Jesus, in Luke's Gospel, fall into three areas.

The destruction of the Temple

READ LUKE 21:5–6

Jesus spoke about the destruction of the Jerusalem Temple at several points in Luke's Gospel. The temple was destroyed by the Romans in AD70 – that is a fact.

Jerusalem had rejected Jesus. In rejecting Jesus, Jerusalem had rejected *salvation*. Jesus said that the city would be judged because of this. Not one stone of the Temple, the symbol of the Jewish faith, would be left standing.

Troubles and persecutions

READ LUKE 21:7–19

Jesus was still teaching in the Temple before his arrest. Some people asked him about the end-times.

This is what Jesus said about the end-times:

- false Messiahs would come
- wars and revolutions would take place

- there would be earthquakes, famines and plagues
- terrifying things would fall out of the sky

This is what Jesus said about his followers:

- they would be arrested and persecuted
- they would be tried and put in prison, and some would be put to death
- they would be helped and comforted in their troubles by Jesus' Spirit
- they would be betrayed, even by their own families and friends.

Terrible things happened to the early Christians. They were persecuted, betrayed and killed for what they believed in. Following Jesus had a price to pay – often a follower's own life. These prophetic words of Jesus must have comforted the early Christians in their troubles.

These words may have been a *real* prophecy – Jesus actually spoke them. Or Luke might have pictured Jesus as speaking these words. Luke wanted the early church to feel that Jesus knew what was going to happen to them and that he would be with them.

When persecution came, Christians in Rome met secretly in the catacombs under the city. This was one of their secret signs, marked on the walls.

- **Fact**

In AD64 there was a terrible fire in Rome. The Emperor Nero blamed the Christians for the fire and many of them were put to death.

- **Fact**

From AD66–70 the Jews waged a war against the Romans. This ended with the complete destruction of the Jerusalem Temple.

- **Fact**

In AD69 there were *four* Roman Emperors in one year. The battles and bloodshed during those months were terrible.

- **Fact**

From AD81–96 the Roman Emperor Domitian persecuted the Christian church terribly. Many Christians suffered and were killed.

These events must have helped convince the early church that Jesus would come back soon. But Jesus did not come back physically and he has not returned in bodily form. Even so, Jesus' words would have given comfort to the early Christians – they experienced his Spirit with them.

Jesus speaks of the destruction of Jerusalem

READ LUKE 21:20–24

Again Jesus spoke words that he had said elsewhere in Luke's Gospel. They were a warning that terrible times were coming.

Elsewhere in Luke's Gospel:

- Jesus speaks of his love for Jerusalem (Luke 13:31–35)
- Jesus weeps over Jerusalem (Luke 19:41–44)

In AD70 the Romans captured Jerusalem and destroyed the Temple, taking their loot back to Rome. The Arch of Titus in Rome shows some of the booty from the Temple, including the great seven-branched candlestick.

- Jesus warns the women of the coming destruction on his way to the cross (Luke 23:27–31)

Because Jerusalem had rejected Jesus, the source of salvation, the city would be judged.

Even though many people (including the early Christians) have tried to tie these prophecies to particular historical events, Jesus' *general message* is that things will get worse – much, much worse – and then he will return.

FOLLOW UP

Question time

1. Some scholars say that Jesus' delay in coming again was a problem in the early church and that Luke has tried to help Christians keep their faith. Complete the following sentences:

Some say that Luke helped solve this crisis by writing about the ____________ and the ____________ as though they were two events that would be ____________ in time.

Luke wrote not one book but two – ____________ and the ____________.

The first one is about ____________. The other is about ____________.

To do

Form a 'buzz group' of between four and six people. You are going to find out what the group thinks about predicting the future.

Get a large sheet of paper or card and print in bold letters the title: CAN THE FUTURE BE PREDICTED? Each member of the group can now write in any direction and in any colour on the paper. Write 'Yes' sentences or 'No' sentences all over the page – e.g. Yes, because ____________, or No, the future can't be predicted because ____________. Give examples of stories you have read or heard.

When you have finished, either discuss the different views held or swap your sheet with another group and discuss their opinions. What evidence is there for these sorts of beliefs? Do people who believe in prophecy or prediction live differently from those who do not believe?

Jesus and the Second Coming

Jesus had predicted the end-times. He said those days will be terrible. There would be wars and revolutions. There would be suffering and death. Then Jesus' words changed. He began to talk about the second coming, when he would come again. This time Jesus would not come as a weak, earthly man, but as a powerful, heavenly being. The glory that Jesus showed to Peter, James and John on the mount of transfiguration would be seen by everyone.

Jesus talked about the end-times while he was still teaching in the Temple. In fact, Jesus' words about his coming again are the last recorded words of his teaching in the Temple before he was betrayed and arrested.

Will the world end in a great nuclear explosion? Many people fear so, and accidents like that at Chernobyl make us feel very insecure.

Warnings of the future

Look at the following passages:

- **The unbelieving towns**

READ LUKE 10:13–16

This is a passage about *judgment*. The Jewish towns will be judged because they have rejected Jesus – the Gentile towns, however, will be saved. Here Jesus is talking about what will happen at the end of the world.

- **The demand for a miracle**

READ LUKE 11:29–32

Jesus is angry here. The people demand a miracle, but they do not see the real meaning of Jesus – that he is the Messiah. The Queen of Sheba (a Gentile woman ruler), and Nineveh (a Gentile city), will be saved – while the Jews will be judged for refusing to recognize their salvation.

Notes

– **The miracle of Jonah** was when Jonah was swallowed by a large fish – and then escaped. Similarly, Jesus will be in a tomb – and then rise up again.
– Jonah preached to **Nineveh** – an evil and Gentile city. The city believed Jonah's message and was not destroyed.
– **The Queen of Sheba** was a famous queen. She came to listen to Solomon, one of Israel's great kings, because she had heard he was so wise. According to Luke, Jesus here claims that he is greater than Solomon.

- **Watchful servants**

READ LUKE 12:35–40

Jesus teaches his followers that they must be constantly on the watch. Jesus will return at a time and place nobody knows and his followers must be ready for him. The early Christians felt that Jesus was coming almost immediately. These words probably had more force for them than for Christians today.

- **Understanding the time**

READ LUKE 12:54–56

Jesus is angry with the crowd. He tells them they know what the weather will be like by looking at the sky. They can read the signs. What the crowd cannot do is to read the signs of the times. They do not recognize that Jesus is the Messiah. They cannot see that the Kingdom of God is near.

- **The coming of the Kingdom**

READ LUKE 17:22–37

In this long passage:
– Jesus predicts his suffering and death
– Judgment will fall on the world quickly and suddenly
– Some people will be saved; others will be left.

This is *apocalyptic* writing. Jesus is talking here about the end of the world and what will happen. Jesus does not say *when* these things will happen. What is important is that the end will be sudden, dramatic and powerful.

The teaching in the Temple

Jesus' teaching in the Temple ends with his talking about his coming again. This teaching falls into three sections:

In this passage, Luke is using Jewish sources:

- **The Son of Man** is a title that Jesus (and only Jesus) used of himself. Either it is simply a way of saying 'I', or Jesus is referring to the heavenly being (the 'Son of Man') talked about in Daniel chapter 7.

- **Noah** was ordered by God in the Old Testament to build a boat – an ark. Noah put two kinds of every animal in the world into the ark. Then, with his wife, sons and their wives, Noah waited. There was a flood. Everyone in the world was drowned except Noah and his family. God did this because the people of that time were so wicked – but God promised he would not send such a flood again.

- **Lot** was a good man who lived in Sodom, a wicked city. God saved Lot, but destroyed Sodom. God had ordered Lot and his family to flee from the city, but not to look back as they went. Lot's wife, however, looked back. Because she disobeyed, she was turned into a pillar of salt.

Jesus uses these stories of judgment from the Old Testament to talk about the end of the world.

- **The coming of the Son of Man** 1

READ LUKE 21:25–28

Just as terrible things are going to happen *in the world* at the end, so terrible things will begin to happen *in heaven*. At the end of this, the Son of Man (Jesus) will appear in power. That will be the final sign that salvation is near.

- **The lesson of the fig-tree** 2

READ LUKE 21:29–32

The fig-tree is found everywhere in Israel. Jesus says that when the leaves of the fig-tree appear, it is obvious that summer is coming. In the same way, when there are wars on earth and strange happenings in heaven, this will be a sign that Jesus is about to come again. Verse 32 perhaps refers to the coming destruction of Jerusalem and the Temple.

● **The Need to Watch** **3**

READ LUKE 21:34–38

Jesus tells the people listening to him that they must always be on the alert. Jesus will come again *suddenly*, when no one is expecting it. His followers must always be ready to be saved, and not to be judged.

Jesus' followers must realize that their real home is not on earth, but in heaven. They must not become too caught up in the worries and activities of this life.

Jesus' teaching is clear at this point:
– things will get worse
– salvation is near
– always be ready
– Jesus will come when you least expect it.

It may have been that the early Christians did hope that the end had come in AD70 when the Jerusalem Temple was destroyed. But that was not the case.

What *did* happen was that Jesus' followers slowly formed themselves into the Christian church.

Finally, the great Roman Empire that had persecuted the Christians became Christian itself (in the 4th century AD), and the good news of Jesus travelled over the whole world.

Some Christians believe that Jesus *will* come again. Others think that these apocalyptic writings are *pictures*. They will not come true in historical events.

What *is* true is that we all live between the claim of Jesus' resurrection – and the end of the world.

FOLLOW UP

Question time

1. What does Jesus say about his second coming? Refer to Luke 21:25–38 for your answer.

2. How important is it for Christians to believe in the second coming of Christ today? Would such a belief help or hinder a person's faith?

3. Outline Jesus' teaching in the Temple under three headings:
● the coming of the Son of Man
● the lesson of the fig tree
● the need to watch.

To do

Discuss in your class people's fears about THE END. Is this just scary talk, or is it a distinct possibility? How might different Christians understand such a possibility? If the world ended tomorrow who would you hold responsible and why? In what ways can we influence our own future?